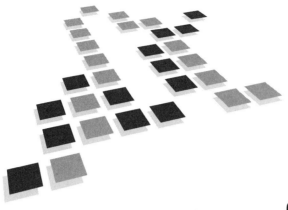

The Essentials
of Political Analysis

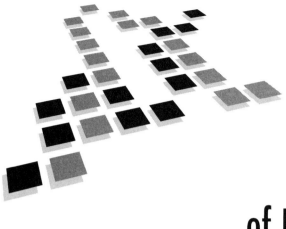

The Essentials
of Political Analysis

Second Edition

Philip H. Pollock III
University of Central Florida

CQ PRESS

A Division of Congressional Quarterly Inc.
Washington, D.C.

CQ Press
1255 22nd Street, NW, Suite 400
Washington, DC 20037

Phone, 202-729-1900; toll-free, 1-866-427-7737 (1-866-4CQ-PRESS)

Web: www.cqpress.com

CQ Press gratefully acknowledges the permission granted by Pippa Norris, John F. Kennedy School of Government, Harvard University, for the use of selected variables in the Shared Global Database at www.pippanorris.com.

Cover design: Malcolm McGaughy

♾ The paper used in this publication exceeds the requirements of the American National Standard for Information Sciences—Permanence of Paper for Printed Library Materials, ANSI Z39.48-1992.

Printed and bound in the United States of America

09   08   07   3   4   5

Library of Congress Cataloging-in-Publication Data

Pollock, Philip H.
  The essentials of political analysis / Philip H. Pollock III.— 2nd ed.
    p. cm.
  Summary: "Presents the logic and practice of political analysis—including concepts, measurement, and hypothesis testing. Covers basic statistical skills, correlation and least squares regression, and binary logistic regression. Provides examples, key terms, and exercises and is accompanied by a workbook"—Provided by publisher.
  Includes bibliographical references and index.
  ISBN 1-56802-997-7 (alk. paper)
  1. Political science—Research—Methodology—Textbooks.   I. Title.

JA86.P65 2005
320'.072—dc22
                                                              2005004460

To my parents,
Philip H. Pollock Jr.
and Rhoda A. Pollock

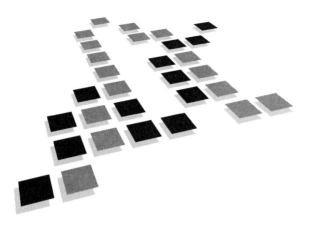

Contents

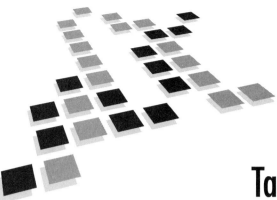

Tables and Figures

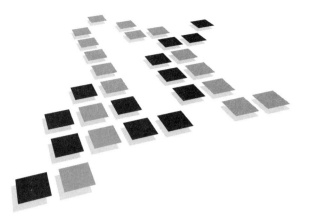

Preface

As an instructor of courses in research methods and data analysis for more than twenty-five years, I have found that political science students often confuse research methods with statistics. "I'm really not a statistics person" is a familiar student refrain. Indeed, many students see political science as a refuge from majors in which quantitative skills play a more prominent role, and they view a course in methods, which is often required, as a rite of passage, not as a fundamental foundation for the substantive courses in the curriculum.

I thus began seeking ways to overcome this anxiety about methods, to get students past their initial apprehension and allow them to learn and apply essential principles of political analysis. I found that the abundant use of examples greatly enhances students' abilities to comprehend and internalize important concepts. I also observed that students become much more adept at describing political variables and interpreting relationships between them if they learn elemental graphing techniques. Accordingly, *The Essentials of Political Analysis* contains numerous hypothetical and actual examples, and the chapters instruct in the interpretation of graphic displays of variables and relationships. In addition to drawing on phenomena from U.S. politics, this second edition also includes new examples from comparative politics and international relations. The narrative encourages students to stop and think about the examples, and the exercises at the end of each chapter permit students to apply their newly acquired skills. Adopters of the first edition will find more exercises in this volume, including six new exercises with a comparative/IR focus.

First-edition adopters will also note another major change: a new chapter on binary logistic regression. Of course, logistic regression has been around for a while, but over the past several years the technique has gained heightened currency, enough so in my judgment to warrant treatment in an introductory methods text. Chapter 8 now covers the basics of the simple binary model: how to convert probabilities to odds and logged odds; how maximum likelihood estimation arrives at model estimates; how to specify and interpret logistic regression models with multiple independent variables; and how to present results in terms of probabilities. Because the lexicon of logistic regression may not be familiar to students, I have tried to use to good pedagogical advantage the analogy between logistic regression and ordinary least squares regression (covered in Chapter 7).

Amid these revisions and enhancements, the basic structure of the text remains unaltered. Chapters 1 through 4 emphasize the logic and practice of political analysis, delving into concepts, measurement, description, hypothesis testing, and control. These four chapters deal very little with statistics. Chapters 5 and 6 cover basic statistical skills—sampling, inference, statistical significance, and measures of association. Chapter 7 covers correlation and ordinary least squares regression, including a discussion of dummy variable regression and interaction effects in multiple regression analysis. As noted, the newly minted Chapter 8 provides introductory treatment of binary logistic regression. In the belief that brevity confers certain advantages—concise chapters are more easily digestible by neophyte student researchers—I have tried to provide clear and accessible discussions of major topics in political research. I hope that instructors wishing to supplement this book with additional readings or lecture material will find the fundamentals adequately covered here.

ORGANIZATION OF THE BOOK

The introduction to *The Essentials of Political Analysis* addresses another observation about students: They sometimes confuse statements of fact with statements of value. Display a table showing the distribution of public opinion on gay marriage, for example, and students will want to debate whether same-sex marriage is right or wrong. At first, anyway, they will be less interested in discussing what empirical factors might cause people to hold different opinions on this issue. The introduction examines the distinction between facts and values, and it attempts to show how empirical analysis expands our knowledge of politics and how it can help to elevate debates about values. It also covers the main elements of the scientific approach to politics.

Chapter 1 instructs students in how to describe political concepts with empirical language, introduces them to problems of validity and reliability, and provides an extended discussion of levels of measurement. Interestingly, identifying the level of measurement of a variable seems to be a sticking point for many students. Chapter 2 covers the logic of explanation in political science. Here students learn to distinguish a good explanation from a poor one, discover how to frame a hypothesis, and consider the basic elements of research design in political analysis. Chapter 3 provides a nonstatistical discussion of central tendency and dispersion and illustrates the main vehicles of hypothesis testing: cross-tabulation and mean comparison analyses. Nonlinear relationships commonly occur in political analysis, so Chapter 3 also discusses some prevalent curvilinear patterns. Chapter 4 covers making controlled comparisons—isolating the effect of the independent variable on the dependent variable, controlling for a rival cause. Students will gain the interpretative tools they need to identify spurious relationships, additive relationships, or interaction in complex empirical relationships. Thus these chapters encourage students to think empirically about concepts and variables, to write testable hypotheses, to perform bivariate analyses, to visualize relationships, and to construct and interpret controlled comparisons. These chapters will engage students in the real world of research, where they can discover the creative pleasures that come from thinking up explanations, applying empirical rigor, and offering interpretations.

Chapters 5 and 6 aim to instill an appreciation for the essential supporting role of statistical knowledge in political analysis. Chapter 5 covers sampling and inference. I have found that the concept of the standard error of a sample statistic, the bedrock foundation of inferential statistics, is among the most difficult for students to grasp. Chapter 5 uses an extended hypothetical example to illustrate this idea and shows how political researchers use informal rules of thumb, as well as normal estimation and the Student's t-distribution, to find the confidence interval of a sample statistic. In Chapter 6 students build on these inferential skills, learning how to test the statistical significance of an observed relationship against the null hypothesis. Chapter 6 also discusses measures of association for nominal and ordinal variables, with special emphasis on proportional reduction in error techniques.

While writing Chapters 5 and 6, I assumed that many instructors would complement their courses with hands-on computer analysis of real-world data. Thus these chapters emphasize the practical side of interpreting the results of data analysis and de-emphasize the calculation of statistical formulas. Chapter 7 draws on several examples to illustrate the essential properties of bivariate and multiple regression and shows students how to use nominal or ordinal variables as independent variables in regression analysis. Chapter 8 similarly uses hypothetical and actual data to introduce binary logistic regression. The goal in Chapters 7 and 8 is to demystify these techniques by showing their logical connections with methods that students have learned in earlier chapters. A final section in Chapter 7, for example, shows students how to use multiple regression to model interaction, a pattern they learned to identify and interpret in Chapter 4. The discussion of maximum likelihood estimation in Chapter 8 makes the link to chi-square, covered in Chapter 6. Chapter 9, the book's concluding chapter, returns to the theme of distinguishing facts from values, encouraging students to use their new skills to enrich their descriptions and analyses of the political world.

ORGANIZATION OF CHAPTERS AND SPECIAL FEATURES

The Essentials of Political Analysis is organized around a time-honored pedagogical principle: Foreshadow the topic, present the material, and then review the main points. Each chapter opens with a bulleted list of learning objectives, followed by an illustrative example or a schematic road map of the chapter's contents. Key terms appear in bold type throughout the text, and each chapter closes with a summary and a list of the key terms, which are referenced with page numbers. For example, as students begin Chapter 1, "The Measurement of Concepts," they will be made aware of its six objectives: identifying the three stages of the measurement process, clarifying the meaning of concepts, writing a conceptual definition, addressing problems of validity and reliability, using variables to measure concepts, and identifying levels of measurement. The chapter then reminds students of the ubiquity of conceptual questions in political science—for example, "Are women more liberal than men?"—and asks them to consider how political researchers might address these questions. Following the discussion of the six objectives, the text recapitulates each topic and references each key term.

Abundant tables and figures—about eighty in all—illustrate methodological concepts and procedures. I used hypothetical data in some instances, but most are based on my analyses of the National Election Studies, the General Social Surveys, a dataset containing variables on a large number of countries, and data on the fifty states. Chapter 1, for example, incorporates data from the 2000 National Election Study to illustrate the discussion of construct validity. Most of the end-of-chapter exercises ask students to analyze actual data as well. A solutions manual is available to instructors.

AN SPSS COMPANION TO POLITICAL ANALYSIS

The Essentials of Political Analysis can be used as a stand-alone text in a political science methods course, but alternatively it is possible to supplement it with the workbook, *An SPSS*

Companion to Political Analysis, which I developed to serve as a tutorial to data analysis using SPSS. The workbook shows students how to use SPSS to perform the techniques covered in the text: obtaining descriptive statistics, conducting bivariate and multivariate cross-tabulation and mean comparison analyses, running correlation and regression, and performing binary logistic regression. The workbook also includes chapters on statistical significance and measures of association, as well as the SPSS data transformation procedures. A final chapter of the *SPSS Companion* provides examples of research projects and helps students as they collect and code data, do original analysis, and write up their findings.

The workbook offers five SPSS-compatible datasets: the 2000 National Election Study, the 2002 General Social Survey, and datasets on the fifty states, 114 countries, and members of the U.S. Senate. Students work through each chapter's guided examples—using computer screen-shots for graphic support—and then apply their new skills in the end-of-chapter exercises. The workbook accommodates the full version of SPSS as well as the student version and virtually any release—SPSS 11.5 or earlier or SPSS 12.0 or later. The instructor's solutions manual provides answers for the full and student versions. Just as *The Essentials of Political Analysis* helps students become critical and competent consumers of political research, the *SPSS Companion* instructs them in how to use a powerful data analysis package as they pursue their own research interests.

ACKNOWLEDGMENTS

I owe thanks to a number of friendly critics for many of the changes and improvements in this edition. Pete Furia of Wake Forest University pointed me toward a clearer discussion of validity and reliability (in Chapter 1) and encouraged a fuller description of patterns of interaction (in Chapter 4). Indeed, I have added a fair amount of content to Chapter 4, and to reflect reviewers' preferences, changed much of its terminology. I thank Johanna Kristin Birnir of the State University of New York at Buffalo for finding a key error in my definition of skewness (in Chapter 3), which I trust has been corrected satisfactorily. The perceptive comments of James Hanley of the University of Illinois at Springfield led me to rectify confusion about the relationship between sample size and random sampling error (in Chapter 5). I owe special thanks to William Claggett of Florida State University for encouraging me to write this book and for providing many helpful suggestions on the second edition, including detailed criticisms of the new Chapter 8 on logistic regression.

At the University of Central Florida, I am blessed with generous and talented colleagues. Thanks to the guidance of Bruce Wilson and Kerstin Hamann, the second edition contains many more examples and end-of-chapter exercises on comparative politics. I also thank Terri Susan Fine and Bernadette Jungblut for their keen insights and timely suggestions. Joel Lefkowitz of the State University of New York at New Paltz and his students provided many helpful comments on an early draft of the first edition, and Jay DeSart of Utah Valley State College helped me point the early chapters in the right direction. I also acknowledge the assistance of the book's anonymous reviewers and hope that the finished product meets with their approval. Any errors that remain are mine alone.

Everyone at CQ Press has been extraordinarily patient and encouraging. I thank Charisse Kiino, acquisitions editor, who helped me get this project off the ground and guided me along through its completion. I am grateful to development editor Michelle Tupper, whose sense of clarity and precision has made this a book of which I am proud, and to Chris Karlsten and Tracy Villano, who were responsible for the production and copy editing, respectively, of the first edition. For this second edition, my thanks go to copy editor Amy Marks, who tirelessly edited and improved my prose, and Joan Gossett, who was responsible for production this time around.

Others contributed in different ways to this book. I am indebted to Theodore J. Eismeier of Hamilton College, who taught me, through many years of productive collaboration, how to meld creative thinking with empirical analysis. Finally, I thank the two most important people in my life, Erin Suzanne Greene and Lauren DeCara Pollock, for their forbearance, inspiration, and love.

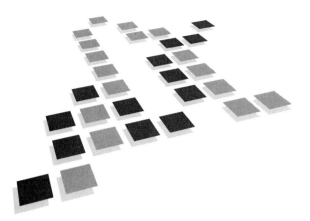

Introduction

The tight presidential contests of 2000 and 2004 provoked commentators, citizens, and scholars to raise new questions, or resurrect old ones, about the U.S. electoral system. Some observers defended the merits of the electoral college. Others advocated reform, perhaps a change to a process based on direct election. What political values shape the present system? What would be the likely consequences of reform? Other observers focused on issues that were narrower, if no less thorny. For instance, some analysts argued that confusing ballot designs and antiquated voting machines were to blame for a large number of miscounted votes in some Florida counties in 2000. Is this true? Are some voting technologies more prone to error or more vulnerable to fraud than other technologies? In 2004, dramatic and unforeseen increases in voter turnout in many states created a different set of problems— long lines, frayed tempers, and questions about the competence and efficiency of election supervisors. How might the voting process be reformed to enhance participation and minimize errors?

The recent elections did not corner the market on interesting or controversial questions. For example, over the past 25 years or so women have become much more likely than men to support the candidate of the Democratic Party. What accounts for this shift? Does the Democratic policy agenda appeal more strongly to women than to men? If so, which policies? We also know that people who earn lower incomes are more likely than higher-income people to vote Democratic. If women, on average, earn lower incomes than men, then maybe the "gender gap" is really an "income gap." If one were to compare women and men with similar incomes, would the gap still show up?

Of course, challenging and important issues are not confined to U.S. politics. During your lifetime, for example, the cold war ended and the Soviet Union collapsed, ending nearly half a century of predictability in patterns of power and internal governance. Emerging independent states have made new claims of national legitimacy. Yet as undemocratic governments dissolve, one might ask, what are the prospects that democratic forms will replace them? Is democratic development pushed along by economic relationships, such as free markets and open competition? What roles do political institutions, cultural beliefs, or ethnic antagonisms play? How would one define a democratic political system anyway?

These are the sorts of questions political scientists ask all the time. Researchers observe the sometimes chaotic political scene and create explanations for what they see. They offer hypotheses about political relationships and collect facts that can shed light on the way the political world works. They exchange ideas with other researchers, discuss the merits of different explanations, refine some explanations and discard others. Sometimes political scientists describe "What if?" scenarios, using established facts or workable assumptions to make predictions about future facts. (If the presidential electoral system were based on direct election, what would be the likely consequences?) Sometimes the facts that researchers seek are already there, waiting to be described and measured. (What is the income difference between women and men?) Scholars may disagree on the meaning of important ideas, and they discuss the measurement of complex concepts. (How would one define democracy?) Through it all, political scientists learn to be dispassionate yet skeptical—debating hypotheses, offering alternative explanations or measurements, questioning analyses and results, illuminating political relationships.

WHAT THIS BOOK IS (AND IS NOT) ABOUT

In this book you will learn essential empirical methods for doing your own political analysis and for critically evaluating the work of others. The first four chapters deal with the logic behind political research. In Chapter 1 we consider how to think clearly about political concepts, and we weigh the tradeoffs and problems involved in measuring concepts in the real world. In Chapter 2 you will be introduced to the essential features of explanation in political science, and you will learn to tell a good explanation from a poor one. Chapters 3 and 4 have a more practical bent—how to describe variables, test hypotheses, and take into account rival explanations. Even in these chapters, however, the emphasis is on the logic of *how* one goes about adducing facts and evaluating relationships. You will find that the great enterprise of political research has much to do with thinking about concepts, looking at relationships between variables, creating explanations, figuring out patterns, and controlling for competing processes. Political research, you will discover, is *not* statistics.

Yet you will also find that basic statistical knowledge is a key resource for the researcher—and for the consumer of political research. Suppose, for example, that you were interested in describing the size of the gender gap among voting-age adults. Although you would not enjoy the uncommon luxury of observing the entire population of women and men you wanted to study, you would have access to a sample, a smaller group of women and men drawn at random from the larger population. Two questions would arise. First, how closely does the gender gap in the sample reflect the true gender gap in the unseen population? And second, how strong is the relationship between gender and partisanship? The answer to the first (and more important) question lies in the domain of inferential statistics, the essentials of which are covered in Chapter 5 and part of Chapter 6. The answer to the second question requires a working knowledge of the most commonly used measures of association, also discussed in Chapter 6. In Chapter 7 we consider linear regression analysis, one of the more sophisticated and powerful methods having wide application in political research. And in Chapter 8 you will learn to use and interpret logistic regression, a specialized but increasingly popular technique among political scientists. This book uses a lot of examples, many of which are based on mass-level surveys of U.S. public opinion. Of course, your own substantive interests may lie elsewhere: comparative politics, international relations, public policy, judicial politics, state government, or any of a number of other areas of political research. Rest assured, the essential principles apply.

FACTS AND VALUES IN PERSPECTIVE

Political scientists long have argued among themselves about the great divide between two sorts of questions: questions of fact, *what is,* and questions of value, *what ought to be.* Often this distinction is plain and elementary. To ask whether or not wealth is equally distributed in the United States is to raise a question of fact, a question that can be addressed through definition and measurement. To ask whether or not wealth ought to be more equally distributed is to raise a question of value, a question that cannot be answered by empirical analysis. Sometimes, however, the is-ought distinction is not so clear. I might say, for example, that gun ownership is more widespread in the United States than in other countries, and I might assert further that the incidence of gun ownership is connected to gun-related crime. I might therefore offer the opinion that gun ownership ought to be restricted or banned. Fact or value? A bit of both. My opinion about gun restrictions is based on assertions about the real world, and these assertions are clearly open to empirical examination. What is the evidence for the connection between guns and crime? Are there plausible alternative explanations? You can see that, to the extent that a value judgment is based on empirical evidence, political analysis can affect opinions by shaping the reasons for holding them. Put another way: Regardless of your personal opinions about political issues, it is important to remain open to new facts and competing perspectives.

Separating one's personal opinion on an issue from objective and open-minded analysis is often easier said than done—and it requires discipline and practice. After all, politics is serious business. And it is interesting *because* it involves differing opinions and the clash of competing values. Consider the discussions and arguments you engaged in or listened to in the aftermath of the terrorist attacks of September 11, 2001. In debating the domestic implications of the attack, arguments often focused on how life in the United States *ought to* change. Many students advocated an emphasis on security—restricting immigration, permitting government authorities more latitude in detaining and arresting suspected terrorists, relaxing legal protections against searches and seizures. Other students were skeptical of such measures. They argued that the basic civil liberties of all citizens would be endangered, that the government would interpret such powers too broadly and begin to restrict any speech or activity it deemed a security risk.

There can be no doubt that you hold an opinion on this subject. How can political analysis help resolve this very serious issue? To be sure, the logic and methods you learn in this book will not show you how to "prove" which competing value—a belief in the desire for security or a belief in civil liberties—is "correct." Yet even in this highly charged debate, the protocol of political research can guide your search for the empirical bases of opinions and value judgments. What specific security vulnerabilities did the terrorists exploit? What existing laws need stricter enforcement? What new laws may be required? How has the U.S. government behaved toward its citizens during past national crises? Might not this historical data inform our current predictions about what the government will do? These questions, and countless others that you can think of, are not easily answered. But they are questions of fact, and, at least in principle, they are answerable. This book is designed to help you frame and address such questions.

THE SCIENTIFIC APPROACH

There is one other way that learning about political research can nurture your ability to analyze political relationships and events—and even to elevate the level of your own political arguments about values. This has to do with an unspoken norm that all scientists follow: *Remain open, but remain skeptical.* All science, political science included, seeks to expand our understanding of the world. To ensure that the pathway to knowledge is not blocked, we must allow entrance to all ideas and theories. Suppose, for example, that I claim that the incidence of property crime is tied to the phases of the moon. According to my "moon theory," crime increases and recedes in a predictable pattern, increasing during the new moon and decreasing during the full moon. Laughable? Maybe. But the "remain open" tenet of scientific inquiry does not permit me to be silenced. So the moon theory gains entrance.

Once on the pathway, however, any idea or theory must follow some "be skeptical" rules of the road. There are two sorts of rules. Some rules deal with evaluating questions of fact. These are sometimes called "What?" questions. Other rules deal with evaluating questions of theory. These are sometimes called "Why?" questions.

On questions of fact, scientific knowledge is not based on common sense, mysticism, or intuition. It is based on empirical observation and measurement. These observations and measurements, furthermore, must be described and performed in such a way that any other scientist could repeat them and obtain the same results. Scientific facts are empirical and reproducible. Thus if I were to claim that the moon theory occurred to me in a dream, my results would be neither empirical nor reproducible. I would fail the fundamental rules for evaluating "What?" questions. If, by contrast, I were to describe an exhaustive examination of crime rate figures, and I could show a strong relationship between these patterns and phases of the moon, then I am still on the scientific path. Another researcher, following in my procedural footsteps, would get the same results.

On questions of theory, scientific knowledge must be explanatory and testable. An idea is explanatory if it describes a causal process that connects one set of facts with another set of facts. In science, explanation involves causation. If I were to propose that moon phases and crime rates go together because criminals are reverse werewolves, only coming out when the moon is new, I would be on shaky ground. Obviously I would be relying on a fact that is neither empirical nor reproducible, plus my "explanation" would lack any sense of process or causation. But suppose I said that criminals, like all individuals, seek to minimize the risks associated with their chosen activity. A full-moon situation would represent greater risk, a greater probability of being seen and arrested. A new-moon situation would represent lower risk, a lower probability of being detected. This idea is explanatory. Using plausible assumptions about human behavior, it describes why the two sets of facts go together. One level of the causal process (greater risk) produces one outcome (lower crime rates), whereas a different level of the causal process (lower risk) produces another outcome (higher crime rates).

An idea is testable if the researcher describes a set of conditions under which the idea would be rejected. A researcher with a testable idea is saying, "If I am correct, I will find such and such to be true. If I am incorrect, I will not find such and such to be true." Suppose a skeptical observer (skeptics abound in the scientific world!), upon reading my moon theory, should say: "Your explanation is very interesting. But not all full-moon situations involve higher risk as you have defined it. Sometimes the sky is heavily overcast, creating just as much cover for criminal activity as a new-moon situation. What would the crime rate be in full moon–overcast situations?" This observer is proposing a test, a test I must be willing to accept. If my idea is correct, I should find that full moon–overcast conditions produce crime rates similar to new-moon conditions. If my idea is incorrect, I would not find this similarity. Suppose my idea fails this test. Is that the end of the road for the moon theory? Not necessarily. But I would have to take my failure into account as I rethink the causal process that I proposed originally. Suppose my idea passes this test. Would that confirm the correctness of my theory? No, again. There would be legions of skeptics on the pathway to knowledge, offering alternative theories and proposing new tests.

CONCLUSION

As you can see, political research is an ongoing enterprise. Political analysis requires clarity, questioning, intellectual exchange, and discipline. Yet it also involves openness, creativity, and imagination. Compared with politics itself, which is enormously dynamic and frequently controversial, political analysis may seem rather stodgy. The basic logic and methods— measuring and describing variables, coming up with theories, testing hypotheses, understanding statistical inference, gauging the strength of relationships—have not changed in many years. (For example, one of the techniques you will read about, chi-square, has been in use for over a century.) This is a comforting thought. The skills you learn here will be durable. They will serve you now and in the future as you read and evaluate political science. You will bring a new critical edge to the many other topics and media you encounter—election or opinion polls, journalistic accounts about the effects of medical treatments, or policy studies released by organizations with an axe to grind. And you will learn to be self-critical, clarifying the concepts you use and supporting your opinions with empirical evidence.

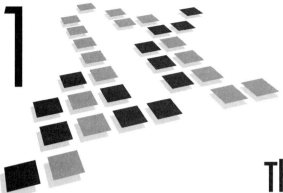

1

The Measurement of Concepts

LEARNING OBJECTIVES

In this chapter you will learn:
- The three stages of the measurement process in political research
- How to clarify the meaning of concepts
- How to write a definition for a concept
- How to identify and address problems of reliability and validity
- How to use variables to measure concepts
- How to identify different levels of measurement for variables

Think for a moment about all the political variety in the world. People vary in their party affiliation: Some are Democrats, some Republicans, and many (self-described Independents) profess no affiliation at all. Some nations are democracies, whereas others are not. Even among democracies there is variety: parliamentary systems, presidential systems, or a combination. Would-be presidential nominees run the ideological gamut from conservatism to liberalism. Each of the terms just mentioned—party affiliation, democracy, conservatism, liberalism—refers to ideas that help us discuss and describe the world. It is virtually impossible to converse about politics without using ideas such as these. Ideas, of course, are not concrete. You cannot see, taste, hear, touch, or smell "partisanship," "democracy," or "liberalism." Each of these is a **concept**, an idea or mental construct that represents phenomena in the real world. Some concepts are quite complicated, and their labels seem a bit intimidating: "globalization," "alienation," "post-modernism." Others, such as "political participation" or "social status," are somewhat simpler.

Simple or complicated, concepts are everywhere in political debate, in journalistic analysis, in ordinary discussion, and, of course, in political research. How are concepts used? In partisan or ideological debate—debates about values—concepts can evoke powerful symbols with which people easily identify. A political candidate, for example, might claim that his or her agenda will ensure "freedom," create "equality," or foster "volunteerism." These are evocative ideas, and they are meant to be. In political research, concepts are not used to stir up value-laden symbols. Quite the opposite. In empirical political science, concepts refer to facts, not values. So when political researchers discuss ideas like "freedom," "equality," or "volunteerism," they are using these ideas to summarize and label observable phenomena, characteristics in the real world.

The primary goals of political research are to describe concepts and to analyze the relationships between them. A researcher may want to know, for example, if social trust is declining or increasing in the United States, whether political elites are more tolerant of dissent than are ordinary citizens, or whether economic development causes democracy. The tasks of describing and analyzing concepts—social trust, political elites, tolerance of dissent, economic development, democracy, and any other concepts that interest us—present formidable challenges. A **conceptual question**, a question expressed using ideas, is frequently unclear and thus is difficult to answer empirically. A **concrete question**, a question expressed using tangible properties, can be answered empirically. The challenge is to somehow transform concepts into concrete terms, to express vague ideas in such a way that they can be described and analyzed.

"Are women more liberal than men?" What is the answer: yes or no? "It depends," you might say, "on what you mean by liberal. Do you mean to ask if women are more likely than men to support abortion, gun control, government support of education, spending to assist poor people, environmental protection, affirmative action, gay rights, funding for drug rehabilitation, or what? Do you mean all of these things, some of these things, none of these things, or completely different things?" That is the challenge for the political researcher. The same concept can refer to a variety of different characteristics. "Liberal," for some, may mean support for gun control. For someone else, the concept might refer to support for environmental protection. Still others may think that support for government spending to assist poor people is the real meaning of liberalism.

Researchers want to describe concepts, such as "liberal" or "liberalism," and they seek to answer conceptual questions, such as "Are women more liberal than men?" But to answer a conceptual question, the researcher first must define the concept in unambiguous language that everyone understands. The researcher must then describe an instrument for measuring the concept in the real world and, finally, obtain empirical measurements of the concept. These three stages—defining a concept, describing how it is to be measured, and obtaining measurements—are the three stages of the measurement process in political research.

Figure 1-1 shows a schematic of the measurement process. A **conceptual definition** restates a concept in unambiguous terms. It clearly describes the concept's properties, and it communicates the subjects (people, nations, states, and so on) to which the concept applies. An **operational definition** describes the instrument to be used in measuring the concept, for putting a conceptual definition "into operation." It provides a procedural blueprint, a measurement strategy. A **variable** records the measurement of the concept. It is the empirical reading we end up with when we implement the operational definition.

In this chapter we consider each stage in the measurement process. First, we discuss how to define a concept. In thinking about concepts and defining them, the researcher keeps an eye trained on the empirical world: What are the measurable characteristics of this concept? Second, we look at problems that emerge when researchers decide on an operational definition. In describing a measurement strategy, the researcher keeps an eye trained on the conceptual world: Does this operational definition accurately reflect the definition of the concept? Third, we look at variables, the empirical measurements of concepts. At this stage, the researcher focuses on precision: How precisely does this variable measure the concept?

Figure 1-1   The Measurement Process

Concept ⟶ Conceptual definition ⟶ Operational definition ⟶ Variable

STAGE ONE: HOW TO DEFINE A CONCEPT

The conceptual definition stage of the measurement process involves two closely related activities: clarifying the empirical properties of a concept and writing a definition of the concept. In clarifying a concept, the researcher makes an inventory of the concept's properties and decides which of these properties represents the best way to measure the concept. This decision, as we shall see, often requires difficult tradeoffs. After clarifying a concept, the researcher writes down a definition of the concept. In this written definition, the researcher communicates the subjects to which the concept applies and suggests a measurement strategy. Let's discuss these steps by working through an extended example.

Clarifying a Concept

Suppose you are interested in studying the effects of religion on politics in the United States. You may wonder, for example, whether religion has declined or increased in importance to various groups. Are young people less religious than older people? Are low-income people more religious than high-income people? Do women have higher levels of religiosity than men? Do less religious people hold different political opinions than more religious people? Notice two things about these questions. First, each is a conceptual question, because each uses the intangible terms *religious* or *religiosity*. Conceptual questions, as we have seen, do not readily admit to empirical, measurable answers. However, we know that the conceptual term "religiosity" represents a concrete characteristic of people. After all, when we say that a person or group of people is "religious," we must have some attributes or characteristics in mind. Second, each question asks whether religiosity varies between groups of people, whether some people have more or less of these attributes or characteristics than other people. When we ask if some people are more religious than others, we must be thinking of characteristics that differ or vary between people. Some have more and others have less of these characteristics. Thus, to clarify a concept, we need to identify characteristics that are concrete and that vary. The term "religiosity" refers to a characteristic or set of characteristics that vary between people. What, exactly, are these characteristics?

A mental exercise can help you to identify characteristics that are concrete and that vary. Think of two subjects, one having a great deal of the concept's characteristics and the other having none of the characteristics. What images of a very religious person do you see in your mind's eye? Of a very nonreligious person? In constructing these images, be open and inclusive. Here is an example of what you may come up with:

A religious person:	A nonreligious person:
Always attends religious services	Never attends religious services
Opposes abortion	Favors abortion
Says religion is the "most important thing in life"	Says religion is "not important at all"
Prays regularly	Never prays
Believes in a supreme deity	Does not believe in a supreme deity
Supports school prayer	Opposes school prayer

Thinking up polar opposites is an open-ended, creative process, and it always produces the raw materials from which a conceptual definition can be built. Once the inventory is made, however, we need to become more critical and discerning. Consider, for example, the second characteristic. According to the list, a religious person "opposes abortion" whereas a nonreligious person "favors abortion." Think about this for a moment. Are opinions about abortion really part of the concept of religiosity? Put another way: Can we think about what it means to be religious or nonreligious without thinking about opinions on abortion? You would probably agree that we could.

This is a common problem that occurs when we clarify a concept. We often come up with traits that seem to fit well with the portraits of our imaginary subjects but are not essential to the concept. The opposing characteristics "supports school prayer" and "opposes school prayer" provide another example. In brainstorming the concept of religiosity, we wanted to capture its essence, so we needed to cast a wide, creative net. We were open and inclusive. But in honing the concept, we need to be more critical. Can you think about the essential characteristics of a religious person and a nonreligious person without considering opinions on school prayer? To be sure, religiosity may be related to opinions on political issues such as abortion and school prayer, but the concept is itself distinct from these opinions.

Now let's reconsider our newly abbreviated inventory:

A religious person:	A nonreligious person:
Always attends religious services	Never attends religious services
Says religion is the "most important thing in life"	Says religion is "not important at all"
Prays regularly	Never prays
Believes in a supreme deity	Does not believe in a supreme deity

Each of these four attributes would seem to be properties of the concept. But continue to be critical. Examine the list carefully. Suppose you had to choose one attribute that best captures the essential difference between a religious person and a nonreligious person. Which one would you choose—and why? You may have noticed that two characteristics— "always/never attends religious services" and "prays regularly/never prays"—refer to how people act, their behavior. The other characteristics—"says religion is 'the most important thing in life'/'not important at all' " and "believes/does not believe in a supreme deity"—refer to what people say about their beliefs. What do you think? Are the acts of attending services and praying the core characteristics of a religious person? And is an individual who engages in neither activity a clear example of a nonreligious person? Or is the expression of deep belief the key to religiosity?

This is a difficult choice, but it is just the sort of choice political researchers often must make. Political research begins with concepts and asks how these concepts might be clarified and measured empirically. Suppose we should decide to use one of the behavioral differences between our mirror-image individuals, the frequency with which they attend religious services, as the essential characteristic of religiosity. In doing so, we would be choosing to ignore other aspects of the concept.

Conceptual thinking requires such tradeoffs, because it requires that we abstract from a vague idea its most essential empirical features. Unlike the common usage of the word, in which an abstract idea is often considered cerebral and complex, in political science **abstraction** is the process of clarifying a concept by describing its most essential features. These observable characteristics, such as those produced by our mental exercise on the concept of religiosity, are sometimes called indicators, appropriately enough, because they give us a tangible indication of an intangible construct. The next step in connecting concepts and measurement is to lay a solid foundation, an unambiguous conceptual definition.

A Template for Writing a Conceptual Definition

A conceptual definition must, at a minimum, communicate three things:

1. The variation within a characteristic
2. The subjects or groups of subjects to which the concept applies
3. How the characteristic is to be measured

Following is a workable template for stating a conceptual definition that meets all three requirements:

> The concept of _____ is defined as the extent to which _____ exhibit the characteristic of _____ .

For religiosity, we would fill in our template as follows:

> The concept of <u>religiosity</u> is defined as the extent to which <u>individuals</u> exhibit the characteristic of <u>attending religious services</u>.

The first term, *religiosity*, when combined with the words "the extent to which," restates the concept's label and communicates the polar-opposite variation at the heart of the concept. The second term, *individuals*, states the subjects to whom the concept applies. The third term, *attending religious services*, suggests the concept's measurement. Let's consider the template in more detail.

By referring to a subject or group of subjects, a conceptual definition conveys the units of analysis. A **unit of analysis** is the entity (person, city, country, county, university, state, bureaucratic agency, etc.) we want to describe and analyze, the entity to which the concept applies. Units of analysis can be either individual-level or aggregate-level. When a concept describes a phenomenon at its lowest possible level, it is using an **individual-level unit of analysis**. Most polling or survey research deals with concepts that apply to individual persons, perhaps the most common individual-level units of analysis you will encounter. Individual-level units are not always persons, however. If you were conducting research on the political themes contained in the Democratic and Republican Party platforms over the past several elections, the units of analysis would be the individual platforms from each year. Similarly, if you were interested in finding out whether environmental legislation was a high priority in Congress, you might examine each bill that is introduced as an individual unit of analysis.

Much political science research deals with the **aggregate-level unit of analysis**, which is a collection of individual entities. Neighborhoods or census tracts are aggregate-level units, as are congressional districts, states, and nations. A university administrator who wondered if student satisfaction is affected by class size would gather information on each class, an aggregation of individual students. Someone wanting to know whether states with lenient voter registration laws had higher turnout than states with stricter laws could use legal statistics and voting data from fifty aggregate-level units of analysis, the states. Notice that collections of

Table 1-1 Individual Opinions and Aggregate Opinion at Two Points in Time

	Favor increased spending?	
Level	*Opinion at time 1*	*Opinion at time 2*
Individual		
A	Yes	No
B	No	Yes
C	Yes	No
D	No	Yes
Aggregate	2 Yes, 2 No	2 Yes, 2 No

individual entities, and thus overall aggregate levels, can vary in size. For example, both congressional districts and states are aggregate-level units of analysis—both are collections of individuals within politically defined geographic areas—but states usually represent a higher level of aggregation, because they are composed of more individual entities. Notice too that the same concept often can be defined at both the individual and aggregate levels. Dwell on this point for a moment. Just as religiosity can be defined for individual persons, religiosity can be defined for states as the level of religious observance manifested by all state residents. For statistical reasons, however, the relationship between two aggregate-level concepts usually cannot be used to make inferences about the relationship at the individual level. If you were to find, for example, that high-religiosity states have higher voter turnouts than low-religiosity states, you could not conclude that highly religious individuals are more likely to vote than less religious individuals.

A classic problem, known as the **ecological fallacy**, arises when an aggregate-level phenomenon is used to make inferences at the individual level. By way of illustration, consider a hypothetical group composed of four individual people, A, B, C, and D. Suppose someone wants to investigate this group's opinion on social welfare spending at two points in time. Did the group's opinion grow more favorable toward spending, did the group become more opposed, or has group opinion remained stable over time? This question is framed at the aggregate level. It asks about the opinion of a collection of four individual entities, all members of the group taken as a whole. Now consider Table 1-1, which reports the "results" of the investigation.

Clearly, the group's opinion did not change at all. Aggregate opinion on whether social welfare spending should be increased was divided evenly between "Yes" and "No" responses at time 1, and it was evenly divided at time 2. So aggregate opinion remained stable. Can we infer from this observation that individual opinions were stable? Clearly not. A change in individual A's opinion from "Yes" to "No" was offset by a change in individual B's opinion from "No" to "Yes." Individuals C and D made a similar switch. Total opinion, then, did not change, but individual opinions changed a lot.

Indeed, scholars who study American public opinion at the aggregate level find remarkable stability. Aggregate opinion changes slowly, not ordinarily given to capricious ups and downs. Scholars who study public opinion at the individual level find remarkable instability, a shifting of opinions from one point in time to the next.[1] Obviously, a proper conceptual definition needs to specify the units of analysis. The researcher must be clear about the units in which he or she is interested.

STAGE TWO: OPERATIONAL DEFINITIONS

In suggesting how the concept is to be measured, a conceptual definition points the way to a clear operational definition.[2] An operational definition describes explicitly how the concept is to be measured empirically. Just how would we determine the extent to which people attend religious services? Would we stand at the church entrance and count heads? Would we develop a questionnaire and interview people? Which people? Would we talk to them face-to-face or over the phone, or would we send the survey through the mail? What questions would provide us with a faithful measurement of each respondent's level of religious observance? This stage of the measurement process, the stage between conceptual definition and operational definition, is often the most difficult to traverse. To illustrate some of these difficulties, we describe an example from public opinion research, the study of the concept of political tolerance.

Political tolerance is important to many students of democracy because, arguably, democratic health can be maintained only if people remain open to different ways of thinking and solving problems. If tolerance is low, then democratic procedures will be weakly supported, and the free exchange of ideas might be threatened. Political tolerance is a rather complex concept, and a large body of research and commentary is devoted to it.[3] For our more limited purpose here, consider the following conceptual definition:

> The concept of political tolerance is defined as the extent to which individuals exhibit the characteristic of expressing a willingness to allow basic political freedoms for unpopular groups.

Awkward syntax aside, this is a serviceable definition, and it has been the starting point for a generation of scholars interested in studying the concept. Beginning in the 1950s, the earliest research "operationalized" political tolerance by asking large numbers of individuals if certain procedural freedoms (for example, giving a speech or publishing a book) should be extended to members of specific groups: atheists, communists, and socialists. This seemed like a reasonable operational definition because, at the time at least, these groups represented ideas outside the conformist mainstream and were generally considered unpopular. And the main finding was somewhat unsettling: Whereas those in positions of political leadership expressed high levels of tolerance, the public-at-large appeared much less willing to allow basic freedoms for these groups.

Later research, however, pointed to important slippage between the conceptual definition, which clarified and defined the important properties of political tolerance, and the operational definition, the procedure used to measure political tolerance. The original investigators had themselves chosen which unpopular groups were outside the mainstream, and these groups tended to have a left-wing or left-leaning ideological bent. The researchers were therefore gauging tolerance only toward those groups. A better measurement strategy, one more faithful to the concept, would allow respondents *themselves* to name the groups they most strongly oppose—that is, the groups most unpopular with or disliked by each person being surveyed. Individuals would then be asked about extending civil liberties to the groups they had identified, not those picked beforehand by the researchers. Interestingly, this superior measurement strategy led to equally unsettling findings: Just about everyone, elites and non-elites alike, expressed rather anemic levels of political tolerance toward the groups they liked the least.

Measurement Error

In deciding how to measure a concept, researchers seek an instrument that maximizes the congruence or "fit" between the concept and the empirical measure of the concept. The researcher asks, "Does this operational instrument measure the characteristic that I intend for it to measure? If so, does it measure *only* that characteristic? Or might it also be gauging a characteristic that I did not intend for it to measure?" Students of political tolerance are interested in asking individuals a set of questions that accurately gauge their willingness to extend freedoms to unpopular groups. The first measurement of tolerance did not accurately measure this characteristic. Why not? Because it was measuring a characteristic that it was not supposed to measure: individuals' attitudes toward left-wing groups. To be sure, the original measurement procedure was tapping some intended characteristic of tolerance. After all, a thoroughly tolerant person would not be willing to restrict the freedoms of any unpopular group, regardless of the group's ideological leanings, whereas a completely intolerant person would express a willingness to do so. When the conceptual definition was operationalized, however, an unintended characteristic, individuals' biases toward leftist groups, also was being measured. Thus the measurement strategy created a poor fit, an inaccurate link, between the concept of tolerance and the empirical measurement of the concept.

Two sorts of error can distort the linkage between a concept and its empirical measure. Serious problems arise when **systematic measurement error** is at work. Systematic error introduces consistent, chronic distortion into an empirical measurement. Often called measurement bias, systematic error produces operational readings that consistently mismeasure the characteristic the researcher is after. The original tolerance measure suffered from systematic measurement error, because subjects with liberal ideological leanings were consistently (and incorrectly) measured as more tolerant than were ideologically conservative subjects. Less serious, but still troublesome, problems occur when **random measurement error** is present. Random error introduces haphazard, chaotic distortion into the measurement process, producing inconsistent operational readings of a concept. To appreciate the difference between these two kinds of error, and to see how each affects measurement, consider an example.

Suppose that a math instructor wishes to test the math ability of a group of students. This measurement is operationalized by ten word problems covering basic features of math. First let's ask, "Does this operational instrument measure the characteristic that the instructor intends for it to measure?" Well, it seems clear that *some* part of the operational measure will capture the intended characteristic, students' actual knowledge of math. But let's press the measurement question a bit further: "Does the instructor's operational instrument measure *only* the intended characteristic, math ability? Or might it also be gauging a characteristic that the instructor did not intend for it to measure?" We know that, quite apart from mathematical competence, students vary in their verbal skills. Some students can read and understand the math problems more quickly than others. Thus the exam is picking up a characteristic it is not supposed to measure—verbal ability.

You can probably think of other characteristics that would "hitch a ride" on the instructor's test measure. In fact, a large class of unintended attributes are often at work when human subjects are the units of analysis. This phenomenon, dubbed the **Hawthorne effect**, inadvertently measures a subject's response to the knowledge that he or she is being studied. Test anxiety is a well-known example of the Hawthorne effect. Despite their actual grasp of a subject, some students become overly nervous simply by being tested, and their exam scores will be systematically depressed by the presence of test anxiety.[4]

Notice two aspects of the kind of unintended characteristics we have been discussing. First, characteristics such as verbal ability and test anxiety are durable, not likely to change very much over time. If the test were administered again the next day or the following week, the test scores of the same students, those with fewer verbal skills or more test anxiety, would yield consistently poor measures of their math ability. Think of two students, both having the same levels of mathematical competence but one having less verbal ability than the other. The instructor's operational instrument will report a persistent difference in math ability between these students when, in fact, no difference exists. Second, this consistent bias is inherent in the measurement instrument. When the instructor constructed a test using word problems, a measure of the unwanted characteristic, verbal ability, was built directly into the operational definition. This is how systematic error affects the measurement process. Systematic error produces consistently inaccurate measures of a concept. The source of systematic error resides—often unseen by the researcher—in the measurement strategy itself.

Now consider some temporary or idiosyncratic factors that might come into play during the instructor's math exam. Some students may be ill or tired whereas others may be well rested. Students sitting near the door may be distracted by commotion outside the classroom whereas others, sitting farther away, are unaffected. Commuting students may have been delayed by traffic congestion caused by a fender-bender near campus, and so, arriving late, they may be pressed for time. The instructor may make errors in grading the tests, accidentally increasing the scores of some students and decreasing the scores of others.

These factors are not durable. They are not consistent across students, and they may or may not be present in the same student if the test were administered again the next day or the following week. Chaotic, unexpected events—commotion, broken pencils, annoying distractions—certainly can affect the operational readings of a concept, but they are not built into the operational definition itself. Rather, these factors intrude from outside the instrument. This is how random error affects the measurement process. Idiosyncratic events and characteristics introduce haphazard, external "noise" that may temporarily and inconsistently affect the measurement of a concept. Temporary factors that are picked up by an operational measure produce inconsistent measures of a concept.

Reliability and Validity
We can effectively use the language of measurement error to evaluate the pros and cons of a particular measurement strategy. For example, we could say that the earliest measure of political tolerance, though perhaps having a small amount of random error, contained a large amount of systematic error. And the hypothetical math instructor's measurement sounds like it had a dose of both kinds of error—measurement bias introduced by systematic differences between students in verbal ability and test anxiety, and random error that intruded via an array of haphazard occurrences. Typically, researchers do not evaluate a measure by making direct reference to the amount of systematic error or random error it may contain. Instead they discuss two criteria of measurement: reliability and validity. However, reliability and validity can be understood in terms of measurement error.

The **reliability** of a measurement is the extent to which it is a consistent measure of a concept. A reliable measure gives the same reading every time it is taken. Applying the ideas we just discussed, we see that a completely reliable measure is one that contains no random error. A measure need not be free of systematic error to be reliable. It just needs to be consistent. Consider a nonsensical example that nonetheless illustrates the point. Suppose a researcher gauges the degree to which the public approves of government spending by using a laser measuring device to precisely record respondents' heights in centimeters, with higher numbers of centimeters denoting stronger approval for spending. This researcher's measure would be quite reliable, because it would contain very little random error and would therefore be consistent. But it would clearly be gauging a concept completely different from opinions about government spending. In a more realistic vein, suppose the math instructor recognized the problems caused by random occurrences and took steps to greatly reduce these sources of random error. Certainly his measurement of math ability would now be more consistent, more reliable. However, it would not reflect the true math ability of students, because it would still contain systematic error. More generally, although reliability is a desirable criterion of measurement—any successful effort to purge a measure of random error is a good thing—it is a weaker criterion than validity.

The **validity** of a measurement is the extent to which it records the true value of the characteristic the researcher intends to measure. A valid measure provides a clear, unobstructed link between a concept and the empirical reading of the concept. Framed in terms of measurement error, the defining feature of a valid measure is that it contains no systematic error, no bias that consistently pulls the measurement off the true value. Suppose a researcher gauges opinions toward government spending by asking each respondent to indicate his or her position on a 7-point scale, from "spending should be increased" on the left to "spending should be decreased" on the right. Is this a valid measure? Below we see that a measure's validity is harder to establish than is its reliability. But it seems reasonable to say that this measurement instrument is free from systematic error and thus would closely reflect respondents' true opinions on the issue. Or suppose the math instructor tries to alleviate the sources of systematic error inherent in his test instrument—switching from word problems to a format based on mathematical symbols, and perhaps easing anxiety by shortening the exam or lengthening the allotted time. These reforms would reduce systematic error, strengthen the connection between true math ability and the measurement of math ability, and thus enhance the validity of the test.

Suppose we have a measurement that contains no systematic error but contains some random error. Would this be a valid measure? Can a measurement be valid but not reliable? Although we find conflicting scholarly answers to this question, let's settle on a qualified yes.[5] Instead of considering a measurement as either not valid or valid, think of validity as a continuum, with "not valid" at one end and "valid" at the other. An operational instrument that has serious measurement bias, lots of systematic error, would reside at the "not valid" pole, regardless of the amount of random error it contains. The early measure of political tolerance is an example. An instrument with no systematic error and no random error would be at the "valid" end. Such a measure would return an accurate reading of the characteristic that the researcher intends to measure, and it would do so with perfect consistency. The math instructor's reformed measurement process—changing the instrument to remove systematic error, taking pains to reduce random error—would be close to this pole. Now consider two measures of the same concept, neither of which contains systematic error, but one of which contains less random error. Because both measures vanquish measurement bias, both would fall on the "valid" side of the continuum. But the more consistent measure would be closer to the "valid" pole.

Approaches to Evaluating Reliability and Validity

To evaluate the quality of a measurement, the researcher must answer two questions: (1) What kind of error is at work? and (2) To what extent is it affecting the measurement process? In the case of systematic error, these questions are difficult to answer. The researcher might be able to identify the sources of systematic error and suggest how it is affecting measurement, but the size of this effect usually remains unknown. In the case of random measurement error, these questions are addressed more easily. Odd as it may sound, researchers always assume that some random error is in play. As a practical matter, idiosyncratic factors are simply too numerous to identify and eliminate. As a statistical matter, however, the amount of random noise in a measurement can be estimated with a fair degree of confidence. Methods for evaluating the reliability of a measurement are designed around this assumption: If a measurement is reliable, it will yield consistent results, give or take an acceptable amount of random measurement error. What constitutes an "acceptable amount" of random error? This question is addressed in Chapter 5, when we discuss the role of random processes in political research. For now, let's take a brief look at some practical approaches to evaluating reliability. We then turn to the more difficult problem of evaluating validity.

The **test-retest method** is an intuitive approach to assessing reliability: Apply the measure once, and then apply it again to the same group of subjects. Thus the math instructor would give the exam, record the scores, and then administer the test again at a later time. If the measurement is reliable, then the two results should be the same or very similar. If a great deal of random measurement error is present, then the two results will be very different. The use of this method on human subjects, of course, has a clear limitation, particularly if the measurement instrument is a survey questionnaire or a test aimed at evaluating skills. Suppose the math instructor administers the ten-item test, administers it again the following week, and then assesses reliability by comparing the two scores. Upon seeing the test a second time, most students will remember the questions, and others may have figured out the answers during the interval between the tests. So the process of being measured the first time will affect the second measurement. Researchers have devised some ways to work around this problem. The **split-half method**, for example, is based on the idea that an operational measurement obtained from half of the test items should be the same as the measurement obtained from the other half. Using the split-half method, the math instructor would test for reliability by seeing if students' scores on five of the questions were the same as their scores on the other five questions.[6]

Reliability is an important and sought-after criterion of measurement. Most of the standardized tests you have encountered—or will encounter—are known for their reliability. The SAT, the Law School Admission Test (LSAT), the Graduate Record Examination (GRE), among others, all return consistent measurements. But of course the continuing and often controversial debate about such tests does not center on their reliability. It centers, instead, on their validity: Do these exams measure what they are supposed to measure and only what they are supposed to measure? Critics argue that because many of these tests' questions assume a familiarity with white, middle-class culture, they do not produce valid measurements of aptitudes and skills. Recall again the earliest measurements of political tolerance, which gauged the concept by asking respondents whether basic freedoms should be extended to specific groups: atheists, communists, and socialists. Because several different studies used this operationalization and produced similar findings, the measure was a reliable one. The problem was that a durable unintended characteristic, the respondents' attitudes toward left-wing groups, was "on board" as well, giving a consistent if inaccurate measurement of the concept. The challenge of assessing validity is to identify durable unintended characteristics that are being gauged by an operational measure, that is, to identify the sources of systematic error.

Validity is a thorny issue in political research, because no set procedure exists for establishing the validity of a measurement. To be sure, some sources of systematic error, such as verbal skills or test anxiety, are widely recognized threats to validity. These sources can be identified, and steps can be taken to ameliorate their effects. In most situations, however, less well-known sources of systematic error might be affecting validity. How can these problems be identified? There are two general ways to evaluate validity.

In one approach, the researcher closely examines an operational procedure and relies on informed judgment. "On the face of it," the researcher asks, "are there good reasons to think that this measure is not an accurate gauge of the intended characteristic?" This is the **face validity** approach. In the other approach, the researcher examines the empirical relationships between a measurement and other concepts to which it should be related. Here the researcher asks, "Does this measurement have relationships with other concepts that one would expect it to have?" This is the **construct validity** approach. Let's look at an example of each approach.

Responses to the following agree-disagree question have been used by survey researchers to measure the concept of political efficacy, the extent to which individuals believe that they can have an effect on government: "Voting is the only way that people like me can have any say about how the government runs things." According to the question's operational design, a person with a low level of political efficacy would see few opportunities for influencing government beyond voting and thus would give an "agree" response. A more efficacious person would feel that other avenues exist for "people like me" and so would tend to "disagree." But examine the survey instrument closely. Using informed judgment, address the face validity question: Are there good reasons to think that this instrument would not produce an accurate measurement of the intended characteristic, political efficacy? Think of an individual or group of individuals whose sense of efficacy is so weak that they view any act of political participation, including voting, as an exercise in political futility. At the conceptual level, one would certainly consider such people to have a low amount of the intended characteristic. But how might they respond to the survey question? Quite reasonably, they could say "disagree," a response that would measure them as having a large amount of the intended characteristic. Taken at face value, then, this survey question is not a valid measure.[7]

This example underscores a general problem posed by threats to validity. An informed observer sometimes can identify potential sources of systematic error and suggest how this error is affecting the operational measure. Thus people with low and durable levels of efficacy might be measured, instead, as being politically efficacious. However, it is difficult to know the size of this effect. How many people are being measured inaccurately? A few? Many? Again, unlike random measurement error, systematic measurement error cannot be estimated with any degree of confidence.

The second approach to evaluating validity, construct validity, assesses the association between the measure of a concept and another concept to which it should be related. This is a reasonable approach to the problem. For example, if the GRE is a valid measure of students' readiness for graduate school, then GRE scores should be strongly related to subsequent grade point averages earned by graduate students. If the GRE is an inaccurate measure of readiness, then this relationship will be weak.[8]

Here is an example from political science. For many years, the National Election Study has provided a measurement of the concept of party identification, the extent to which individuals feel a sense of loyalty or attachment to one of the major political parties. This concept is measured by a 7-point scale. Each person is classified as a Strong Democrat, Weak Democrat, Independent-leaning Democrat, Independent–no partisan leanings, Independent-leaning Republican, Weak Republican, or Strong Republican. Applying the face validity approach, this

Table 1-2 The Relationship Between Party Identification
and Campaign Activity

Party identification	Percentage engaging in at least one campaign activity[a]
Strong Democrat	53
Weak Democrat	34
Independent-leaning Democrat	43
Independent	28
Independent-leaning Republican	47
Weak Republican	43
Strong Republican	57

Source: Nancy Burns, Donald R. Kinder, Steven J. Rosenstone, Virginia Sapiro, and the National Election Studies, *American National Election Studies 2000: Pre- and Post-election Survey*, 2nd version (Ann Arbor: University of Michigan, Center for Political Studies [producer], 2001; Inter-university Consortium for Political and Social Research [distributor], 2002).

[a] Campaign activities include the following: trying to influence the vote choice of others; displaying a button, sticker, or sign; going to meetings or rallies; performing campaign work; contributing money to a candidate; contributing money to a party; contributing money to any other political group that supported or opposed candidates.

measure is difficult to fault. Following an initial gauge of direction (Democrat, Independent, Republican), interviewers meticulously lead respondents through a series of probes, recording gradations in the strength of their partisan attachments: strongly partisan, weakly partisan, independent-but-leaning partisan, and purely independent.[9] Durable unintended characteristics are not readily apparent in this measurement strategy. But let's apply the construct validity approach. If the 7-point scale accurately measures strength of party identification, then it should bear predictable relationships to other concepts.

For example, we would expect strongly partisan people, whether Democrats or Republicans, to engage in much campaigning during an election—displaying bumper stickers, wearing buttons, trying to persuade others how to vote, attending rallies, or perhaps donating money to one of the parties. By the same token, we would expect weak partisans to engage in fewer of these activities, independent "leaners" fewer still, and independents the fewest of all. That is the logic of construct validity. If the 7-point scale is a valid measure of partisan strength, then it should relate to clearly partisan behaviors, campaign activities, in an expected way. How does the concept of party identification fare in this test of its validity?

Table 1-2, based on information from the 2000 National Election Study, shows the empirical relationship between the 7-point party identification measurement and a measurement of campaigning. The numbers in the table were calculated by figuring out the percentage of Strong Democrats who engaged in at least one campaign activity during the election, the percentage of Weak Democrats who engaged in at least one activity, and so on for each of the groups along the party identification scale. Notice that, as expected, people at the strongly partisan poles, Strong Democrats and Strong Republicans, were the most likely to report campaign behavior. More than half of each of these groups engaged in at least one campaign act. And, again as expected, pure independents were the least likely to engage in partisan activity. But, beyond these expectations, is anything amiss here? Notice that Weak Democrats, measured as having stronger party ties than independent-leaning Democrats, were less likely to campaign than were independent-Democratic "leaners." A similar comparison at the Republican side of the scale—Weak Republicans compared with Independent-Republican "leaners"—shows the same thing: Weak partisans behaved in a less partisan manner than people measured as Independent with partisan leanings.

Scholars who have examined the relationships between the 7-point scale and other concepts also have found patterns similar to that shown in Table 1-2.[10] In applying the construct validity approach, we can use empirical relationships such as that displayed in Table 1-2 to evaluate an operational measure. What would we conclude from this example about the validity of this measurement of partisanship? Clearly the measure is tapping some aspect of the intended characteristic. After all, the scale "behaves as it should" among strong partisans and pure independents. But how would one account for the unexpected behavior of weak partisans and independent leaners? What durable unintended characteristic might the scale also be measuring? Some have suggested that the scale is tapping two durable characteristics: one's degree of partisanship (the intended characteristic) and one's degree of independence (an unintended characteristic). These scholars believe that the two concepts, partisanship and independence, should be measured separately.[11] There is, to put it mildly, spirited debate on this and other questions about the measurement of party identification.[12]

Rest assured that debates about validity in political science are not academic games of "gotcha," with one researcher proposing an operational measure and another researcher marshaling empirical evidence to shoot it down. Rather, the debate is productive. It is centered on identifying potential sources of systematic error, and it is aimed at improving the quality of widely used operational measures. It bears emphasizing, as well, that although the problem of validity is a concern for the entire enterprise of political analysis, some research is more prone to it than others. A student of state politics could obtain a valid measure of the concept of state-supported education fairly directly, by calculating a state's per-capita spending on education. A congressional scholar would validly measure the concept of party cohesion by figuring out, across a series of votes, the percentage of times a majority of Democrats opposed a majority of Republicans. In these examples, the connection between the concept and its operational definition is direct and easy to recognize. By contrast, researchers interested in individual-level surveys of mass opinion, as the above examples illustrate, often face tougher questions of validity.

STAGE THREE: VARIABLES

The operational definition of a concept provides a blueprint for its measurement. When we follow through on the plan, when we construct what the blueprint describes, we end up with a variable. A variable is an empirical measurement of a characteristic. Recall the example of religiosity, which we defined as the extent to which individuals exhibit the characteristic of attending religious services. What would be an empirical measurement of religiosity? How would we measure the characteristic of attendance at religious services? As a measurement strategy, suppose we devise a questionnaire and administer it to a large number of individual persons, our units of analysis. One of the questions in the survey, which we name "self-reported frequency of attendance at religious services," asks respondents to choose the answer that best reflects their attendance: Do they attend "weekly," "almost weekly," "once or twice a month," or "yearly," or do they "never attend?" This is our measurement blueprint. The label, "self-reported frequency of attendance at religious services," is the name of the variable on which we want to obtain measurements. By examining responses to the survey question, we will be able to place the units of analysis into five different categories: "weekly," "almost weekly," "once or twice a month," "yearly," or "never." These five different categories are the values of the variable. The first respondent might say "once or twice a month," whereas the second respondent says "never." These two respondents have different values on the same variable, named "self-reported frequency of attendance at religious services." Similarly, Democrat, Republican, and Independent are three values of the variable named "party identification"; Northeast, Midwest, South, and West are four values of a variable named "region"; less than high school, high school, some college, and college graduate are four values of a variable named "level of education."

Students often are confused about the distinction between a variable's name and the variable's values. Suppose you are collecting information on the height, in inches, of each of your classmates. What is the variable's name? What are its values? If you have difficulty sorting this out, think of one unit of analysis and ask this question, "What is this unit's _____?" The word that completes the question is always the name of a variable. You would ask, "What is this classmate's height?" So the term that completes the question, *height,* is the name of the variable. The answer to the question is always a value. So, for example, "67 inches" is one of the values of the variable named height.[13]

Some variables, such as age, may take on many values.[14] Others, such as race, have only a few possible values. However, a variable must have at least two possible values. Beyond this fundamental requirement, however, variables can differ in how precisely they measure a characteristic. Suppose you were purchasing a car and had the choice of two speedometers. One reported speed in a familiar way, by a dial that pointed to the car's speed in miles per hour. The other (a less expensive option, we assume) consisted of a dash-mounted sign that flashed the words *slow* or *fast*. Measurements of the variable, speed, that were made by the "slow-fast" speedometer would produce two possible values and so would meet the minimum requirement for a variable. But we clearly would prefer the instrument that made more precise distinctions. We would prefer an instrument that had a higher level of measurement.

Levels of Measurement

Researchers distinguish three levels—three "degrees of precision"—with which a variable measures an empirical characteristic. Nominal variables are the least precise. A **nominal-level variable** has values that communicate differences between subjects on the characteristic being measured. We might measure religious denomination by four values: Protestant, Catholic, Jewish, and other religion. The values of the variable tell us that subjects having one value, such as Protestant, differ from subjects that have another value, such as Catholic. This would be a nominal-level variable, since each value represents a different category of the measured characteristic. Ordinal variables are more precise than nominal-level variables. An **ordinal-level variable** has values that communicate relative differences between subjects on the characteristic being measured. Support for abortion measured by three values—oppose, neutral, and support—would be an ordinal-level variable, because each value measures the variable in relation to other values of the variable. How much more support is "neutral" than "oppose?" The values do not tell us the exact difference, but they do permit us to say that a subject who is neutral is more supportive than a subject who is opposed and is less supportive than a subject who supports abortion. Interval variables give the most precise measurements. An **interval-level variable** has values that communicate exact differences between subjects on the measured characteristic. Age measured in years, for example, is an interval-level variable, since each of its values—18 years, 24 years, 77 years, and so on—measures the exact amount of the variable. How much difference exists between a subject with 24 years and a subject with 18 years? Exactly 6 years. Interval-level variables are considered the "highest" level of measurement because their values impart precise information and permit the researcher to gauge fine differences between units of analysis.[15]

When constructing a variable, the researcher seeks the highest possible degree of precision. Simply by their nature, some characteristics are easier than others to measure precisely. Some characteristics can be quantified readily. Such characteristics can be measured by a common scale of standard units that everyone understands. If someone were to ask you, "What distance do you drive each day?" your response could be gauged easily by an interval-level value, such as "16 miles." Notice that this value is a not simply a number. It is a number that uses a standard unit of measurement, miles, that communicates the exact quantity of the characteristic. The researcher would easily determine that your response is different from someone else's answer (such as "15 miles"), that you drive farther each day (because 16 miles is greater than 15 miles), and that the two responses are separated by exactly one unit on a commonly recognized scale (1 mile). That is the field mark of an interval-level variable. The values of an interval-level variable allow you to gauge exact differences between subjects on a measured characteristic.

It is not difficult to think of interval-level variables in everyday life: the liquid volume of a can of soda, the length of a semester, the score of a baseball game, the percentage of one's time devoted to studying. When political researchers are using aggregate-level units of analysis, interval variables are common, as well. A student of state politics might measure the percentage of eligible voters who turned out in the gubernatorial election, the number of days before an election that state citizens may register, or the size (in dollars) of the state's education budget. A student of comparative politics might record the number of years that the same regime has been in power in a country, or the percentage of the country's budget spent on national defense. A student of interest groups may want to know membership size, number of years since the group's founding, or the cost of joining.

When political researchers are analyzing individual-level units of analysis, such as survey respondents, nominal-level variables and ordinal-level variables are much more common than interval-level variables. There are two reasons for this situation. First, many characteristics of interest are by nature not quantifiable. Gender, race, and religious denomination are examples of such characteristics. These attributes are measured by variables having nominal-level values. Second, some characteristics are quantifiable, at least in principle, but they lack a known scale that would permit interval-level measurement. One's level of political interest, whether one supports or opposes gun control, whether one approves or disapproves of homosexuality, and whether one cares or doesn't care about the outcome of an election are all examples of such characteristics. These attributes are measured by variables having ordinal-level values. It is important to be clear about the distinction between nominal and ordinal levels of measurement.

Consider an example of a nominal variable. If someone were to ask you, "In what region of the country do you live?" your response could not be gauged by an interval-level value, such as "98 units" of region. The idea looks silly. And it is. Region is not quantifiable. Your response would have to be measured by a category, such as "Northeast." This value would permit the researcher to distinguish you from people who gave different responses, such as "South," "West," or "Midwest," but clearly it would make no sense to say that you have more of the characteristic, "more region," than any other person. That is the distinguishing feature of a nominal-level variable. The values of a nominal-level variable allow you to say that two units of analysis have different values—and nothing more.

Now consider an ordinal-level variable. If someone asked, "Do you approve of the way the president is handling the economy?" your response still could not be gauged by a quantitative value, such as "98 units" of approval. Just as with region, your answer would be measured by a category, such as "Yes, approve." And, just as with region, this value would enable the researcher to differentiate you from people who gave the other response, "No, do not approve." Now, does it also make sense to say that a person who responds "Yes, approve" is relatively more approving than a person who responds "No, do not approve"? Yes, it makes perfect sense. That is the distinguishing feature of an ordinal-level variable. The values of an ordinal variable allow you to say that two units of analysis have different values *and* that one unit has relatively more (or less) of the measured characteristic.

Ordinal-level variables abound in political research, especially survey research. Questions gauging approval or disapproval of government policies or social behaviors—handgun registration laws, immigration reform, welfare spending, abortion rights, homosexuality, marijuana use, child-rearing practices, and virtually any others that you can think of—are almost always framed by ordinal categories. Ordinal-level measures are abundant, at least in part, because many political concepts do not have a known underlying metric. For example, there may be quantifiable "units of political tolerance," much like there are quantifiable units of age, but at present we do not know what those units are or how to measure them. We can, however, compare subjects on the basis of their relative levels of tolerance.

The dearth of interval-level variables—and the abundance of characteristics that permit ordinal measurement—has fostered the development of ever more sophisticated ordinal scales in survey research. Generally, an ordinal scale is constructed by adding up a number of ordinal measurements of the same characteristic, thus producing a single variable that makes more precise distinctions between units of analysis. For example, since 1972 the General Social Survey has asked respondents a series of questions eliciting their opinions about abortion. The interviewer begins with this prompt: "Please tell me whether or not you think it should be possible for a pregnant woman to obtain a legal abortion if . . ." The interviewer then names six different conditions, to which the respondent separately answers "Yes" or "No": "If there is a strong chance of serious defect in the baby?" "If she is married and does not want any more children?" "If the woman's health is seriously endangered by the pregnancy?" "If the family has very low income and cannot afford any more children?" "If she became pregnant as a result of rape?" "If she is not married and does not want to marry the man?" An individual answering "Yes" to any of these questions can be said to be more favorable toward abortion rights than a person answering "No." So each item, by itself, is an ordinal-level measure of support for abortion rights. An ordinal-level "abortion rights support scale" could be constructed by summing the number of "Yes" responses for each person who was interviewed, thus creating a new variable. This new variable would gauge finer differences between respondents. A respondent might say "Yes" to none of the conditions, one condition, two conditions, all the way up to six conditions. The researcher would be able to say that a person with, for example, four "Yes" responses is relatively more supportive of abortion rights than a person with three "Yes" responses.

The widespread use of ordinal scales in political research raises an issue that is not often discussed but ought to be mentioned here. Notice that, because each of the six items comprising the abortion scale is an ordinal-level variable, the abortion scale must be ordinal-level as well. This is because the six conditions do not measure standard "units" of support for abortion rights in the same way that years are standard units of age or dollars are standard units of income. Think about this. Is a "Yes" response to "If the woman's health is seriously endangered by the pregnancy?" equivalent to a "Yes" response to "If she is married and does not want any more children?" Does each of these questions measure the same unit of support for abortion rights? They do not. Confusion arises on this point because the abortion scale, along with other widely used ordinal scales, have values that are numeric. The "Yes" responses of one person, for example, might add up to a scale value of "3," whereas another person's may sum to a value of "4." However, these values do not make interval-level distinctions. They do not use a standard unit to communicate the exact amount of the characteristic. They represent relative amounts of the measured characteristic. Having said that, it is an open secret in political science that survey researchers often treat ordinal scales as if they were interval-level variables.

Clearing Up Confusion over Levels of Measurement

Students often ask two questions about levels of measurement. The first question is a practical one: "How can I tell whether a variable is interval, ordinal, or nominal?" The second question has a more skeptical bent: "Why does it matter?" Turning first to the second question, we say that a variable's level of measurement determines the appropriate technique for describing and analyzing it. The more precise the level of measurement, the more powerful is the description and analysis. This idea will become much clearer when you begin to analyze variables and evaluate the relationships between them.

The first question is of more immediate concern. The main source of confusion about a variable's level of measurement usually centers on the distinction between the variable's name and the variable's values. A variable's name will tell you the characteristic being measured by the variable. But, generally speaking, a variable's values will tell you the variable's level of measurement. To determine level of measurement, focus on the values of the variable. Think of two units of analysis having different values on the variable. Ask yourself this question: Do the values allow me to calculate the exact difference between the two subjects on the measured characteristic? If the answer is "Yes," then the variable is measured at the interval level. If the answer is "No," ask another question: Do the values allow me to say that one subject has more of the measured characteristic than the other subject? If the answer is "Yes," then the variable is measured at the ordinal level. If the answer is "No," then the variable is measured at the nominal level. Let's apply these steps to an example.

Survey researchers and demographers are interested in measuring geographic mobility, the extent to which people have moved from place to place during their lives. What values are used to measure this variable? Typically, respondents are asked this question: "Do you currently live in the same city that you lived in when you were 16 years old? Do you live in the same state but a different city? Or do you live in a different state?" So the values are "same city," "same state but different city," and "different state." Look at these values and follow the steps. Think of two subjects, each of whom has a different value on the variable. Do the values allow you to calculate the exact difference between subjects on the measured characteristic? No, the values are not expressed in units of geographic mobility. So this is not an interval-level variable. Do the values allow you to say that one subject has more of the measured characteristic than another subject? Can you say, for example, that someone who still lives in the same city has more or less of the characteristic, geographic mobility, than someone who now lives in the same state but in a different city? Yes, the second subject has been more geographically mobile than the first. Because the values permit us to tell the relative difference between the subjects, this variable is measured at the ordinal level of measurement.

Most of the time for most of the variables you will analyze, these steps will lead you to the correct conclusion about a variable's level of measurement. As political scientists exchange ideas and debate explanations for political phenomena, they develop the comforting habit of using many of the same variables to measure the same characteristics at the same levels of measurement. This practice defines a common ground, a set of shared measurement standards that allows political scientists to communicate in the same terms. We turn in the next chapter to a consideration of the creative essence of political research: the development of explanations and the logic of testing them.

SUMMARY

In this chapter we introduced the essential features of concepts and the measurement process. We have seen that, because the same concept may refer to many different characteristics, conceptual questions are frequently unclear and are difficult to answer empirically. The main challenge of the measurement process in political research is to transform conceptual questions into concrete questions—questions that can be answered empirically. The researcher begins by abstracting the essential empirical properties of a concept. The researcher then writes a conceptual definition, which communicates variation within a characteristic, the units of analysis to which the concept applies, and how the concept is to be measured. In measuring a concept, the researcher seeks a valid measure, a measure that gauges the intended characteristic, as spelled out in the conceptual definition, and does not gauge any unintended characteristics. Finally, the researcher wants to measure a characteristic with the highest possible degree of precision. Some characteristics, as we have seen, can be measured by interval-level values, whereas others are best measured at the ordinal or nominal level of measurement.

KEY TERMS

abstraction (p. 10)
aggregate-level unit of analysis (p. 11)
concept (p. 7)
conceptual definition (p. 8)
conceptual question (p. 8)
concrete question (p. 8)
construct validity (p. 18)
ecological fallacy (p. 12)
face validity (p. 18)
Hawthorne effect (p. 14)
individual-level unit of analysis (p. 11)
interval-level variable (p. 21)

nominal-level variable (p. 21)
operational definition (p. 8)
ordinal-level variable (p. 21)
random measurement error (p. 14)
reliability (p. 15)
split-half method (p. 17)
systematic measurement error (p. 14)
test-retest method (p. 17)
unit of analysis (p. 11)
validity (p. 16)
variable (p. 8)

EXERCISES

1. The concept of *democracy* is a source of continuing debate among political scientists. How might one define democracy? The concept may seem a bit vague, but certainly one can imagine countries that have a high level of democracy and countries that have a low level of democracy.

    A. Think of two countries, one that has all of the characteristics you would associate with democracy and one that has none of these characteristics. Using the table below as a guide, list three polar-opposite characteristics.

A country with a high level of democracy	A country with a low level of democracy

    B. Examine the list you have made. In your judgment, which one of these characteristics best represents the essential difference between countries with a high level of democracy and countries with a low level of democracy? Write a paragraph explaining your choice.

    C. Using the characteristic you have chosen, complete this conceptual definition: The concept of democracy is defined as the extent to which _____ exhibit the characteristic of _____.

2. In this chapter we discussed the ecological fallacy. What is the ecological fallacy? Illustrate the ecological fallacy, using an example other than that used in this chapter.

3. In this chapter we discussed two types of measurement error: systematic error and random error. Define each of these terms.

4. Mutt Jeffley wants to weigh his dog. He proceeds as follows: While holding the dog he steps onto a bathroom scale and records the weight. Just to make sure he got it right, he immediately repeats the procedure: While holding the dog he steps onto the scale a second time and again records the weight. Would Mutt's measurement of the dog's weight be reliable? Why or why not? Would Mutt's measurement of the dog's weight be valid? Why or why not?

5. As we discussed in this chapter, political scientists who are interested in survey research often must deal with tough issues of validity. A survey question may tap an intended characteristic, but it also may gauge an unintended characteristic. Validity problems can sometimes be identified using the face validity approach. Below are three hypothetical survey questions. For each one (i) identify an unintended characteristic being measured by the question and (ii) rewrite the survey question to improve its validity.

    Example. Intended characteristic: Whether or not an individual voted in the 2004 election. Survey question: "Thinking about the 2004 election, some people did their patriot duty and went to the polling place to vote on Election Day. Others were too unpatriotic to vote. How about you—did you vote on Election Day?"

        (i) Unintended characteristic: Individuals' feelings of patriotism. Not wanting to appear unpatriotic, citizens who did not vote may respond that they did vote.

        (ii) Improved rewrite: "Thinking about the 2004 election, some people voted in the election, whereas other people did not vote. How about you—did you vote in the 2004 election?"

    A. Intended characteristic: Environmental beliefs. Survey question: "Would you agree or disagree with the following statement: It is the federal government's responsibility to protect and improve the environment."

    B. Intended characteristic: Attitudes toward Social Security reform. Survey question: "Some politicians, mostly Republicans, have proposed that the Social Security system be replaced with a system that allows people to invest in the stock market. Other politicians, mostly

Democrats, oppose the Republican plan. Would you support or oppose replacing the Social Security system with a system that allows people to invest in the stock market?"

C. Intended characteristic: Attitudes toward dealing with crime. Survey question: "Some people think that the way to solve crime is to have harsher punishment for criminals. Others think that the way to solve crime is to improve our educational system. What do you think—should we have harsher punishment for criminals or should we improve our educational system?"

6. Seven variables are listed below. The variables' values for two subjects follow in parentheses. For each variable, state whether it is being measured at the nominal, ordinal, or interval level.
   A. State's enforcement of speed limits (State 1: lenient; State 2: strict)
   B. Individual's region of residence (Individual 1: South; Individual 2: West)
   C. Voting district's ballot technology (District 1: optical scan; District 2: punch card)
   D. Individual's commute time (Individual 1: 39 minutes; Individual 2: 14 minutes)
   E. Individual's approval of laws permitting gay marriage (Individual 1: Strongly disapprove; Individual 2: Disapprove)
   F. Timing of individual's presidential vote decision (Individual 1: before the primary elections; Individual 2: during the primary elections)
   G. Country's government type (Country 1: parliamentary democracy; Country 2: military dictatorship)

2

Explanations and Hypotheses

LEARNING OBJECTIVES

In this chapter you will learn:
- How to distinguish an acceptable explanation from an unacceptable explanation
- The difference between an independent variable and a dependent variable
- How to write a hypothesis stating the relationship between an independent variable and a dependent variable
- The importance of rival explanations and alternative hypotheses in political research
- Different research designs used to test hypotheses

The first goal of political research is to define and measure concepts. And you now know the three stages in the measurement process: clearly defining the concept to be measured, determining how to measure the concept accurately, and selecting variables that measure the concept precisely. We begin the measurement process with a vague conceptual term and we end up with an empirical measurement of a concrete characteristic. The measurement process thus is designed to answer "What?" questions. *What* is political tolerance, and *what* is a valid measurement of this concept? The definition and measurement of concepts is an essential goal. But it is not the only goal.

This chapter concerns the second goal of political research: to propose and test explanations for political phenomena. This goal is not defined by *what*? It is defined by *why*? *Why* are some people more politically tolerant than other people? The empirical landscape is teeming with "Why?" questions. In fact, such questions occur to us quite naturally whenever we observe some difference between people. Why do some people attend religious services weekly whereas others never attend? This is the sort of intellectual activity you engage in all the time—trying to explain the behavior of people and things you observe in the world. Some observed phenomena seem trivial and merely pique our curiosity. Why do some students prefer to sit in the back of the class whereas others prefer the front? Other phenomena occasion more serious thought. News footage of opposing groups of pro-life protesters and pro-choice demonstrators confronting each other outside an abortion clinic, for example, might raise the question: Why is one group so vociferously opposed to abortion and the other so ardently in favor of keeping it legal? Or consider the fact, routinely noted by political commentators, that only about half of all eligible voters show up at the polls on Election Day. Why do some people vote whereas others do not? And, thinking of elections, why do some voters cast their ballots for the Democrat, some for the Republican, and still others for third-party candidates?

All of these questions—and any other "Why?" questions you can think of—have two elements. First, each question makes an explicit observation about a characteristic that varies. Each cites a variable. Explanation in political research begins by observing a variable—a difference between subjects that we want to understand. Individuals' abortion beliefs are "pro-life" or "pro-choice." Students' seating preferences vary between "back" and "front." Voting turnout takes on the values "voted" or "did not vote." And so on, for any "Why?" question. Second, each question implicitly requests a causal explanation for the observed differences. Each can be recast into the form "What causes differences between subjects on this variable?" What causes differences between people in abortion beliefs? What causes differences between students' seating preferences? What causes differences between eligible voters in turnout? Explanation in political research involves causation. An explanation for differences in turnout, for example, might propose that education plays a causal role. As people's level of education increases, they become more aware of politics, and they develop a sense of political efficacy, a belief that they can have an impact on political outcomes. Thus, by this proposed explanation, education causes awareness and efficacy to increase, which cause turnout to increase. This explanation proposes that education is causally linked to turnout.

Proposing explanations defines the creative essence of political research. It is creative because it invites us to think up possible reasons for the observed differences between subjects. It allows us to range rather freely in our search, proposing causal variables that come to mind and describing how those variables might account for what we see. Proposing explanations, however, is not an "anything goes" activity. An explanation must be described in such a way that it can be tested with empirical data. It must suggest a **hypothesis**, a testable statement about the empirical relationship between cause and effect. The education-turnout explanation, for example, suggests a hypothetical relationship between education and voting. If the explanation is correct, then people with less education will vote at lower rates than people with more education. If the explanation is not correct, then level of education and turnout will not be empirically related.[1]

A hypothesis, then, is a conditional statement. It tells us what we should find when we look at the data. When we examine the relationship using empirical data, we are testing the hypothesis. Testing hypotheses defines the methodological essence of political research. It is methodological because it follows a set of procedures for determining whether the hypothesis is incorrect. Several different sets of procedure may be used. All of them, however, share a common methodological feature: They set up a comparison. How would we test the education-turnout hypothesis? Using empirical data, we would compare the turnout rate of people having less education with the turnout rate of people having more education. It is this empirical comparison that tests the hypothesis.

Thus three activities—proposing an explanation for a variable, stating a hypothesis, and testing the hypothesis—are the three stages of the explanatory process in political research. Figure 2-1 shows a schematic of the explanatory process. In this chapter we consider each stage.

Figure 2-1 The Explanatory Process

Variable ⟶ Explanation ⟶ Hypothesis ⟶ Test

First, we look at how to construct an explanation for a variable. Observing variables in political life, as we have already seen, seems to be a natural and straightforward activity. And essentially it is. In the context of an explanation, however, we view a variable in a particular way—as the effect of some unknown cause. The variable that represents the effect in a causal explanation is called the **dependent variable**. We consider how to propose an acceptable or "good" explanation for a dependent variable and how to avoid unacceptable or "poor" explanations. An acceptable explanation often requires a fair amount of thought—and perhaps some imagination. An acceptable explanation has to be plausible and always requires a long paragraph. Odd as it may sound, however, an acceptable explanation does not have to be correct. In fact, most of the examples of good explanations in this chapter were constructed without any regard for their correctness. The distinguishing feature of an acceptable explanation is not its correctness or incorrectness, but whether it can be *tested* to find out if it is incorrect.

In the second section of this chapter we discuss how to frame a hypothesis. A hypothesis is directly based on the explanation that has been proposed. In framing a hypothesis, the researcher selects a variable that represents the casual factor in the explanation. Like any variable, this variable measures differences between subjects on a characteristic. In the context of an explanation, however, we view this variable in a particular way—as the cause of the dependent variable. The variable that represents a causal factor in an explanation is called the **independent variable**. A hypothesis is a testable statement of the proposed relationship between the independent variable, which measures the cause, and the dependent variable, which measures the effect. A hypothesis states that, as subjects' values on the independent variable change, their values on the dependent variable should be found to change, too, and in just the way suggested by the explanation. Hypotheses are the workhorses of explanation in political science. In this chapter you will learn a foolproof template for writing a testable hypothesis.

In the third section of this chapter we discuss how to design a test for a hypothesis. Here you will learn to appreciate a fact of life for the political researcher: For every explanation we propose, and for every hypothesis we test, there are alternative causes, rival explanations, for the same phenomena. These rival explanations create a problem, because they undermine our ability to evaluate the effect of the independent variable on the dependent variable. Is the independent variable affecting the dependent variable, as our explanation suggests, or is some other variable at work, distorting our results and leading us to erroneous conclusions? Our ability to rule out worrisome alterative explanations depends on the power of our research design, the procedures we use in testing our hypotheses.

STAGE ONE: FROM VARIABLE TO EXPLANATION

Most of us are quite adept at discovering interesting variables. Several examples appeared at the beginning of this chapter. Political scientists observe and measure variables all the time. Consider this: Many people in the United States support a ban on handguns, and many people oppose such a ban. Individuals' opinions on this issue, in fact, are about evenly divided between the two values of the variable: "favor" and "oppose." [2] If we were to cast this variable, support for a handgun ban, into a "Why?" question, it becomes a dependent variable, the measurement of a characteristic we wish to explain: "Why do many people favor a ban and many people oppose one? What causes differences between people on this dependent variable?" Many of us get stymied right away. "That's easy," you might suggest, "People favor a ban because they support gun control. People oppose a ban because they don't support gun control." This is not an enlightening answer, because it is a tautology—a circular statement that is necessarily true. Good explanations are never circular. Here is a second try. "Gun opinions have something to do with gender. Women and men have different opinions about gun control." This answer is more hopeful. It cites another variable, gender, and it says that this new variable has "something to do with" the dependent variable, gun control opinions. But this statement is still a poor explanation. The connection it makes between two characteristics—gender and opinions—is far too vague. Good explanations are never vague. In what way, exactly, do gender differences cause or produce different gun control opinions? And what is the tendency of this effect? Do women tend to oppose gun control, whereas men tend to be in favor of it? Or do tendencies run the other way, with women more in favor than men? A good explanation connects two variables and provides a detailed description of the causal linkages between them. A good explanation requires some thinking. And it requires some writing:

> Attitudes toward political issues like gun control are products of deeply ingrained socialization practices in American culture. The socialization process is applied differently to males and females. Males engage in competitive play, often involving make-believe weapons, and they are taught that solving problems often requires the use of force. For females, cooperative play and care-giving activities are the norm in our society. Females are taught that problems are best resolved through dialogue and discussion, not force. As a result of these two different types of childhood socialization, males and females enter adulthood with different predispositions on many political issues that represent the use of force: fighting wars versus engaging in diplomacy, punishing criminals versus addressing the social problems that cause crime, or opposing gun control versus favoring a ban on guns. Therefore, females will be more likely than males to favor a handgun ban.

This explanation is far better than the earlier attempts. What makes this a good explanation? First, it describes a connection between the dependent variable, gun control opinions, and a causal variable, gender. In the context of an explanation, the causal variable is called the independent variable: Differences in gun control opinions depend on differences in gender.[3] Second, it asserts the tendency of this difference. As the values of the independent variable change from male to female, the dependent variable will change in a specific way: Women will be more likely than men to favor gun control.[4] Third, it is testable. If we find that females and males do not differ in their gun control opinions, then we can seriously question or discard the explanation. So the explanation connects an independent variable with a dependent variable, asserts the tendency of the connection, and suggests a testable empirical relationship.

But clearly the explanation does more than simply propose a testable empirical relationship. It says that the relationship between gender and gun control opinions is one consequence of a general causal process, the socialization process, which instills and reinforces different cultural values in males and females. For males, these values are "competitive," and for females they are "cooperative." These different values give rise to different predispositions toward several political issues—attitudes toward the military, opinions about solving crime, as well as gun control. Thus the explanation suggests the existence of other relationships in the empirical data. A scholar of childhood socialization should observe differences between boys and girls in the ways they interact and resolve conflicts. A scholar of public opinion should find that men are more inclined than women to favor the use of military force. Men should be more favorably disposed toward policies that emphasize punishing criminals as opposed to solving social problems that lead to crime. Now, do we know if any of these assertions are correct? No, we don't. But each of these relationships is testable. Each suggests what we should find if the explanation is correct. A good explanation describes a general causal process that suggests several testable relationships. A good explanation arouses curiosity: "Well, *what else* should we find?"

Many very interesting explanations in social science began in just the way illustrated by this example. A researcher observes a phenomenon, develops a causal explanation for it, and then asks, "What else should I find?" In his provocative book *Bowling Alone*, Robert Putnam begins with a seemingly innocuous observation: Although the pastime of bowling has steadily increased in popularity among individuals over the past several decades, the number of bowling leagues has declined precipitously.[5] So the individual enjoyment of the sport has increased, but the collective enjoyment of the sport has declined. This observation, as one reviewer of Putnam's work says, may be "a matter of no small concern to bowling-alley proprietors whose revenues depend heavily on the convivial sharing of beer and pretzels." [6] But is the decline in organized bowling being produced by a general causal process that has other consequences? Putnam argues, in part, that generational change, the replacement of older generations with younger cohorts, is causally linked to the erosion of community and social groups of all kinds. People born in the years preceding World War II, the "long civic generation," are more likely than younger generations to engage in organized social interaction. The effects of generational change can be seen in the lost vitality of all sorts of community groups—parent-teacher associations, civic booster groups, charitable organizations, religious congregations, and, of course, bowling leagues. Older cohorts are more likely than younger generations to favor these social activities. The effects can also be seen in the sorts of activities that are on the rise—"check book memberships" in far-flung groups that do not require social interaction, disembodied Internet "chat," and, of course, the individual enjoyment of bowling. Older cohorts are less likely than younger people to favor these activities. Thus, Putnam connects a dependent variable, the decline of bowling leagues, with an independent variable, the changing age composition of American society. He describes the tendency of the relationship: Older generations are more likely than younger generations to join bowling leagues. More important, Putnam develops a general explanation that suggests many other relationships between generation and membership in different sorts of organizations. Much of his book is devoted to examining these relationships to find out whether they are correct.[7]

Consider another example that demonstrates well the role of creativity and imagination in thinking up explanations. Malcolm Gladwell's book *The Tipping Point* also begins with a single, curious observation—about shoes. Hush Puppies, comfortable if unstylish suede footwear, suddenly began appearing on the feet of young and well-appointed males on the streets and in the clubs of Manhattan, where Gladwell lives and works. Where did this strange trend originate? Gladwell did some checking around. By 1994, Hush Puppies sales had dipped to 30,000 pairs, sold mostly in mom-and-pop retail stores. Wolverine, the shoes' manufacturer, considered the brand all but dead. But later that year Hush Puppies began showing up in an unlikely place, resale shops in Manhattan's Soho and Greenwich Village districts. In 1995, sales rocketed to 430,000 pairs—then to over 1.5 million pairs in 1996—and Hush

Puppies became the accessory of choice among New York's fashion elite. "How does a thirty-dollar pair of shoes," Gladwell wonders, "go from a handful of downtown Manhattan hipsters and designers to every mall in America in the space of two years? . . . Why is it that some ideas or behaviors or products start epidemics and others don't?" [8]

Gladwell proposes that the Hush Puppies fad was the end result of the same sort of causal process that produces epidemics of infectious diseases. Ideas, consumer products, and biological bugs all require the same causal conditions in order to spread "successfully." For one thing, a small group of highly infectious people, whom Gladwell calls "connectors," must transmit the infection to many other people beyond a closely knit community. In the case of sexually transmitted diseases, such as the AIDS-causing virus HIV, connectors are highly promiscuous individuals who have weak personal ties to their many partners. In the case of an idea or fad, connectors are people who have an extraordinary number of casual social contacts. These contacts may or may not know each other directly, but they all know the connector.[9] Thus, Gladwell links a dependent variable, the success or failure of contagion, to an independent variable, the presence or absence of connectors. He asserts that his causal explanation helps to account for a host of social results, from the Hush Puppies craze and the precipitous decline in New York's crime rate to the persistence of teen smoking, suicide epidemics, and even the resounding success of Paul Revere's fabled midnight ride.[10] Interesting and imaginative, to be sure. But is Gladwell's explanation testable?

From the standpoint of proposing a testable relationship, Gladwell's explanation for the success of Paul Revere's famous word-of-mouth campaign is especially instructive. Of course, Paul Revere fits the description of classic connector, "a fisherman and a hunter, a card-player and a theater-lover, a frequenter of pubs and a successful businessman," an organizer and communicator, a recognized and trusted link between the secret and disparate revolutionary societies that emerged after the Boston Tea Party.[11] It is little wonder that he successfully mobilized local militia in the towns along his route. What makes Gladwell's explanation convincing, though, is that it also accounts for the *failure* of Revere's comrade in arms, William Dawes, a fellow revolutionary who set out on the same night, carrying the same alarming message over the same distance and similar countryside and through the same number of towns. The same "disease"—the news that the "Redcoats are coming!"—and the same context—vigilant local militia awakened in the middle of the night—produced a completely different result: A mere handful of men from Dawes's circuit showed up to fight the British the next day. "So why," Gladwell asks, "did Revere succeed where Dawes failed?" [12] William Dawes, like Revere, was a committed and courageous revolutionary. Unlike Revere, however, Dawes was not socially well-connected. He was an ordinary person with a normal circle of friends and acquaintances, known and trusted by only a few people, all of whom were within his own social group. This historical event thus provides a test of Gladwell's explanation. One value of the independent variable, the presence of a connector, produced one value of the dependent variable, the successful contagion of an idea. A different value of the independent variable, the absence of a connector, produced a different value of the dependent variable, the failure of contagion.

STAGE TWO: FROM EXPLANATION TO HYPOTHESIS

All of these examples illustrate the creative aspect of proposing explanations. Within the generous boundaries of plausibility, researchers can describe causal explanations that link cause with effect, specify tendency, and suggest a variety of other consequences and relationships. Yet we have also seen that any relationship suggested by an explanation must be testable. A testable relationship is one that tells us what we should find when we examine the data. A testable relationship proposes a hypothetical comparison. The gender–gun opinions explanation tells us what we should find when we examine the gun control opinions of men and women. It suggests a hypothetical comparison. If we separate subjects on the values of the independent variable, gender, and compare values on the dependent variable, gun control opinions, we should find a difference: Women will be more likely than men to fall into the "favor" category of the dependent variable.

The deceptively simple necessity of proposing a testable comparison is central to the methodology of political research. This comparison is formalized by a hypothesis, defined as a testable statement about the empirical relationship between an independent variable and a dependent variable. The hypothesis tells us exactly how different values of the independent variable are related to different values of the dependent variable. Here is a hypothesis for the relationship between gender and gun control attitudes:

> In comparing individuals, those who are women will be more likely to favor a handgun ban than will those who are men.

This hypothesis makes an explicit, testable comparison. It tells us that when we compare units of analysis (individuals) having different values of the independent variable (gender), we will observe a difference in the dependent variable (gun control opinions). What is more, the hypothesis reflects the tendency of the relationship. As the values of the independent variable change, from male to female, the dependent variable changes from less support to more support for a handgun ban. This example suggests a template for writing any hypothesis:

> In comparing [units of analysis], those having [one value on the independent variable] will be more likely to have [one value on the dependent variable] than will those having [a different value on the independent variable].

Let's look at a different example, using different units of analysis and different variables, and see if the template works.

Suppose a student of comparative politics observes interesting variation in this dependent variable: the percentage of countries' voting-age populations who turn out in national elections, such as parliamentary or congressional elections. In fact, turnouts range widely—from less than 50 percent in some countries to over 80 percent in others. The researcher proposes the following explanation:

> Potential voters think of their ballots in the same way that potential investors think of their dollars. If people believe that they will get a good return on their money, then they are more likely to invest. If people view a potential investment as having weak prospects, then they will be less likely to commit their money. By the same token, if individuals think that their votes will elect the parties they support and produce the policies they favor, then they will be more likely to turn out. If, by contrast, eligible voters do not believe their ballots will have an impact on the outcome of the election or on the direction of public policy, they are more likely to stay home. Just as stocks vary in how well they translate dollars into return on investment, countries differ in how well their electoral systems translate voters' preferences into legislative representation. Many countries

use some form of proportional representation (PR). In a PR system, a political party is allocated legislative seats based on the percentage of votes it receives in the election. So a party that represents a specific policy or point of view—an environmental party, for example—can gain political power in a PR system. Countries using proportional representation are likely to have multiple parties that afford voters a wide array of choices. And the turnouts in these countries will be high, because voters will see a strong link between their votes and their impact on government. Other countries use some form of a plurality system. In a plurality system, only the party that receives the most votes wins representation in the legislature. A party receiving less than a plurality of the vote—again, such as an environmental party—ends up with no representation. Countries using plurality systems will have fewer political parties that offer blunt choices on a large array of issues. And turnouts in these countries will be low, because voters will perceive a weak link between their votes and their impact on government.

This explanation describes several causal linkages. Countries vary in how directly their electoral systems convert citizens' votes into legislative power. Proportional representation systems foster multiple parties, giving citizens more choices and greater impact. Plurality systems produce fewer parties, giving individuals fewer choices and lesser impact. The explanation connects a dependent variable, voter turnout, with an independent variable, type of electoral system, and it tells us how the two variables are related. Using the template, we can use this explanation as the basis for a hypothesis:

> In comparing *countries*, those having *PR electoral systems* will be more likely to have *higher voter turnout* that will those having *plurality electoral systems*.

The independent and dependent variables are easily identified, and the tendency of the hypothetical relationship between them is clear. The hypothesis tells us what to compare—turnouts in countries having PR systems with turnouts in countries having plurality systems—and what we should find: Turnouts should be higher in countries having PR systems. As we observe a change in the values of the independent variable, from PR systems to plurality systems, the dependent variable should change from higher turnouts to lower turnouts. So the template works.

By becoming familiar with this format, you can learn to identify—and avoid—some common mistakes in writing hypotheses.[13] Examine the following statements:

A. In comparing individuals, some people are more likely to donate money to political candidates than are other people.
B. Highly religious people vote at high rates.
C. In comparing individuals, gender and abortion attitudes are related.
D. Because of important cultural changes that began in the 1960s, many current political conflicts are based on generational differences.

Statement A is not a poor hypothesis. It simply is not a hypothesis! It describes one variable, whether or not people donate money to political candidates, but it does not state a relationship between two variables. A hypothesis must compare values on a dependent variable for subjects that differ on an independent variable. Statement B is a poor hypothesis because it does not make an explicit comparison. Highly religious people vote at high rates compared with whom? Such a comparison may be implied, but it is never a good idea to leave the basis of comparison unstated. Statement C is defective because it fails to state the tendency of the relationship. In what way, exactly, are gender and attitudes related? As we have seen, an acceptable explanation does more than simply connect two variables. A good hypothesis tells us exactly how different values of the independent variable are related to different values of the dependent variable. Statement D actually sounds interesting, and it would certainly be a conversation-starter. Stimulating as it is, however, statement D is much too vague to qualify as a testable hypothesis. Vague hypotheses can always be traced to vague explanations. And good explanations are never vague. What is meant by "cultural changes"? What is the dependent variable? What is the independent variable? How would we describe the causal process that connects them?

A good explanation, as we have seen, always describes a causal process, a causal linkage or series of linkages that connects the independent variable with the dependent variable. These linkages, in turn, suggest the existence of other testable relationships. Let's consider an example that is especially rich in causal linkages. This example helps illustrate an additional, important point about explanations and hypotheses.

Students of presidential elections have long discussed and debated explanations for the different choices that individual voters make between candidates. A typical "Why?" question asked by scholars: "Why do some voters vote for the incumbent president whereas others vote for the challenger?" In 1992, for example, though many people voted for the incumbent, George Bush, many more chose the challenger, Bill Clinton. In 1996, incumbent Clinton attracted more votes than his challenger, Bob Dole.

> When it comes to making a vote choice, people look at how good a job the incumbent has done in managing the economy. Most voters don't have a great deal of knowledge about political or social problems, but they do know one thing: whether their personal financial situation has improved or gotten worse while the incumbent has been in office. If things have gotten better for them, they attribute this to the good job the incumbent has done in handling the economy and thus are likely to vote for the incumbent candidate. By contrast, if their economic situation has gotten worse, they will blame the incumbent's poor handling of the economy, and they are likely to support the challenging candidate. As one of President Clinton's advisers memorably put it, "It's the economy, stupid." Differences in voters' economic situations cause differences in their vote choices.

This explanation describes the values of an independent variable, voters' economic situations having either "gotten better" or "gotten worse," and it connects this independent variable to the dependent variable, a vote choice for the incumbent candidate or a vote for the challenger. It suggests the following hypothesis:

> In comparing voters, those whose economic situations have gotten better will be more likely to vote for the incumbent candidate than will voters whose economic situations have gotten worse.

The explanation also describes a causal linkage between the independent variable and the dependent variable. Voters evaluate their own situations, thumbs up or thumbs down, tie this evaluation to the incumbent's management skills, and then cast their votes accordingly. Thus the independent variable affects another variable, favorable or unfavorable opinions about the incumbent's job performance in handling the economy, which in turn affects the dependent variable. This causal linkage suggests *two* additional hypotheses:

> In comparing voters, those whose economic situations have gotten better will be more likely to have favorable opinions about the incumbent's handling of the economy than will voters whose economic situations have gotten worse.

> In comparing voters, those who have favorable opinions about the incumbent's handling of the economy will be more likely to vote for the incumbent than will those who have unfavorable opinions.

The first hypothesis says that voters' opinions about the incumbent's handling of the economy depend on voters' economic situations. In the first hypothesis, the job performance variable is the dependent variable. The second hypothesis says that vote choice depends on opinions about job performance. So, in the second hypothesis, the job performance variable is the independent variable. In using an explanation to construct different hypotheses, we might cast the same variable as the dependent variable in one hypothesis and as the independent variable in another hypothesis.

This example is not at all unusual. Many explanations in political science describe an **intervening variable**—a variable that acts as go-between or mediator between an independent variable and a dependent variable. Intervening variables often are of central importance in describing *how* the independent variable is linked to the dependent variable. If someone were to ask how individuals' economic situations and their vote choices are linked, the task of explaining the connection would fall to the intervening variable—voters' opinions about the incumbent's job performance. What is more, if the explanation is correct, then the two additional hypotheses—that voters' economic fortunes affect their opinions about job performance and that opinions about performance affect vote choice—should stand up to empirical scrutiny. Finally, remember that a variable is not inherently an intervening variable. A variable assumes the role of intervener in the context of an explanation that describes a causal process.

STAGE THREE: FROM HYPOTHESIS TO TEST

In his book *Data Analysis for Politics and Policy*, Edward R. Tufte recounts the story of a famous surgeon, a pioneer in the technique of vascular reconstruction, who delivered a lecture to medical school students on the large number of patients saved by the surgical procedure:

> At the end of the lecture, a young student at the back of the room timidly asked, "Do you have any controls?" Well, the great surgeon drew himself up to his full height, hit the desk, and said, "Do you mean did I not operate on half of the patients?" The hall grew very quiet then. The voice at the back of the room very hesitantly replied, "Yes, that's what I had in mind." Then the visitor's fist really came down as he thundered, "Of course not. That would have doomed half of them to their death." God, it was quiet then, and one could scarcely hear the small voice ask, "Which half?" [14]

Humiliating as it may have been, the young questioner's skepticism was precisely on-point. If the famous surgeon wished to demonstrate the effectiveness of his surgical technique, then he would have to make a comparison. He would have to compare values of the dependent variable, survival rates, for patients who had different values on the independent variable—patients who had received the surgery and patients who had not received the surgery. As it was, the surgeon was reporting values of a dependent variable from observations that he made on a test group. A **test group** is composed of subjects who receive a treatment that the researcher believes is causally linked to the dependent variable. In this case, the test group was composed of patients who had received the surgical procedure. But the surgeon had no basis for comparison. He had no control group. A **control group** is composed of subjects who do not receive the treatment that the researcher believes is causally linked to the dependent variable. In this case, the control group would be composed of patients who had not received the surgical procedure. Without data from a control group, there is simply no way he could have known whether the independent variable had any effect on the dependent variable.

What is more, to get an accurate assessment of the effectiveness of the surgery, the medical researcher would have to make sure that the patients in both groups, the test group and the control group, were identical in every other way that could affect the dependent variable. Thus, for example, patients in both groups would need to be identical or very similar in age, medical history, current prognosis, and so on. Why put such stringent conditions on testing the effect of the surgery? Because each of these factors represents a **rival explanation**, an alternative cause for different values of the dependent variable. If patients in the test group were younger and in currently better health than patients in the control group, for example, then it could be these differences, not the surgery, that explain their better rates of survival. Only by making these other factors equal, by controlling them and neutralizing their effects, can we isolate the effect of the independent variable on the dependent variable.

This anecdote is a cautionary tale for political researchers because we face the same problem of controlling for rival explanations. The political world is a complicated place. For every explanation we describe, there is a competing explanation that accounts for the same dependent variable. Recall the earlier explanation proposing that gender is causally linked to opinions about gun control. Let's say that we test the hypothesis that women will be more likely than men to favor a handgun ban. And suppose we find that, sure enough, a much larger percentage of females than males support gun control. Imagine that, after reporting these results to a large group of students, one student asks: "Do you have any controls? Women are more likely to be Democrats and men are more likely to be Republicans. Since Democrats are stronger gun-control advocates than Republicans, maybe the dependent variable is being caused by partisan differences, not gender differences. You might be making a big mistake, confusing the effect of gender with the effect of party. Did you control for partisanship?" This imaginary questioner has proposed a plausible rival explanation, an alternative cause for the same dependent variable, gun control opinions.

Our ability to isolate the effect of an independent variable on a dependent variable—to neutralize the effects of rival causes—depends on the power of our **research design**, an overall set of procedures for evaluating the effect of an independent variable on a dependent variable. Some research designs are "strong." They are strong in the sense that they control for the possible effects of all plausible rival explanations. Research that follows a **true experimental design** fits into this category. Other designs are "weak." They are weak in the sense that they control for some rival explanations, but they do not control for other plausible causes of the dependent variable. Research that follows the **controlled comparison design** fits into this category. Still other research designs fall between these two poles, retaining some features of the true experimental design but remaining vulnerable to rival explanations. Research that follows the **natural experimental design** falls into this category.[15]

The true experiment is the standard protocol in the natural sciences. Natural experiments are somewhat more common in the social sciences, and controlled comparisons are by far the most common design in social science, including political science. However, true experimental procedures are not unknown in political science. By understanding the true experimental research design and considering an example from political science, we can gain an appreciation of the problems of control faced in political research.

The True Experiment

A true experiment allows the investigator to manipulate the test group and control group in such a way that, in the beginning, both groups are virtually identical. The investigator then measures the dependent variable for both groups. This is called the pre-measurement phase. The two groups then receive different values of the independent variable. This is the treatment phase—typically, the test group gets some "treatment" while the control group does not. In the post-measurement phase, the dependent variable is measured again for both groups. Since, by design, the independent variable is the only way the groups differ, any observed differences in the dependent variable can be attributed directly to the independent variable and cannot be attributed to any other cause.

Two aspects of the true experimental research design—equalizing the test and control groups and pre-measuring the dependent variable—are the keys to its strength. In true experiments using human subjects, the individuals themselves do not choose the group, test or control, to which they will belong. Why not? Individuals who choose the test group may be different (in age, sex, race, etc.) from individuals who choose the control group. These different attributes may, in turn, affect the dependent variable. True experiments eliminate such alternative explanations by randomly assigning subjects to each group. **Random assignment** means that each subject has an equal chance of being picked for the test or control, and it guarantees that both groups are virtually the same.[16]

Why pre-measure the dependent variable? Shouldn't the random assignment of subjects be sufficient to eliminate alternative causes? Not necessarily. Suppose that, despite random assignment and other efforts to eliminate competing explanations, the control group's value on the dependent variable changes between the pre-measurement and the post-measurement. This could happen for a variety of reasons that are difficult to control—for example, the natural human response to the knowledge of being studied. Since these potentially confounding conditions can be plausibly attributed to the test group as well, the researcher can get a good idea of how much the test group changed, over and above any changes observed in the control group.

Classic research on the effect of mass media on public opinion provides an excellent example of the true experimental research design in political science. The general questions and controversies about news media may be familiar to you. Does network news bias stories toward one ideological perspective? Do reporters and newscasters ignore issues they find less important and emphasize events more in keeping with their agendas? If so, does such bias and selectivity affect the opinions of the viewing public? Is this effect large or small?

Focus, for now, on one role the media might play—that of agenda setter. Agenda setting is the idea that the issues covered by media stories become the issues that the public thinks are most important, the problems that raise urgent concerns and should be high on the list of society's priorities. Here is an explanation for how agenda setting might affect the public:

> A person learns about social problems and political issues in different places and from different people in his or her life—family, friends, and coworkers, for instance. If these people are talking about a particular problem, such as crime or the environment, then the person perceives that problem as being more important than other problems. The most influential sources of information are the major media outlets, particularly broadcast media. For people who pay attention to broadcast news programs, the kind of issues covered by the media will be perceived as most important. People who pay less attention, by contrast, will find those issues to be less important.

This explanation suggests the following hypothesis:

> In comparing individuals, those who are exposed to issues covered by the media will be more likely to perceive those issues as important than will those who are not exposed to issues covered by the media.

In this case, the independent variable is level of media exposure. The dependent variable is the level of perceived importance of the issues covered in media stories. The explanation proposes that media exposure is the cause and perceived importance of media stories is the effect.

The test of this hypothesis might seem straightforward. Why not simply compare people who watch a lot of television news (a test group) with people who watch very little (a control group) and see if the test group puts greater importance on the issues being covered by the media? One reason this will not work, of course, is the familiar chicken-or-egg problem: Perhaps the media are covering stories that, according to their market research, viewers *already* think are important. Broadcasting is a business, and a highly competitive one at that. Couldn't one plausibly suggest that the media's managers, like any corporate managers, would try to determine which issues and problems are most important to people, and then cover those stories? This is a plausible rival explanation. This rival says that causality runs in the opposite direction—perceived importance determines media exposure—and it suggests the same relationship as the agenda-setting explanation.

In their study of media, Shanto Iyengar and Donald Kinder designed a series of true experiments that controlled for this competing explanation.[17] They began by randomly assigning subjects to a test or control group. In the pre-measurement phase, both groups were given a list of eight national problems—defense, inflation, illegal drugs, the environment, and so on—and asked to rank them from most important to least important. Each of the groups then gathered to watch the news each night for 6 days. The individuals in one group, the control subjects, were shown a regular newscast. For the other group, the test subjects, the researchers used state-of-the-art video equipment and editing techniques to insert stories dealing with a specific national problem. At the end of the 6 days, subjects were again asked to rank the eight issues in terms of importance. The results were stunning. Compared with the control subjects, whose rankings did not change appreciably from beginning to end, individuals who had been shown the doctored newscasts dramatically altered their lists of priorities. For example, in one instance where the investigators had interspliced stories about defense preparedness, test subjects promoted defense from sixth to second place, whereas control subjects reported no change in their assessments of the importance of this national problem.[18]

Iyengar and Kinder's findings are convincing. They followed strict procedures that did not permit rival explanations—particularly the troublesome chicken-or-egg rival—to account for their results. Neutralizing rival explanations, however, required a lot of "creative control." They created and controlled everything in the research environment: the assignment of subjects, the pre-measurement instrument, the independent variable, and the post-measurement instrument. Because the experimental research design imposes such a large degree of creative control, the results obtained from true experiments are internally valid. **Internal validity** means that, within the conditions artificially created by the researcher, the effect of the independent variable on the dependent variable is isolated from other plausible explanations. And one would have to say that, within the conditions created by Iyengar and Kinder, the effect of media exposure on the perceived importance of media stories was isolated and precisely measured.

However, whether or not true experiments can be externally valid is more problematic. **External validity** means that the results of a study can be generalized—that is, its findings can be applied to situations in the nonartificial, natural world. When people watch the news each evening, do they travel to a university campus, check in with a professor or graduate student, and then watch television with a group of strangers? To be sure, Iyengar and Kinder went to considerable lengths to re-create natural circumstances—putting subjects at ease, providing a comfortable living-room setting, encouraging casual conversation, and so on. Even so, some inferential distance exists between the true experimental finding that "viewers exposed to news devoted to a particular problem become more convinced of its importance" to the real-world conclusion that "[n]etwork news programs seem to possess a powerful capacity to shape the public's agenda." [19]

Drawbacks aside, the true experiment represents the gold standard in research procedure. For most research questions in political science, however, true experimental methods are not feasible—or they are simply impossible. Usually we study units of analysis as we find them, as they occur "naturally" in society and politics. Obviously, many naturally occurring independent variables of potential interest, such as age or sex or education level, cannot be manipulated. More generally, one and usually both of the experiment's key strengths—random assignment to the test or control group and pre-measurement of the dependent variable—are beyond the researcher's control.

The Natural Experiment

In the natural experimental design, the researcher studies two groups—a test group and a control group, pre-measures the dependent variable for both groups, applies a "treatment" to the test group, and then measures the dependent variable again for both groups. But one main distinction exists between a natural experiment and a true experiment. In a natural experiment, the subjects themselves select the group to which they will belong—test or control. This distinction can make a big difference, because subjects who find their way into each group might differ in some way other than the independent variable. These other differences represent potential rivals, alternative causes for the dependent variable.

Consider the following example of a natural experiment. A recent study designed to test the academic effectiveness of Internet-enhanced instruction set up two sections of the same course, introductory American National Government, for which students could choose to enroll.[20] Both sections had the same instructor, the same textbook, the same assigned readings, and the same exams. One section of the course was structured in the conventional way. Students in this section, the control subjects, attended lectures twice a week, interacted in the usual manner with each other and with the instructor, and were given traditional assignments. The other section of the course relied more heavily on the Internet. Students in this section, the test subjects, met face-to-face only once a week. The remaining time was used for Internet-enhanced learning activities, computer-based quizzes, and forum discussions. Both groups were given a pretest measuring basic knowledge of political concepts and facts, and both were tested again at the end of the term.

This study was designed to control several factors that plausibly affect student learning. Because both sections had the same instructor, textbook, readings, and exams, any observed differences in the dependent variable, student knowledge of basic concepts and facts, could not be attributed to these alternative causes. But all natural experiments are vulnerable to **selection bias,** bias that occurs when the subjects who find their way into the test group differ from subjects who find their way into the control group—and these differences, in turn, affect the dependent variable. In the course schedule, consulted by students during registration, one section of American National Government was listed as having two 1-hour-and-15-minute class meetings per week. The other section was listed as meeting one day a week for 1 hour and 15 minutes, and it included this notation: "For above course: Web enhanced; reduced class time. WWW access, browser & e-mail skills required." Did the students who selected the test section differ from students who selected the control? Did these uncontrolled differences affect the dependent variable?

The two groups of students were indeed quite different. Compared with their counterparts in the Internet section, students who enrolled in the conventional lecture setting had more academic experience, were more likely to be political science majors, and professed greater interest in and attentiveness to politics. Thus, the independent variable, traditional instruction versus Internet-enhanced instruction, was applied to two very different student audiences. This study, like many natural experiments, had a selection bias problem: From the beginning of the study, the control group was predisposed to perform better than the test group.

Although in natural experiments subjects find their own ways into the research setting, the investigator can exercise some methodological leverage over the problems this creates. Since the natural experimental design requires pre-measurement of the dependent variable, the researcher can compare these measurements for the test and control groups. A large difference between the test and control groups alerts the researcher to the selection problem. And, because the design requires post-measurement of the dependent variable, the researcher can gauge changes in the dependent variable for both groups. By and large, however, the investigator must search for naturally occurring differences between the test and control groups, find out how these uncontrolled variables are affecting the dependent variable, and then try to neutralize their effects. This is accomplished by matching test and control subjects as closely as possible on these alternative causal variables, and then comparing their values on the dependent variable. After these procedures were followed in the study of Internet-enhanced instruction, the findings actually showed better performance of the Internet students on the dependent variable.

The Controlled Comparison

"In what ways, other than the independent variable," the researcher always must ask, "do the test group and the control group differ? How else are they not the same?" In those uncommon instances when we are doing a true experiment, this question has a clear answer: "Except for the independent variable, the test group and the control group are indistinguishable." For most of us most of the time, however, the "How else?" question defines life in the real world of political research. Ordinarily, in testing the effect of an independent variable on a dependent variable, we do two things. First, we make the comparison suggested by our hypothesis. Second, we make a controlled comparison, holding constant other variables suggested by rival explanations and hypotheses. In Chapter 3 we consider the mechanics of the first step, making comparisons. There you will learn how to make comparisons and test hypotheses using real data. In Chapter 4 we discuss the second step, controlled comparisons. There you will learn how to set up controlled comparisons with real data, and you will learn how to interpret what these comparisons reveal. In the remainder of the present chapter, we use mostly hypothetical data to demonstrate the logic behind the controlled comparison research design.

As a point of departure, recall the gender-based explanation of gun control opinions introduced earlier in this chapter. That explanation, which we will call the "gender explanation," proposed that a causal process, childhood socialization, encouraged different political predispositions in males and females. These predispositions were causally linked to different opinions about gun control among adult men and women. It was hypothesized that, in comparing individuals, women will be more likely than men to favor a handgun ban. This comparison, using actual data from the 1996 National Election Study, is a real eye-opener: Over 57 percent of women, but only 33 percent of men, favor a ban. What do you think? Should we regard these findings as confirming the correctness of the gender explanation? Doing so, obviously, would be jumping the gun.

The "How else?" question is the unofficial mantra of political research. And it needs to be repeated every time we test a hypothesis. How else, other than gender, are the two groups— men and women—not the same? Might these other, unexamined differences account for differences in gun control attitudes? Consider a rival explanation, which we will call the "partisanship explanation." This explanation also accounts for differences between people in their attitudes toward a handgun ban:

> When people enter early adulthood, they have only very basic orientations toward politics. Partisanship is one of these orientations. In much the same way that people adopt the religious denomination of their parents, people tend to adopt the party loyalties of their parents. A person who is raised in a Democratic household is likely to identify with the Democrats, whereas a person who is raised in a Republican household is likely to become a Republican. These partisan orientations may be basic, but they become useful later in life when people are deciding their positions on important political issues. Democrats will look at the issue positions of Democratic opinion leaders—Democratic members of Congress, for example—and adopt those issue positions themselves. Republicans will look to Republican opinion leaders. Gun control is a good case in point. Gun control is one issue that has increasingly divided Democratic and Republican opinion leaders. Democratic opinion leaders, from the presidential and congressional levels to states and local governments, have advocated stricter measures. Republicans, who often call for tougher enforcement of existing laws, have opposed new gun control measures. The opinions of ordinary citizens have followed this lead. Therefore, the following hypothesis seems plausible: In comparing individuals, Democrats will be more likely than Republicans to favor gun control.

Table 2-1 Respondents Favoring Handgun Ban, by Gender, Controlling for Partisanship (percent)

Gender	Favors handgun ban	
	Democrat *(Group 1)*	Republican *(Group 2)*
Female	DF	RF
Male	DM	RM

The partisanship explanation describes a general causal process and suggests the existence of several empirical relationships. It links a dependent variable, opinions on gun control, to an independent variable, party affiliation. The test of the hypothesis centers on a simple comparison—the percentage of Democrats favoring a handgun ban compared with the percentage of Republicans. And this comparison, again using data from the 1996 National Election Study, reveals a large difference: Over 53 percent of Democrats, but only 38 percent of Republicans, support such a ban.

More important, the partisanship model suggests a plausible answer to the "How else?" question. Men and women may also differ in their partisan attachments. If females are more likely to be Democrats, and males are more likely to be Republicans, then this difference—not gender-based issue positions—could explain the observed difference in gun attitudes between men and women. How would we go about neutralizing this rival? Think about this for a moment. Suppose we observed a group of men and women, all of whom were Democrats. If the gender explanation is correct, then female Democrats should be more likely to favor a ban than male Democrats. If the gender explanation is incorrect, then there will be no difference between genders on the dependent variable. Now imagine another group of men and women, all of whom are Republicans. Again, if the gender explanation is correct, female Republicans will be more in favor of gun control than will male Republicans. If the gender explanation is off base, we will not observe this gender difference. That is the logic of controlled comparison. We neutralize the effects of a rival cause by holding it constant—by not permitting it to operate. Obviously, any difference in gun opinions between female Democrats and male Democrats cannot be caused by partisan differences—everybody's a Democrat.

Table 2-1 lays out a framework for testing the effect of gender on gun ban attitudes, holding partisanship constant. In this basic design, we are holding the partisanship explanation constant by defining groups of subjects who do not differ in their party affiliations. All of the people in Group 1 are Democrats and all in Group 2 are Republicans. This permits gender differences, the female-male comparison, to operate within each of the groups. The symbols DF, DM, RF, and RM represent the percentages of subjects who favor a handgun ban. So DF stands for the percentage of Democratic females who favor a ban, DM represents the percentage of Democratic males who support a ban, and so on.

We can compare the percentage of Democratic females (DF) who favor a handgun ban with the percentage of Democratic males (DM) who favor a ban. And we can compare the percentage of Republican females (RF) with the percentage of Republican males (RM). And in doing so we can be sure of this: Any gender differences in gun attitudes observed within each partisan group cannot be attributed to differences in partisanship. That much is clear. But notice this bonus. In dividing up subjects like this, we are also obtaining the information we need in order to hold gender constant and allow partisanship to operate. By comparing

Table 2-2 Respondents Favoring Handgun Ban, by
Gender; Partisanship Explanation Incorrect (percent)

| | Favors handgun ban | |
| | *Democrat* | *Republican* |
Gender	*(Group 1)*	*(Group 2)*
Female	60	60
Male	45	45

Note: Hypothetical data.

percentage DF with percentage RF—and making the same comparison between percentage DM and percentage RM—we can evaluate the effect of party, controlling for gender. So, by this logic, any partisan differences in gun attitudes observed within each gender group cannot be attributed to differences in gender. Do the gender explanation and the partisanship explanation yield different answers about what all these comparisons should reveal?

Continue to concentrate on the logic. Suppose, first, that the gender explanation is correct and the partisanship explanation is incorrect. If this were the case, what percentages for DF, DM, RF, and RM would we expect to find? What would these numbers look like? You might come up with something like Table 2-2. These mocked-up numbers show that gender continues to explain gun control opinions after party affiliation has been controlled. A much higher percentage of female Democrats than male Democrats favor gun control in this scenario. And a much higher percentage of female Republicans than male Republicans support a ban. Plus, partisanship plays no explanatory role. Holding gender constant and looking for partisan differences reveals no differences at all. Both groups of women, Democrats and Republicans, are equally supportive at 60 percent. Both groups of males are the same, too, since 45 percent of each group favors a handgun ban.

Now imagine some values for DF, DM, RF, and RM that would reveal the partisanship explanation to be correct and the gender explanation incorrect. Table 2-3 would certainly fill the bill. Here, the data have turned against the gender idea. Holding party constant, gender differences drop to zero. For Democrats, the percentage of females (60) minus the percentage of males (60) is zero. For Republicans, the percentage of females (45) minus the percentage of males (45) is zero. Partisanship is doing all of the explanatory work. Looking only at the numbers for women, female Democrats (60%) are far more likely to favor gun control than are female Republicans (45%). Ditto for males: A large percentage point difference exists between Democratic men and Republican men.

Table 2-3 Respondents Favoring Handgun Ban, by
Gender; Partisanship Explanation Correct (percent)

| | Favors handgun ban | |
| | *Democrat* | *Republican* |
Gender	*(Group 1)*	*(Group 2)*
Female	60	45
Male	60	45

Note: Hypothetical data.

Table 2-4 Respondents Favoring Handgun Ban, by Gender; Gender and Partisanship Explanations Correct (percent)

	Favors handgun ban	
Gender	Democrat (Group 1)	Republican (Group 2)
Female	65	55
Male	40	30

Note: Hypothetical data.

"Wait a minute!" you might object, "If you compare female Democrats with male Republicans, you find a huge difference between the sexes." This sort of comparison, which might seem reasonable, underscores a crucial point about making controlled comparisons. In evaluating rival explanations, the only meaningful comparisons are comparisons between groups of subjects who differ on one independent variable but share the same value on the other independent variable. That is a hard-and-fast rule. In this example, the only revealing comparisons are those between men and women who share the same party affiliation and Democrats and Republicans who have the same gender.

Another objection, however, has a great deal of merit. Isn't it plausible that *both* explanations might be correct? After all, the partisanship explanation and the gender explanation may be rivals, but they are not mutually exclusive. Perhaps gender socialization, which occurs early in life, shapes general dispositions toward issues like gun control. The role of partisan opinion leaders might alter basic dispositions, but the imprint of gender could persist into adulthood. Plausible enough. And, since we are not yet dealing with actual opinions about gun control, we can make the data cooperate with this idea. What hypothetical percentages for DF, DM, RF, and RM would support both explanations? Consider Table 2-4. What happens when we control for party and let gender operate? Clearly gender has a big effect within Group 1 and Group 2. Bringing up the topic of guns to a roomful of Democrats would invite a spirited debate between females and males. Similarly, Republicans would not speak with one voice on this issue, since a gun ban is much more popular among female Republicans than among their male counterparts. So the gender explanation works. But partisan differences are important, too. Holding gender constant, female Democrats are more likely than female Republicans to support a tough gun law, and male Democrats are more likely than male Republicans to favor such a law. In this hypothetical scenario, both gender and partisanship contribute to an explanation of gun control opinions.

Or do they? Repeat the mantra: "How else, other than gender and partisanship, do Group 1 and Group 2 differ? Could these other, uncontrolled differences account for opinions on gun control?" Certain regions, such as the South and mountain West, have deeper cultural reservations about gun control than other regions, like the Northeast. Could we describe a plausible explanation and formulate a hypothesis for this independent variable, region? Suppose this new rival, the "region explanation," was correct, the gender explanation was correct, and the partisanship explanation incorrect. How would you design a set of controlled comparisons to evaluate these various explanations? What would the data look like in such a case?

Be reassured that political researchers are not in the habit of dreaming up imaginary numbers to support or undermine rival explanations. (That would raise the investigator's ability to manipulate subjects to an entirely new level!) For now, odd as it may sound, the explanation of gun control attitudes—to which we return in the chapters that follow—is not as important as how we go about discovering the explanation of gun control attitudes. This is the logic of inquiry in the real world of political research. Controlled comparison and the "How else?" mantra define the boundaries of that world.

SUMMARY

In this chapter we introduced the essential ideas behind describing explanations, stating hypotheses, and designing tests for hypotheses that control for alternative explanations. We have seen that political research often begins by observing an interesting variable and then developing a causal explanation for it. An explanation describes how a causal variable, the independent variable, is linked to an effect variable, the dependent variable. Remember that an explanation must describe the causal linkage between an independent variable and a dependent variable, and it must be plausible. An explanation must be testable. It must suggest a hypothesis, a testable statement about the empirical relationship between an independent variable and a dependent variable.

   In testing a hypothesis to see if an independent variable affects a dependent variable, the researcher tries to control for rival or alternative explanations—other plausible causes of the dependent variable. The ability to rule out or neutralize rival causes for a dependent variable depends on the power of the research design being used. In the experimental research design, test subjects differ from control subjects only in the independent variable. Any observed differences in the dependent variable can be attributed directly to the independent variable and cannot be attributed to any other cause. In the natural experimental research design, subjects themselves choose to be in the test group or the control group. Selection bias occurs when the subjects choosing the test group differ from subjects choosing the control group in ways that affect the dependent variable. Selection bias introduces rival causes for the dependent variable. In the controlled comparison research design, the researcher examines the relationship between an independent variable and a dependent variable while holding a rival causal variable constant, controlling its effect on the dependent variable. Any observed relationship between the independent variable and the dependent variable may not be attributed to the variable being controlled. However, there may be other, uncontrolled causes for the observed relationship. The controlled comparison research design is the most common design in political research. After examining the relationship between an independent variable and a dependent variable, the researcher must always ask, "How else, other than the independent variable, are the test group and control group not the same?"

KEY TERMS

control group (p. 38)
controlled comparison design (p. 38)
dependent variable (p. 30)
external validity (p. 41)
hypothesis (p. 29)
independent variable (p. 30)
internal validity (p. 41)
intervening variable (p. 37)

natural experimental design (p. 39)
random assignment (p. 39)
research design (p. 38)
rival explanation (p. 38)
selection bias (p. 42)
test group (p. 38)
true experimental design (p. 38)

EXERCISES

1. The 2000 presidential election again raised questions about the television networks' practice of calling election outcomes early on election night, before the polls have closed. The conventional wisdom is that early declarations depress turnout in areas where the polls are still open. Case in point: All the broadcast and cable networks declared Al Gore the winner in Florida before the polls in Florida's panhandle (which is in the central time zone) had closed. According to the conventional wisdom, panhandle residents who had intended to vote did not go to the polls, which depressed turnout in the panhandle.

   A. Think about the relationship between an independent variable, whether or not people have knowledge of an election's predicted outcome (they either "know" or they "don't know" the predicted outcome) and a dependent variable (they either "voted" or they "did not vote"). The conventional wisdom links one value of the independent variable, "know the predicted outcome," with one value of the dependent variable, "did not vote." For the conventional wisdom to qualify as an acceptable explanation, what else must it describe?

   B. Suppose you believe that knowledge of an election's predicted outcome is causally linked to turnout. Why might differences in knowledge of the outcome cause differences in turnout? Write a paragraph describing the causal linkages between these two variables. Be sure to describe the tendency of the relationship.

   C. Using proper form, state a testable hypothesis for the relationship between the independent variable and the dependent variable.

2. Third-party candidates are something of a puzzle for students of electoral behavior. In presidential elections, most voters cast their ballots for one of the major-party candidates, but many voters support a minor-party candidate, such as Ross Perot in 1992 and 1996 or Ralph Nader in 2000 and 2004. What causes some people to vote for a major-party candidate and some voters to vote for a minor-party candidate? Voters can be measured by one of two values on this dependent variable: major-party voter and minor-party voter.

   A. Think up a plausible independent variable that may explain differences between voters on the dependent variable. Write a paragraph describing an explanation for why some voters support the major parties' candidates and some support the minor parties' candidates. Make sure you connect the causal variable to the dependent variable, and be sure to describe the tendency of the relationship.

   B. Using proper form, state a testable hypothesis for the relationship between the independent variable and the dependent variable.

3. Four statements appear below. For each one (i) identify and describe at least one reason why it is a poor hypothesis and (ii) rewrite the statement in proper hypothesis-writing form. (You may have to embellish a bit, using your own intuition.)

   Example. Income and partisanship are related.

   (i) This statement does not identify the units of analysis. Also, it does not state the tendency of the relationship because it does not say how income and partisanship are related.

   (ii) In comparing individuals, people with lower incomes will be more likely to be Democrats than will people with higher incomes.

   A. In comparing individuals, some people will be more likely to have served in the military than will other people.

   B. Decentralized workplaces have highly satisfied workers.

   C. Because of widespread access to the Internet, people are becoming more isolated from other human beings.

   D. Education and smoking are related.

4. Robert Putnam's research, which was discussed briefly in this chapter, has stimulated renewed interest in the role played by voluntary associations in American democracy. Putnam's work seems to suggest that, when people get involved in groups and help make collective decisions for the group, they develop participatory skills. These participatory skills, in turn, cause people to participate more in politics—voting at higher rates than people who are not involved in any groups. One hypothesis: In comparing individuals, those who belong to voluntary associations will be more likely to vote than will those who do not belong to voluntary associations.
   A. This explanation cites an intervening variable. What is the intervening variable?
   B. Based on the explanation, write a hypothesis in which the intervening variable is the dependent variable.
   C. Based on the explanation, write a hypothesis in which the intervening variable is the independent variable.

5. In this chapter we discussed the methodological principles behind controlled comparison. The basic idea is this: The observed relationship between an independent variable and a dependent variable may be caused by some other, uncontrolled difference between subjects. So we always ask, "How else, besides the independent variable, do the subjects differ?" For each of the three hypotheses below (i) think up a plausible alternative causal variable (other than income!) on which the subjects might differ and (ii) describe how this variable might affect the relationship between the independent variable and the dependent variable.
   Example. In comparing individuals, older people will be more likely to vote Democratic than will younger people.
   (i) Plausible alternative variable: income
   (ii) Older people might have lower incomes than younger people. If people with lower incomes are more likely to vote Democratic than people with higher incomes, then differences in income, not differences in age, could explain the relationship between the independent and dependent variables.
   A. In comparing congressional candidates, candidates who spend more money on their campaigns will be more likely to win than will candidates who spend less money. (Hint for plausible alternative variable: Incumbents generally spend more money than challengers.)
   B. In comparing students, those who arrive late to class will be more likely to receive poor grades than will those who arrive on time.
   C. In comparing individuals, people who have children will be more likely to approve of spanking as a form of discipline than will people who do not have children.

6. Here is a variable: Some people support a government-backed health insurance plan that would cover all citizens whereas others oppose such a plan. This variable has two values: "support government plan" and "oppose government plan." Let's say that one explanation, the "age explanation," suggests this hypothesis: In comparing individuals, those who are old will be more likely to support a government health plan than will those who are young. A rival explanation, the "income explanation," suggests this hypothesis: In comparing individuals, those who have low incomes will be more likely to support a government plan than will those who have high incomes.
   A. Using Table 2-1 as a guide, write down a framework for testing the age explanation, controlling for the income explanation. The symbols in your framework should represent percentages that support a government plan. (The age variable has two values: "young" and "old." The income variable has two values: "low" and "high.")

3

Describing Variables and Making Comparisons

LEARNING OBJECTIVES

In this chapter you will learn:
- How to determine the central tendency of a variable
- How to describe the amount of dispersion in a variable
- How to test hypotheses using cross-tabulation analysis and mean comparison analysis
- How to describe linear relationships between variables
- How to describe curvilinear relationships between variables

It has been said that Dwight Eisenhower, no-nonsense if not particularly energetic president of the United States during the 1950s, greatly valued succinctness and simplicity. The story goes that he asked his staff members to condense their voluminous daily reports into a single typewritten page. (President Eisenhower's detractors claimed that if the summary were any longer than a page, Ike's lips would get tired.) Many of us are not so different from Eisenhower. After all, "boil it down," "get to the point," or "give it to me in a nutshell" are common requests in everyday life. And the summary number most in demand, it seems, is the average.

The world is defined by averages. When your college or university wants to summarize your entire academic career, what one number does it use? What is the average tuition cost of higher education institutions in your state? When people go on vacation, how many days do they typically stay? What is the most popular month for weddings? What make of automobile do most people drive? What is the make most frequently stolen? What is the typical amount paid for a car? Political research, too, has a passion for the typical. How much does a congressional candidate commonly spend on a campaign? Do people who describe themselves as Republicans have higher incomes, on average, than Democrats? What opinion do most people hold on the abortion issue? Affirmative action? Immigration reform?

When it comes to describing variables, averages are indispensable. However, political researchers rarely use the term *average* in the same way it is used in everyday life. They refer to a variable's **central tendency**—that is, its typical or average value. A variable's central tendency may be measured in three ways. The appropriate measure depends on the variable's level of measurement. The most basic measure of central tendency is the **mode**. The mode of a variable is the most common value of the variable, the value that contains the largest number of cases or units of analysis.[1] The mode may be used to describe the central tendency of any variable. For nominal-level variables, however, it is the only measure that may be used. For describing variables with higher levels of measurement—that is, ordinal or interval—the **median** comes into play. The median is the value of a variable that divides the cases right down the middle—with half of the cases having values below the median and half having values above the median. The central tendency of an ordinal-level variable may be measured by the mode or median. For interval-level variables, a third measure, the **mean**, also may be used to describe central tendency. The mean comes closest to the everyday use of the term *average*. In fact, a variable's mean *is* its arithmetic average. When we sum all the cases' individual values on a variable, and divide by the number of cases, we arrive at the variable's mean value. All of these measures of central tendency—the mode, the median, and the mean—are workhorses of description, and they are the main elements in making comparisons and testing hypotheses.

Yet there is more to describing a variable than reporting its measure of central tendency. A political variable also is described by the **dispersion**, or variation, of its values.[2] When we say that opinions on gun control are "polarized," for example, we are describing their variation, the particular way opinions are distributed across the values of the variable—many people support gun control, many people oppose it, and only a few take a middle position. To say that general "consensus" exists among Americans that capitalism is preferable to communism is to denote little variation among people, or widespread agreement on one option over another. When scholars of comparative politics discuss the level of economic equality in a country, they are interested in the variation or dispersion of wealth. Is there little variation, with most economic resources being controlled by a few? Or is the distribution more equitable, with economic resources dispersed across many or most citizens?

In the first part of this chapter we discuss the meaning and appropriate uses of measures of central tendency—mode, median, and mean. We also explore nonstatistical approaches to describing a variable's dispersion.[3] You will find that central tendency and dispersion are not separate aspects of a variable. They work together to provide a complete description of a variable. In the second part of this chapter we demonstrate fundamental methods for testing hypotheses—for implementing the logic of comparison covered in Chapter 2. Again the discussion is nonstatistical.[4] And in the third part of this chapter we consider ways to describe the direction of the relationship between two variables.

DESCRIBING VARIABLES

Let's begin by looking at three variables: region of residence (a nominal variable), frequency of attendance at religious services (an ordinal variable), and age measured in years (an interval variable). In the survey results we are using here, there are four possible values of region (Northeast, North Central, South, and West), and there are five possible values of religious attendance (weekly, almost weekly, once or twice a month, yearly, never). The range of possible ages is huge, from 18 to 99. How did a large group of actual subjects respond when asked how old they are, how often they attend church, and what region they live in?

First consider the nominal and ordinal variables, region and religious attendance. Table 3-1 shows how a large sample of individuals responded to the region question in the 1996 National Election Study. Table 3-2 depicts the religious attendance variable. Each table is a

Table 3-1 Region of Residence (tabular)

Region	Frequency	Percentage
Northeast	260	15.2
North Central	458	26.7
South	642	37.5
West	354	20.7
Total	1,714	100.1

Source: Steven J. Rosenstone, Donald R. Kinder, Warren E. Miller, and the National Election Studies, *American National Election Study, 1996: Pre- and Post-election Survey,* 4th version (Ann Arbor: University of Michigan, Center for Political Studies [producer], 1999; Inter-university Consortium for Political and Social Research [distributor], 2000).

Table 3-2 Attendance at Religious Services (tabular)

Attendance	Frequency	Percentage	Cumulative percentage
Never attend	505	29.5	29.5
Yearly	306	17.9	47.4
Once or twice a month	248	14.5	61.9
Almost weekly	208	12.2	74.1
Weekly	444	25.9	100.0
Total	1,711	100.0	

Source: 1996 National Election Study.
Note: Question: "Do you go to religious services every week, almost every week, once or twice a month, a few times a year, or never?"

frequency distribution, a tabular summary of a variable's values. Frequency distributions are commonly used in data presentations of all kinds—from survey research and journalistic polls to marketing studies and corporate annual reports. The first column of each frequency distribution lists the variable's values. The second column reports the number, or **raw frequency**, of subjects giving each response. The raw frequencies are totaled at the bottom of the column. This is the **total frequency**. The third column reports the percentage of subjects falling into each value of the variable.[5] The equation to figure the percentage for each value is

$$\text{Percentage for each value} = (\text{raw frequency/total frequency}) \times 100.$$

Frequency distributions for ordinal-level variables usually contain an additional column. Unlike nominal variables, which measure differences between cases, ordinal variables tell us the relative amount of the characteristic being measured. This higher level of precision allows us to determine **cumulative percentage**, or the percentage of cases at or below any given value of the variable. So, in Table 3-2, 47.4 percent of respondents attend religious services yearly or never, and 61.9 percent attend once or twice a month or less.

A picture, to use an old cliché, is worth a thousand words. This adage aptly applies to frequency distributions, which are often presented in the form of a **bar chart**, a graphic

Figure 3-1 Region of Residence (graphic)

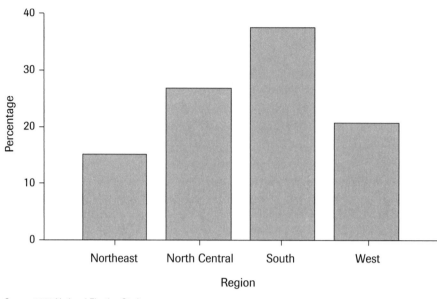

Source: 1996 National Election Study.

display of data. For interval-level variables such as age, as we will see, graphic applications are even more important for describing a variable. Figures 3-1 and 3-2 show bar charts for the frequency distributions of, respectively, region of residence and attendance at religious services. Bar charts are visually pleasing and elegant. The variable's values are labeled along the horizontal axis and percentages (or, alternatively, raw frequencies) along the vertical. So, the height of each bar clearly depicts the percentage or number of cases having that value of the variable.[6]

Examine the frequency distributions and bar charts for a few moments. Suppose you had to write a paragraph about each variable. Religious attendance, in particular, has something of an offbeat appearance. How would you describe it?

> Among the 1,711 respondents, nearly a third (29.5 percent) said they never attend religious services. Although "never attend" was the most common response given by individuals, over a fourth (25.9 percent) were highly observant, attending every week. There appears to be much heterogeneity among people, with sizable percentages in each category of the variable. There may be a tilt toward lower religiosity: Slightly less than half of the sample (47.4 percent) reported either that they attend very rarely (once a year) or never attend.

You will find that, in describing the information contained in a frequency distribution or a graphic, you are naturally drawn toward enriching the description by citing a variable's most prominent features. The sentences above noted two such features: the typical response to the religious attendance question and the extent to which responses were dispersed across the variable's values. In describing a variable's typical or average value we are reporting the distribution's central tendency. In describing variety across the variable's values we are reporting the amount of dispersion in the variable.

Figure 3-2   Attendance at Religious Services (graphic)

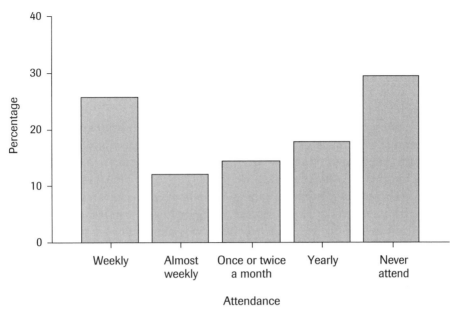

Source: 1996 National Election Study.
Note: Question: "Do you go to religious services every week, almost every week, once or twice a month, a few times a year, or never?"

As noted at the beginning of the chapter, the most basic measure of central tendency is the mode, which is defined as the most common value of a variable. The mode of the religiosity variable (Table 3-2) is "never attend," since the largest percentage of people gave that response. The mode for region (Table 3-1) is "South," the value with the highest percentage. Note that the mode itself is not a percentage or a frequency. It is always a value. A good description takes the following form: "Among the [units of analysis], the mode is [modal value], with [percentage of units] having this value." In the example of region, "Among the 1,714 individuals in the survey, the mode is South, with 37.5 percent having this value."

A frequency distribution having two different values that are heavily populated with cases is called a **bimodal distribution**. Many nominal and ordinal variables have a singular central tendency that is clearly captured by the mode. Region, for example, has a single peak that is easily identified. Religious attendance, by contrast, is a bimodal variable, and a rather interesting one at that. One of its responses ("never") has the highest percentage of cases and, thus, is technically the mode of the distribution. But the flipside response ("weekly") has nearly as many cases, giving the distribution two very prominent, and very different, response categories. You have to exercise judgment in deciding whether a variable is bimodal. Of course, the percentages of the two values should be similar. Also, in the case of ordinal variables, the two modes should be separated by at least one nonmodal category. Because the two modes of religiosity are separated by three response categories ("yearly", "once or twice a month," "almost weekly"), the distribution is clearly bimodal. If, instead, the two modes were "never" and "yearly"—that is, if the responses were concentrated in two similar values—we would want to use a single mode to describe the central tendency of the distribution.

The mode may be used in describing any variable, but for nominal-level variables it is the only measure of central tendency that can be used. Again consider the frequency distribution for region (Table 3-1). Notice that, because region is a nominal variable, the rows could be arranged in any order. It would make just as much sense to list South first, then West, North Central, and Northeast. But for religiosity the situation is different. Since we can order or rank subjects according to their frequency of attendance, it is possible to find a true center of the distribution. For ordinal variables—and for interval variables, too—it is possible to find the value that bisects the respondents into equal percentages, with 50 percent of the cases having higher values of the variable and 50 percent having lower values. The middle-most value of a variable is the median.

The median is one member of a larger family of locational measures referred to as percentiles. Anyone who has taken a standardized college-entrance exam, such as the SAT, is familiar with this family. A **percentile** reports the percentage of cases in a distribution that lie below it. This information serves to locate the position of an individual value relative to all other values. If a prospective college entrant's SAT score puts him in, say, the 85th percentile on the SAT, that person knows that 85 percent of all other test-takers had lower scores on the exam (and 15 percent had higher scores). The median is simply the 50th percentile, the value that divides a distribution in half.

So, what is the median of religious attendance? This is where the cumulative percentage column of Table 3-2 comes into play. We can see that "never" is not the median, since only 29.5 percent of the cases have this value; nor is it "yearly," since 47.4 percent lie at or below this value. Clearly, too, if we jump to "almost weekly" we have moved too high in the order, since 74.1 percent of the respondents are at or below this value. The median is within "once or twice a month," since the true point of bisection must occur in this value. Some researchers put a finer point on the computation of the median, but for our purposes the median of an ordinal variable is the value of the variable that contains the median. Thus we would say that the median is "once or twice a month."

Now take a step back and reconsider the big picture. Would you say that "once or twice a month" is the typical response people gave when asked how frequently they attended religious services? Probably not. The example of religious attendance underscores the importance of considering the amount of variation in a variable before deciding if its measure of central tendency is really average or typical. Here is a general rule: The greatest amount of dispersion for any variable occurs when the cases are equally spread among all values of the variable. Conversely, the lowest amount of dispersion occurs when all the cases are in one value of the variable. If 20 percent of the cases fell into each category of the religiosity variable, this variable would have maximum dispersion—or, to use an ordinary term, complete heterogeneity. If, by contrast, all respondents reported the same level of religious observance, this variable would have no dispersion at all—complete homogeneity. By the same token, the region variable would have maximum dispersion if each of its four values (Northeast, North Central, South, and West) contained 25 percent of the cases, that is, if all of the bars in Figure 3-1 were the same height. It would have no dispersion if one value, such as "West," contained all the cases. Another indication of dispersion, for ordinal variables at least, is provided by comparing the mode and median. If the mode and median are separated by more than one value, then the cases are more spread out than if the mode and median fall in the same value of the variable. By either of these guidelines, religious attendance can be said to have a high degree of dispersion. If dispersion is the most prominent feature of a nominal or an ordinal variable, then it would be misleading to use a mode or median to describe it. In such a case, which the religiosity variable exemplifies, we would base our description on the variable's dispersion.

Odd as it may sound, the median's main strength is that it is impervious to the amount of variation in a variable. It simply locates the middle-most score. For bimodal distributions, as we have just seen, this can be a problem. But for single-peaked distributions, those having one mode, the median's resistance to extremely high or low values is a definite asset—an asset that often stands it in good stead with its interval-level sibling, the mean.

Recall that an interval-level variable gives us precise measurements. Unlike nominal variables, whose values represent differences between subjects, and ordinal variables, whose values represent relative differences between subjects, the values of interval variables communicate the exact amount of the characteristic being measured. What is more, since interval-level variables are the highest form of measurement, each of the "lower" measures of central tendency—the mode and median—also may be used to describe them. Table 3-3 reports the (ungainly!) frequency distribution for the age variable. What is the mode, the most common age? Although it does not jump off the page at you, the most heavily populated value is 35 years of age, with 57 respondents. So 35 is the mode. And what is the median, the middle-most value? Just as with the religiosity variable, we read down the cumulative percentages until we hit the 50th percentile. Since 50.7 percent of the respondents are age 44 or younger, 44 is the median age.

What about the mean? As noted at the beginning of the chapter, the mean is the arithmetic center of an interval-level distribution. The mean is obtained by summing the values of all units of analysis and dividing the sum by the number of units. In calculating the mean age of people responding to the 1996 National Election Study survey, we take the sum of the ages of all respondents (which, according to the computer, is 81,382 years), and then divide this sum by the number of valid responses (1,712).[7] The result: 47.5 years. Now let's get the big picture and see which of the three measures of central tendency—the mode, the median, or the mean—best conveys the typical age.

Figure 3-3 displays a bar chart of the age variable. It was constructed just like the earlier bar charts for region and religious attendance. The values of the variable appear along the horizontal axis. The percentages of respondents falling into each value are reported on the vertical axis. Examine Figure 3-3. How would you describe this variable? It would appear that the respondents are grouped fairly densely between 35 and 40 years of age, tapering off in numbers at about age 30 on the "younger" side and age 50 on the "older" side. You could safely describe this distribution as having one mode. But notice that there are some individuals at the extreme upper values of this variable—creating a longer tail on the right-hand side than on the left-hand side. In fact, the data in Figure 3-3 are skewed—that is, they exhibit an asymmetrical distribution of cases. Distributions with a longer, or skinnier, right-hand tail have a **positive skew**; and those with a skinnier left-hand tail have a **negative skew**. The mean is sensitive to skewness. In the example of age, respondents in the upper values of the variable pull the mean upward, away from the clump of individuals in the 35- to 40-year-old range.

Extreme values may have an obvious effect on the mean, but they have little effect on the median. In keeping with its reputation for disregarding dispersion, the median (age 44) reports the value that divides the respondents into equal-size groups, unfazed by the distribution's positive skew. For this reason, the median is called a **resistant measure of central tendency**, and you can see why it sometimes gives a more faithful idea of the true center of an interval-level variable.

Here is a general rule: When the mean of an interval-level variable is higher than its median, the distribution has a positive skew. When the mean is lower than its median, the distribution has a negative skew. Because the mean age is 47.5 and the median age is 44, the

Table 3-3 Age of Respondents (tabular)

Age	Frequency	Percentage	Cumulative percentage	Age	Frequency	Percentage	Cumulative percentage
18	4	0.2	0.2	56	27	1.6	69.8
19	10	0.6	0.8	57	23	1.3	71.1
20	19	1.1	1.9	58	26	1.5	72.7
21	21	1.2	3.2	59	18	1.1	73.7
22	20	1.2	4.3	60	15	0.9	74.6
23	15	0.9	5.2	61	19	1.1	75.7
24	28	1.6	6.8	62	28	1.6	77.3
25	31	1.8	8.6	63	18	1.1	78.4
26	25	1.5	10.1	64	20	1.2	79.6
27	31	1.8	11.9	65	21	1.2	80.8
28	25	1.5	13.4	66	12	0.7	81.5
29	26	1.5	14.9	67	29	1.7	83.2
30	36	2.1	17.0	68	16	0.9	84.1
31	36	2.1	19.1	69	21	1.2	85.3
32	40	2.3	21.4	70	25	1.5	86.8
33	38	2.2	23.7	71	15	0.9	87.7
34	44	2.6	26.2	72	25	1.5	89.1
35	57	3.3	29.6	73	21	1.2	90.4
36	40	2.3	31.9	74	18	1.1	91.4
37	42	2.5	34.3	75	12	0.7	92.1
38	51	3.0	37.3	76	24	1.4	93.5
39	35	2.0	39.4	77	10	0.6	94.1
40	40	2.3	41.7	78	9	0.5	94.6
41	37	2.2	43.9	79	12	0.7	95.3
42	49	2.9	46.7	80	9	0.5	95.9
43	35	2.0	48.8	81	7	0.4	96.3
44	33	1.9	50.7	82	9	0.5	96.8
45	35	2.0	52.7	83	11	0.6	97.4
46	28	1.6	54.4	84	9	0.5	98.0
47	35	2.0	56.4	85	8	0.5	98.4
48	34	2.0	58.4	86	2	0.1	98.5
49	28	1.6	60.0	87	8	0.5	99.0
50	30	1.8	61.8	88	10	0.6	99.6
51	23	1.3	63.1	89	1	0.1	99.6
52	17	1.0	64.1	91	4	0.2	99.9
53	24	1.4	65.5	92	1	0.1	99.9
54	18	1.1	66.6	93	1	0.1	100.0
55	28	1.6	68.2	Total	1,712	100.0	

Source: 1996 National Election Study.

Figure 3-3 Age of Respondents (graphic)

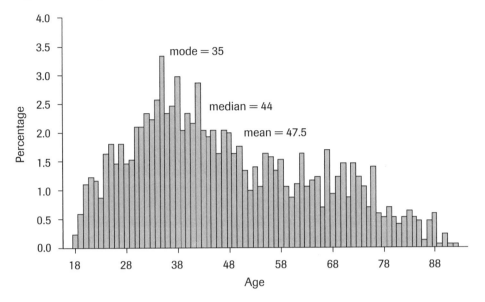

Source: 1996 National Election Study.

distribution depicted in Figure 3-3 has a positive skew. Now, an interval-level variable will always have some skewness. The mean and median are rarely the same. This being the case, should we simply ignore the mean and report only the median of an interval-level variable? How much skewness is too much? Most computer programs provide a statistical measure of skewness that can help the analyst in this regard.[8] As a practical matter, however, you have to exercise judgment in deciding how much is too much.

Consider Table 3-4 and Figure 3-4, which portray the frequency distribution and bar chart of respondents' opinions about government spending on seven programs. The General Social Survey routinely includes a series of questions that ask individuals whether the government is spending "too little," "about the right amount," or "too much" in a number of policy areas.[9] Table 3-4 and Figure 3-4 report the number of programs on which, in the respondents' opinions, the government is spending "too little." This variable can take on any value between 0 (the respondent doesn't think the government is spending too little on any of the programs) and 7 (the respondent thinks the government is spending too little on all seven programs). Higher scores, then, would suggest a more liberal attitude toward spending. Examine the frequency distribution and bar chart. Is this distribution skewed? Yes, it is. The mean, 3.8, is lower than the median and mode (both of which are 4.0), indicating a negative skew. The skinnier tail toward lower values also suggests negative skewness. But make a judgment call. Would it be misleading to use the mean value, 3.8, as the central tendency of this distribution? In this case, the mean serves as a good gauge of central tendency.

SUMMARY GUIDELINES OF DESCRIPTION

As we have seen, describing a variable requires a combination of quantitative knowledge and informed judgment. By way of review, here are some general guidelines for interpreting central tendency and dispersion.

Table 3-4 Number of Programs with "Too Little" Government Spending (tabular)

Number of programs	Frequency	Percentage	Cumulative percentage
0	44	4.0	4.0
1	76	6.9	10.8
2	131	11.8	22.7
3	197	17.8	40.5
4	255	23.0	63.5
5	212	19.2	82.7
6	145	13.1	95.8
7	47	4.2	100.0
Total	1,107	100.0	
Mean = 3.8			

Source: James A. Davis, Tom W. Smith, and Peter V. Marsden, *General Social Surveys, 1972–2002* (Chicago, Ill.: National Opinion Research Center [producer], 2003; Storrs, Conn.: Roper Center for Public Opinion Research, University of Connecticut/Ann Arbor, Mich.: Inter-university Consortium for Political and Social Research [distributors], 2003).
Note: Displayed data are from the 2002 GSS.

Figure 3-4 Number of Programs with "Too Little" Government Spending (graphic)

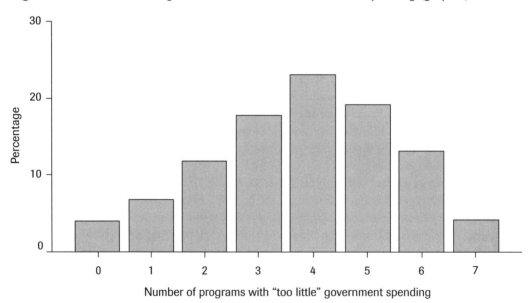

Number of programs with "too little" government spending

Source: James A. Davis, Tom W. Smith, and Peter V. Marsden, *General Social Surveys, 1972–2002* (Chicago, Ill.: National Opinion Research Center [producer], 2003; Storrs, Conn.: Roper Center for Public Opinion Research, University of Connecticut/Ann Arbor, Mich.: Inter-university Consortium for Political and Social Research [distributors], 2003).
Note: Displayed data are from the 2002 GSS.

For nominal variables, find the mode. Using a bar chart as a visual guide, ask yourself these questions: Is the distribution single peaked with a prominent mode? Or is there more than one mode? Visualize what the bar chart would look like if the cases were spread evenly across all values of the variable. What percentage of cases would fall into each value of the variable if it had maximum variation? Compare this mental image to the actual distribution of cases. Would you say that the variable has a large amount of dispersion? A moderate amount? Or are the cases concentrated in the modal value?

For ordinal variables, find the mode and median. Examining the bar chart, mentally construct a few sentences describing the variable. Just as with nominal variables, imagine a "maximum dispersion scenario": Does the actual spread of cases across the variable's values approximate maximum variation? With ordinal variables, you also can compare the modal and median values. Are the mode and median the same, or very close, in value? If so, the central tendency of the variable can be well described by its median. If the mode and median are clearly different values, then it probably would be misleading to make central tendency the focus of description. Instead, describe the variable's dispersion.

For interval variables, find the mode, median, and mean. As we have seen, because frequency distributions for interval variables tend to be inelegant, a bar chart is essential for getting a clear picture.[10] Consider the three measures of central tendency and examine the shape of the distribution. Do the mode, median, and mean fall close to each other on the variable's continuum? If so, use the mean to describe the average value. Is the mean a lot higher or lower than the median? If so, then the distribution may be badly skewed. Describe the source of skewness and use the median as the best representation of the distribution's center.

MAKING COMPARISONS

Political research begins by describing variables, but it does not end there. Our main project, as discussed in Chapter 2, is developing explanations and testing hypotheses—that is, making comparisons. In this part of the chapter, we address two of the most common hypothesis-testing situations. First, we look at how to present and interpret comparisons in which the dependent variable and the independent variable are either nominal or ordinal. Second, we consider situations in which the dependent variable is interval level and the independent variable is nominal or ordinal.[11]

Cross-tabulations

A hypothesis suggests a comparison. It suggests that, if we separate subjects according to their values on the independent variable and compare their values on the dependent variable, we should find a difference. Subjects that differ on the independent variable also should differ on the dependent variable in the hypothesized way. We can now put a finer point on this method. When the dependent and independent variables are nominal or ordinal, hypothesis testing begins by comparing the frequency distributions of a dependent variable for groups of subjects that differ on an independent variable. To illustrate this concept, we will use the hypothesis that was framed in Chapter 2 by the partisanship explanation of gun control. The original hypothesis was as follows: In comparing individuals, Democrats will be more likely than Republicans to favor gun control. The dependent variable, support for gun control, has two possible values: People are either "for" or "against" a handgun ban. The independent variable, partisanship, is an ordinal-level measure, with shadings from "strong Democrat" at one pole to "strong Republican" at the other, and "independent" in between. To simplify the example, we will collapse partisanship into three categories: Democrat, independent, and Republican.[12]

Before looking at the data, try to visualize three side-by-side frequency distributions, one for each partisan group. Imagine a group of subjects, all of whom are Democrats, distributed

Table 3-5 Gun Control Opinions, by Partisanship (cross-tabulation)

Opinion on gun ban	Party identification			Total
	Democrat	*Independent*	*Republican*	
Favor	52.9%	46.6%	37.9%	46.6%
	(314)	(223)	(162)	(699)
Oppose	47.1%	53.4%	62.1%	53.4%
	(280)	(256)	(265)	(801)
Total	100.0%	100.0%	100.0%	100.0%
	(594)	(479)	(427)	(1,500)

Source: 1996 National Election Study.

Note: Question: "Do you favor or oppose a ban on the sale of all handguns, except those that are issued to law enforcement officers?"

across the two values of the dependent variable, "favor" or "oppose," a group of independents distributed across the variable, and a group of Republicans, a percentage of whom favor a ban and a percentage of whom oppose it. Now ask yourself: If the hypothesis were correct, what would a *comparison* of these three frequency distributions reveal?

This mental exercise is the basis for elemental hypothesis testing in political research. Table 3-5, which displays the relationship between partisanship and gun control attitudes, introduces the most common vehicle for analyzing the relationship between two variables, the **cross-tabulation**. A cross-tabulation is a table that shows the distribution of cases across the values of a dependent variable for cases that have different values on an independent variable. A noticeable kinship exists between a frequency distribution and a cross-tabulation. The first column of a frequency distribution shows the values of a variable. Similarly, the first column of a cross-tabulation shows the values of a variable—the values of the dependent variable. The second and third columns of a frequency distribution show how *all* the cases are distributed across the values of a variable and report the percentage falling into each value. Likewise, a cross-tabulation shows how the cases *within each category* of the independent variable are distributed across the values of the dependent variable. So, the first column of numbers in Table 3-5 displays the distribution of the 594 Democrats across the values of the gun control variable, the second column the distribution of the 479 independents, and the third the distribution of the 427 Republicans. Each column contains the raw frequency and percentage of cases falling into each category of the dependent variable. Thus, 314 of the 594 Democrats, which is 52.9 percent, support a ban, 223 of the 479 independents (46.6%) are in favor, as are 162 of the 427 Republicans (37.9%). Notice that the right-most column, labeled "Total," which combines all 1,500 respondents, is the frequency distribution for the dependent variable.

Table 3-5 was constructed by following three rules that should always guide you in setting up a cross-tabulation. The first two rules help you organize the data correctly. The third rule helps you interpret the relationship.

Rule One: Set up a cross-tabulation so that the categories of the independent variable define the columns of the table and the values of the dependent variable define the rows. For each value of the independent variable, the raw frequencies falling into each category of the dependent variable are displayed (by convention, in parentheses), totaled at the bottom of each column.

Rule Two: *Always* calculate percentages of categories of the independent variable. *Never* calculate percentages of categories of the dependent variable. This may sound rigid, but Rule Two is the most essential—and most frequently violated—rule. The partisanship explanation states that the independent variable, party identification, is the cause. The dependent variable, gun opinions, is the effect. As partisanship changes, from Democrat to independent to Republican, gun control attitudes should change—from favor to oppose. Does the balance of opinion change, as the hypothesis suggests, as we move from one level of the causal process to another? To answer this question, we want to know if differences in the causal factor, partisanship, lead to different outcomes, different opinions on gun control. We need to know the percentages of the respondents in each category of the independent variable who favor or oppose gun restrictions. Accordingly, the percentages in each column are based on the column totals, not the row totals. As a visual cue, these percentages are totaled to 100.0 percent at the bottom of each column.

Rule Three: Interpret a cross-tabulation by comparing percentages across columns at the same value of the dependent variable. This is the comparison that sheds light on the hypothesis. We could compare the percentage of Democrats favoring a gun ban with the percentages of independents and Republicans favoring a ban. Alternatively, we could compare the partisan groups across the other category of the dependent variable, "oppose." But we could not mix and match.

These simple rules help avoid some common mistakes. The most serious of these errors, calculating percentages of the dependent variable, already has been pointed out. Another mistake is the tendency to interpret a cross-tabulation by referring to the largest percentages in a column. If I were to say, "While 52.9 percent of the Democrats support gun control, 62.1 percent of Republicans oppose a ban," I certainly would be describing the numbers, but I would not be directly addressing the hypothesis. The hypothesis says that one value of the dependent variable should be different for cases having different values of the independent variable. Hone in on a comparison of percentages across only one value of the dependent variable.

A related error, one that affects the interpretation of the results, occurs when the analyst gets distracted by the absolute magnitudes of the percentages and neglects to make the comparison suggested by the hypothesis. Suppose, for the sake of illustration, that 80 percent of the Democrats favored a gun ban, 70 percent of the independents were in favor, and 60 percent of the Republicans were in favor. In interpreting percentages such as these—percentages that in this case would show high absolute support for gun control in each partisan group—we might be tempted to say, "The hypothesis is wrong. Large majorities of Democrats, independents, and Republicans favor a ban on handguns." This would be an incorrect interpretation. Remember that a hypothesis is a *comparative* statement. It requires a comparison of *differences* in the dependent variable across values of the independent variable. Always apply a comparative standard. Applying this standard to the illustrative 80-70-60 percentages, we would have to say that, as partisanship changes from Democrat to independent to Republican, the percentage of people who support gun control declines.

Let's return to the data in Table 3-5. Does the partisanship hypothesis on gun control appear to be correct? Following the rules, we would focus on the percentage of each partisan group favoring a handgun ban and read across the columns, starting with the Democrats. Democrats are most in favor of a ban (52.9%), independents show somewhat weaker support (46.6%), and Republicans are least likely to favor a ban (37.9%). The pattern is systematic and not inconsistent with the hypothesis. Each time we change the independent variable,

Table 3-6   Smoking, by Income (cross-tabulation)

Smoker?	$13,999 or less	$14,000–$24,999	$25,000–$39,999	$40,000–$59,999	$60,000 or more	Total
	Income category					
Yes	32.5%	27.0%	24.6%	21.8%	16.4%	24.2%
	(90)	(62)	(76)	(58)	(52)	(338)
No	67.5%	73.0%	75.4%	78.2%	83.6%	75.8%
	(187)	(168)	(233)	(208)	(265)	(1,061)
Total	100.0%	100.0%	100.0%	100.0%	100.0%	100.0%
	(277)	(230)	(309)	(266)	(317)	(1,399)

Source: 1996 National Election Study.
Note: Question: "Are you a smoker?"

from Democrat to independent to Republican, the distribution of the dependent variable changes, too, and in the hypothesized way.

Here is another example. A student of health policy is investigating the relationship between income and cigarette smoking. Are poor people more likely than rich people to smoke cigarettes? The policy researcher's hypothesis is as follows: In comparing individuals, people earning lower incomes will be more likely to smoke than will individuals earning higher incomes. Again, before looking at the data, try to visualize a cross-tabulation. You should see groups of people separated into categories of the independent variable, income. Each group will be distributed across values of the dependent variable, smoker or nonsmoker. A certain percentage of the low-income group will be smokers and a certain percentage of higher-income individuals will be smokers. If the hypothesis is incorrect, what will a comparison of these percentages look like? If the hypothesis is correct, what should we find?

Table 3-6 shows the cross-tabulation, constructed according to the rules. The independent variable, a five-value ordinal measure of income, defines the columns. The values of the dependent variable, smoker and nonsmoker, define the rows. The cells of the table contain the raw frequencies and percentages of smokers and nonsmokers for each category of the independent variable, totaled at the bottom of each column. The frequency distribution for the entire sample appears in the right-most column.

How would you interpret the percentages? Obviously, if the hypothesis were incorrect, the percentages of smokers in each category of income should be about the same. But they are not the same at all. Comparing percentages across columns at the same value of the dependent variable—we will focus on the percentage of smokers—reveals an unambiguous pattern. Whereas nearly a third of the lowest income group are smokers, the percentage of smokers drops systematically as income goes up, to 27 percent, then to 25 percent, to 22 percent, and finally to 16 percent among the most affluent respondents. The hypothesis survives. (The smokers may not.)

Mean Comparisons

The same logic of comparison applies in another common hypothesis-testing situation, when the independent variable is nominal or ordinal and the dependent variable is interval. The rules for presenting the comparison, however, are a bit more flexible. For a change of scene,

Table 3-7 Political Rights and Freedoms, by Country Per Capita GDP (mean comparison, format 1)

	Per capita GDP				
	Low	*Medium-low*	*Medium-high*	*High*	Total
Mean score[a]	3.2	6.4	7.4	11.3	7.1
Number of countries	28	28	28	28	112

Source: Per capita GDP based on data compiled by Mike Alvarez, Jose Antonio Cheibub, Fernando Limongi, and Adam Przeworski, *Democracy and Development: Political Institutions and Well-Being in the World, 1950–1990* (Cambridge, U.K.: Cambridge University Press, 2000). Political rights and freedoms score based on data obtained from Freedom House, http://www.freedomhouse.org/.

Note: Displayed data are from 1997.

[a] Score calculated by summing the Freedom House 7-point political rights index and the 7-point civil liberties index. Combined index was rescaled to range from 0 (fewest rights and freedoms) to 12 (most rights and freedoms).

let's consider a hypothesis using countries as the units of analysis. The dependent variable of interest is a measure of the political rights and freedoms enjoyed by countries' citizens. This index can range from 0 (citizens have very few rights and freedoms) to 12 (citizens have many rights and freedoms). As you might guess, countries vary a lot in this respect. Of the 112 countries being analyzed here, almost a quarter scored 3 or lower on the 12-point scale, another quarter scored 11 or 12, with the remaining half spread fairly evenly across the middle ranges of the variable.[13] What causes such huge variation in political freedom across countries? We know that characteristics involving economic development, such as economic growth or education levels, create a social and political environment conducive to the expansion of freedoms. One such measure of development, per capita gross domestic product (per capita GDP), becomes the independent variable in this hypothesis: In comparing countries, those having lower per capita GDP will have fewer political rights and freedoms than will countries having higher per capita GDP.

Perform the mental exercise. Imagine 112 countries divided into four groups on the independent variable: countries with low GDP per capita, countries with medium-low GDP per capita, countries with medium-high GDP per capita, and countries having high GDP per capita. Now for each group of countries, "calculate" a mean of the dependent variable—the mean score on the 12-point political freedoms index for low-GDP countries, for medium-low GDP countries, and so on. Your mental exercise, as before, sets up the comparison we are after. If the hypothesis is correct, will these means be different? If so, in what way?

Table 3-7 displays a mean comparison table, which shows the results of an analysis using actual data. A **mean comparison table** is a table that shows the mean of a dependent variable for cases that have different values on an independent variable. Just as in a cross-tabulation, the values of the independent variable define the columns of the table, and the number of cases in each value appears at the bottom of each column. Thus, 28 countries were classified as low-GDP countries, 28 as medium-low, 28 as medium-high, and 28 as high. The right-most column, labeled "Total," reports information for all the cases, all 112 countries. In the rows of Table 3-7 we find two numbers: the mean of the dependent variable for countries having each value of the independent variable and the raw frequency of countries in each category. So, the mean score on the political rights and freedoms index is 3.2 for low-GDP countries, 6.4 for medium-low countries, 7.4 for medium-high countries, and 11.3 for high-GDP countries.

Table 3-8 Political Rights and Freedoms, by Country Per Capita GDP (mean comparison, format 2)

Country per capita GDP	Mean score[a]
Low	3.2
	(28)
Medium-low	6.4
	(28)
Medium-high	7.4
	(28)
High	11.3
	(28)
Total	7.1
	(112)

Source: Per capita GDP based on data compiled by Mike Alvarez, Jose Antonio Cheibub, Fernando Limongi, and Adam Przeworski, *Democracy and Development: Political Institutions and Well-Being in the World, 1950–1990* (Cambridge, U.K.: Cambridge University Press, 2000). Political rights and freedoms score based on data obtained from Freedom House, http://www.freedomhouse.org/.

Note: Displayed data are from 1997.

[a] Score calculated by summing the Freedom House 7-point political rights index and the 7-point civil liberties index. Combined index was rescaled to range from 0 (fewest rights and freedoms) to 12 (most rights and freedoms).

How would we interpret Table 3-7? Just as in interpreting a cross-tabulation, we would compare values of the dependent variable across values of the independent variable. If the hypothesis were incorrect, we should find that political rights and freedoms scores are about the same in all categories of the independent variable. But what do the data reveal as we move across the columns, from low GDP to high GDP? Clearly, each time we compare countries with higher values of the independent variable to countries with lower values of the independent variable, we find the hypothesized difference: Higher-GDP countries have higher mean values on the dependent variable than do lower-GDP countries.

Table 3-7, which was set up in a manner similar to a cross-tabulation, is a perfectly correct format for making mean comparisons. Most of the mean comparison tables you will encounter, though, are arranged in a different way. Table 3-8 presents the per capita GDP–political rights and freedoms relationship according the most common format. In Table 3-8, the means of the dependent variable, along with the number of cases, appear in a single column, next to the values of the independent variable. By simply reading down the column from low to high values of the independent variable, we can see what happens to the average value of the dependent variable. Either way, Table 3-7 and Table 3-8 tell the same story: As per capita GDP goes up, so do political rights and freedoms. Again, the hypothesis passes muster.[14]

GRAPHING RELATIONSHIPS AND DESCRIBING PATTERNS

The above examples illustrate the mechanics of presenting and interpreting comparisons. And these comparisons have fit neatly into one of two classic patterns. The GDP–political

Figure 3-5 Smoking, by Income (bar chart)

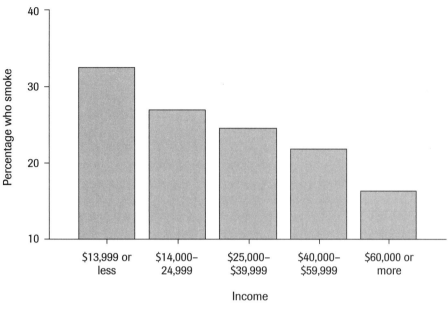

Source: 1996 National Election Study.
Note: Question: "Are you a smoker?"

rights and freedoms relationship is a **positive relationship**: An increase in the independent variable, per capita GDP, is associated with an increase in the dependent variable, political rights and freedoms. The income-smoking relationship is a **negative relationship**: An increase in the independent variable, income, is associated with a decrease in the dependent variable, the likelihood of smoking. Obviously, if the independent variable is a nominal measure, such as region or race or gender, questions about whether the relationship is positive or negative never come up. If the independent variable is measured at the ordinal or interval level, however, we can ask whether the relationship between the independent and dependent variables is positive or negative.

Earlier we saw how bar charts can be a great help in describing variables. An adaptation of the bar chart—along with another form of visual display, the **line graph**—also can help to describe relationships between variables. Figure 3-5 displays a bar chart for the income-smoking cross-tabulation (Table 3-6). As simple as the cross-tabulation is, the bar chart is simpler still. The categories of the independent variable, income, appear along the horizontal axis. This placement of the independent variable is just as it was in the bar charts introduced earlier that were based on the frequency distributions of single variables. In using this graphic form to depict relationships, however, the vertical axis does not represent the percentage of cases falling into each value of the independent variable. Rather, the vertical axis records the percentage of cases in each value of the independent variable that fall into *one* value of the dependent variable—the percentage who smoke. The height of each bar, therefore, tells us the percentage of subjects at each income level who are smokers. As you move along the horizontal axis from low to high income, notice that the heights of the bars decline in a systematic pattern. Figure 3-5 shows the visual signature of a negative or inverse relationship. As the values of the independent variable increase, the value of the dependent variable, the percentage of smokers, decreases.

Figure 3-6 Political Rights and Freedoms, by Country Per Capita GDP (line graph)

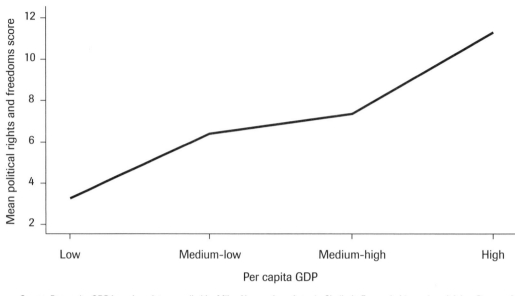

Source: Per capita GDP based on data compiled by Mike Alvarez, Jose Antonio Cheibub, Fernando Limongi, and Adam Przeworski, *Democracy and Development: Political Institutions and Well-Being in the World, 1950–1990* (Cambridge, U.K.: Cambridge University Press, 2000). Political rights and freedoms score based on data obtained from Freedom House, http://www.freedomhouse.org/.
Note: Displayed data are from 1997.

For a hypothesis that has an interval-level dependent variable, such as the per capita GDP–political rights and freedoms relationship (Table 3-7 or Table 3-8), a line graph is often used (Figure 3-6). The basic format is the same as a bar chart. The values of the independent variable, countries' GDP levels, are along the horizontal axis. The vertical axis records the mean of the dependent variable for each value of the independent variable. This graphic rendition of the mean comparison table reveals the visual signature of a positive or direct relationship. As per capita GDP increases, mean scores on the rights and freedoms index go up.

Both the income-smoking relationship and the GDP–political rights and freedoms relationship are linear. In a **linear relationship**, an increase in the independent variable is associated with a consistent increase or decrease in the dependent variable. Linear relationships can be positive or negative. In a negative linear relationship, any time you compare the dependent variable for subjects having different values on the independent variable, you find a negative relationship: The lower value of the independent variable is associated with a higher value of the dependent variable. In the income-smoking bar chart (Figure 3-5), for example, it doesn't matter which two income groups you compare—people making $13,999 or less with people making $25,000 to $39,999, or people in the $14,000–$24,999 category with people whose income is $60,000 or more, or any other comparison you care to make. Each comparison shows a negative relationship. People with lower incomes are more likely to smoke. The same idea applies to positive linear relationships, such as the GDP–political rights and freedoms example. Each time you compare values of the dependent variable for cases having different values on the independent variable, you find a positive relationship: The lower value of the independent variable is associated with a lower value of the dependent variable. A comparison between any two groups of countries in Figure 3-6 will show a positive pattern.

Figure 3-7   Relationship Between Exam Score and Hours Spent Studying

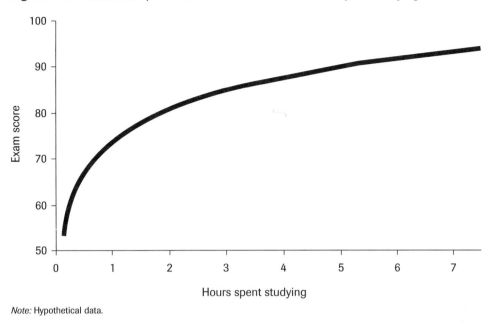

Note: Hypothetical data.

Many relationships between political variables do not fit a clear linear pattern. They are nonlinear or curvilinear. In a **curvilinear relationship**, the relationship between the independent variable and the dependent variable depends on which interval or range of the independent variable is being examined. The relationship depends on which values of the independent variable are being compared. As one moves along the values of the independent variable, comparing values of the dependent variable, one might find a positive relationship; that is, an increase in the independent variable occasions an increase in the dependent variable. But as one continues to move along the independent variable, entering a different range of the independent variable, the relationship may turn negative; that is, as the independent variable continues to increase, the dependent variable decreases. Or a relationship that initially is positive or negative may flatten out, with an increase in the independent variable being associated with no change in the dependent variable. Many other possibilities exist. Let's consider some common curvilinear patterns.

The first pattern is well within your everyday experience. What is the relationship between the number of hours you spend studying for an exam (independent variable) and the grade you receive (dependent variable)? Generally speaking, of course, the relationship is positive: The more you study, the better you do. But is the amount of improvement gained from, say, the first 2 hours spent studying the same as the amount of improvement gained from the fifth and sixth hours spent studying? Perhaps not. Figure 3-7 depicts a hypothetical relationship for this example. Notice that, for the lowest values of the independent variable, between 0 hours and 1 hour, the relationship between the independent and dependent variables is steeply positive. That first hour translates into about a 20-point improvement on the test, from a less-than-lustrous 50 to about a 70. Adding a second hour returns dividends, too, but not as much as the first hour: about 10 additional points. As the hours wear on, the relationship, though still positive, becomes weaker and weaker. The curve begins to flatten out.

Figure 3-8 Relationship Between Turnout and Partisanship

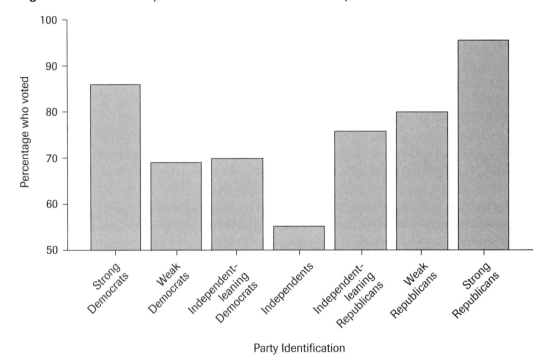

Party Identification

Source: 1996 National Election Study.
Note: Figure 3-8 is based on the following percentages (and number of cases): Strong Democrat, 85.92 percent reported voting (298); weak Democrat, 69.08 percent (304); independent-leaning Democrat, 69.85 percent (199); independent, 55.20 percent (125); independent-leaning Republican, 75.78 percent (161); weak Republican 80.00 percent (230); and strong Republican, 95.52 percent (201). Reported turnout for the entire sample of 1,518 respondents was 77.21 percent.

The common expression, "diminishing rate of return," characterizes this sort of curvilinear relationship.

Another pattern, one often encountered in social research, is the V-shaped (or U-shaped) relationship. For lower values of the independent variable, the relationship is negative. For higher values, the relationship is positive. (The inverted V- or U-shape is based on the same idea: positive in the lower range, negative in the higher range.) Consider Figure 3-8, which displays a bar chart of the relationship between the 7-point party identification scale and reported turnout in the 1996 election. Strong Democrats turned out at a high rate. But, as you can see, as Democratic identification weakens, reported turnout declines, hitting a low point among pure independents. As the scale shades through independent-leaning Republican and weak Republican, the relationship turns positive, finally culminating among respondents who occupy the second "tip" of the V-shape, strong Republicans.[15]

Consider an example of the inverted-V pattern. Suppose a researcher wants to examine the relationship between age (independent variable) and membership in voluntary associations such as charitable organizations and community groups (dependent variable). The researcher divides subjects into five age groups and calculates the mean number of memberships for each category of age. Figure 3-9 displays a line graph of the relationship. Notice that the relationship is positive through the first three categories of the independent variable, peaking among respondents who are 41 to 50 years of age. For the older groups, though, the average declines, creating a negative relationship in this range of the independent variable.

Figure 3-9 Relationship Between Mean Number of Group Memberships and Age

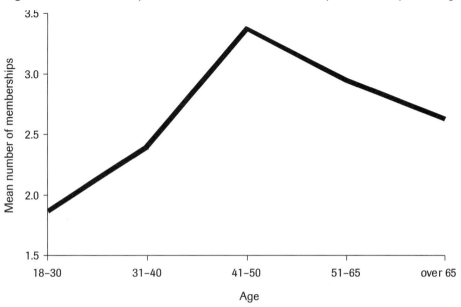

Source: 1996 National Election Study.
Note: Respondents were asked about their memberships in a wide variety of groups. The dependent variable is based on the total number of groups to which individuals said they belonged. The mean number of groups for each age category (and the number of respondents in each age category) were as follows: 18–30, 1.86 memberships (237 respondents); 31–40, 2.39 (378); 41–50, 3.37 (306); 51–65, 2.95 (302); and over 65, 2.63 (303). The mean number of memberships for all 1,526 respondents was 2.67.

Curvilinear relationships are fairly common in political research. And they are always interesting. Sometimes we encounter such relationships while organizing or exploring data, and we then propose and test explanations for them. Why is it, we might ask, that the age-membership relationship is shaped the way it is? Sometimes, however, we may offer explanations that suggest nonlinear relationships. Let's explore this route, beginning with this fact: Some people favor antidiscrimination laws protecting gays, whereas others oppose such laws. What accounts for this fact? Consider two plausible explanations:

Explanation 1: When people are in their youth, they are more open to novel or alternative ideas. They have fewer responsibilities and may entertain beliefs outside society's mainstream. However, as they age, enter the workforce, and raise families, they become more cognizant of traditional views about many social mores, such as sexual orientation. Therefore, people change their opinions throughout their lives, becoming more conservative as they get older.

Explanation 2: Individuals are deeply affected by prevailing social norms and political values during their early adulthood. People socialized during a liberal era, such as the mid-1960s or 1990s, will have more tolerant attitudes on personal freedom issues, such as sexual orientation. People socialized during a more conservative time, like the 1950s or mid-1980s, will hold more traditional views.

The first explanation describes a life-cycle explanation. It would hypothesize the following relationship between the independent variable, age, and the dependent variable, gay rights

Table 3-9 Gay Rights Opinions, by Age (cross-tabulation)

Opinion on gay rights law	Age					Total
	18–30	*31–40*	*41–50*	*51–65*	*over 65*	
Favor	69.2%	60.9%	68.5%	63.4%	59.0%	63.9%
	(157)	(220)	(200)	(177)	(164)	(918)
Oppose	30.8%	39.1%	31.5%	36.6%	41.0%	36.1%
	(70)	(141)	(92)	(102)	(114)	(519)
Total	100.0%	100.0%	100.0%	100.0%	100.0%	100.0%
	(227)	(361)	(292)	(279)	(278)	(1,437)

Source: 1996 National Election Study.

Note: Question: "Do you favor or oppose laws to protect homosexuals against job discrimination?"

attitudes: In comparing individuals, younger people will be less likely to oppose antidiscrimination laws than will older people. The second explanation proposes a generational explanation. It hypothesizes this pattern: In comparing individuals, those coming of age during the 1950s and 1980s will be more likely to oppose gay rights laws than will those socialized during the 1960s and 1990s.

Visualize these different patterns. The life-cycle idea is straightforward. Each time we increase the value of the independent variable—comparing a younger age group with an older age group—the percentage of people in the "oppose" category of the dependent variable should increase. So a positive relationship should exist between age and the likelihood of opposing gay rights. The generational idea requires more reflection. In a simple way, of course, the youngest cohort, those in their twenties or younger, should be more liberal than the oldest cohort, those who are, say, over 65. But there is a definite "flower-power-versus-Reagan era" element in the generational claim. Individuals socialized during the 1960s, who would now be in their forties or early fifties, should be less strongly opposed to gay rights legislation than a younger cohort, those entering political awareness during the 1980s, who are now in their thirties. Interesting. Which explanation, the life-cycle explanation or the generational explanation, better fits the data?

Table 3-9 shows the cross-tabulation that addresses the hypotheses. Figure 3-10 displays a bar chart of the relationship. Focusing on the percentage of each age group in Table 3-9 who oppose a law protecting gays, and reading across the columns from younger to older respondents, what do we find? People in the youngest cohort, those 18 to 33 years of age, are the least likely to oppose, with only 30.8 percent taking this position. The next-oldest group, those 31 to 40, are stronger opponents (39.1%). But notice that the likelihood of opposing a gay rights law then drops to 31.5 percent among respondents 41 to 50, then builds again among the older age groups. Figure 3-10 shows the graphic profile of this pattern very clearly. The 31-to-40 age group sticks out like a sore thumb. These results, one would conclude, come closer to the nonlinear pattern proposed by the generational explanation than the positive relationship implied by the life-cycle explanation.

As this example suggests, you must be alert to the possibility that a political relationship of interest may not follow a classic positive or negative pattern. By carefully examining cross-tabulations and mean comparisons, you can get a clearer idea of what is going on in the relationship. Graphic depictions, such as bar charts and line graphs, offer clarity and simplicity. It is recommended that you always sketch an appropriate graphic to help you interpret a rela-

Figure 3-10 Relationship Between Opposition to Gay Rights Law and Age

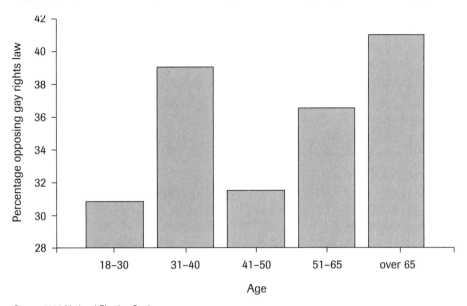

Source: 1996 National Election Study.
Note: Question: "Do you favor or oppose laws to protect homosexuals against job discrimination?"

tionship. Graphic forms of data presentation will become especially useful when you begin to analyze more complicated relationships—when you begin to interpret controlled comparisons. We turn in the next chapter to a discussion of control.

SUMMARY

In this chapter we covered three topics in political analysis: describing variables, making comparisons, and graphing relationships and describing patterns. We have seen that a variable can be described by its central tendency, its typical or average value, and by its dispersion, the distribution of cases across the variable's values. We also have seen that an accurate description often requires informed judgment. By examining the frequency distribution and bar chart of a variable, we can decide which measure of central tendency—the mode, the median, or the mean—best reflects the typical value of a variable. Frequency distributions and graphic displays also help us decide if a variable might best be described by its dispersion or variation.

The cross-tabulation is the most common vehicle for testing a hypothesis about the relationship between nominal or ordinal variables. A cross-tabulation presents side-by-side frequency distributions of the dependent variable for subjects that have different values on the independent variable. To test a hypothesis about the relationship between a nominal or an ordinal independent variable and an interval-level dependent variable, a mean comparison table is used. A mean comparison table compares the mean values of the dependent variable for subjects that have different values of the independent variable.

The relationship between two variables may have a linear pattern. In a linear relationship, an increase in the independent variable is associated with a consistent increase or decrease in the dependent variable. A linear relationship can be positive or negative. Some relationships have nonlinear or curvilinear patterns. In a curvilinear relationship, the relationship between the independent variable and the dependent variable is not the same for all values of the independent variable. Whether one describes the relationship as positive or negative depends on which interval or range of the independent variable is being examined. The analyst might discover nonlinear patterns and develop explanations for them. Sometimes the analyst proposes explanations that imply nonlinear relationships.

KEY TERMS

bar chart (p. 53)
bimodal distribution (p. 55)
central tendency (p. 51)
cross-tabulation (p. 62)
cumulative percentage (p. 53)
curvilinear relationship (p. 69)
dispersion (p. 52)
frequency distribution (p. 53)
linear relationship (p. 68)
line graph (p. 67)
mean (p. 52)

mean comparison table (p. 65)
median (p. 52)
mode (p. 52)
negative relationship (p. 67)
negative skew (p. 57)
percentile (p. 56)
positive relationship (p. 67)
positive skew (p. 57)
raw frequency (p. 53)
resistant measure of central tendency (p. 57)
total frequency (p. 53)

EXERCISES

1. The 1998 General Social Survey asked this question: "How many hours each day do you spend watching television?" Here are the three measures of central tendency for this variable: mode, 2 hours; median, 2 hours; mean, 2.86 hours.
   A. Based on this information, would you say that the distribution of this variable is skewed? If so, does it have a negative skew or a positive skew?
   B. Which is the better measure of central tendency for this variable—the mean or the median? Why?

2. Another question on the 1998 General Social Survey elicited opinions about laws that govern divorce: "Should such laws make a divorce easier to obtain, should the laws remain the same, or should it be more difficult to get divorced?"
   A. Is this variable nominal, ordinal, or interval? Explain.
   B. Here are the raw frequencies for each value: "Easier," 428; "Stay the same," 351; "More difficult," 967. Construct a frequency distribution for this variable. Sketch a bar chart.
   C. Examine the frequency distribution and bar chart. What is the mode? What is the median?
   D. How would you describe the variation in this variable? Would you say that it has a great deal of variation or not much variation? Explain.

3. Senator Foghorn described a political rival, Dewey Cheatum, this way: "Dewey Cheatum is a very polarizing person. People either love him or hate him." Suppose a large number of voting-age adults were asked to rate Dewey Cheatum on a 10-point scale. Respondents could give Cheatum a rating ranging between 1 (they strongly disapprove of him) and 10 (they strongly approve of him).
   A. If Senator Foghorn's characterization of Dewey Cheatum is correct, what would a bar chart of approval ratings look like? Sketch a bar chart that would fit Foghorn's description.
   B. Still assuming that Senator Foghorn is correct, which of the following sets of values, Set 1 or Set 2, is more plausible? Set 1: mean, 5; median, 5; mode, 5. Set 2: mean, 5; median, 5,

mode, 2. Explain your choice. Why is the set of numbers you have chosen more plausible than the other set of numbers?

C. Now assume that the data show Senator Foghorn to be incorrect, and that the following characterization best describes the bar chart of approval ratings: "Dewey Cheatum is a consensus-builder, not a polarizer. He generally elicits positive ratings from most people, and there is little variation in these ratings." Sketch a bar chart that would fit this new description. Invent plausible values for the mean, median, and mode of this distribution.

4. Who thinks that spanking is an appropriate practice for disciplining children? This has become a somewhat controversial question in recent years, as some advocacy organizations have pressed state legislatures to enact tougher child abuse laws. Would such laws be welcomed equally by different demographic groups in society? Consider this hypothesis: In comparing individuals, people with lower levels of education will be more likely to approve of spanking than will people with higher levels of education. The 1998 General Social Survey reports these raw frequencies for approve/disapprove of spanking among respondents in five education categories: Less than high school, 214 approve/52 disapprove; high school, 740/233; junior college, 98/32; bachelor's degree, 223/89; graduate degree, 86/60. (Total sample, 1,361 approve/466 disapprove.)

A. Construct a cross-tabulation from this information. Write a paragraph interpreting the results. What do you think? Do the results support the hypothesis?

B. Sketch a bar chart for this relationship. Put the values of the independent variable, education level, on the horizontal axis. Put the percentage approving of spanking on the vertical axis.

C. How would you describe the relationship in the bar chart? Does it more closely approximate a negative relationship or a positive relationship? Explain your reasoning.

5. Another difficult issue that has surfaced in recent years is the debate over a person's "right to die," whether or not assisted suicide should be permitted by law. One can think of several plausible variables that may shape a person's opinion on this issue. Consider this hypothesis, which is based on the idea that an individual's *own* health affects attitudes toward the right to die: In comparing individuals, people who are in excellent health will be less likely to approve of legalizing the right to die than will people who are in poor health. In the actual data (from the 1998 General Social Survey), the independent variable is measured by four ordinal categories: Respondents are asked if their health is "excellent," "good," "fair," or "poor." Here are the raw frequencies for approve/disapprove of the right to die for each category: excellent, 382 approve/159 disapprove; good, 602/230; fair, 209/88; poor, 63/18.

A. Construct a cross-tabulation from this information. Examine the percentages closely. Write a paragraph describing the relationship. What do you think? Is the hypothesis supported?

B. Sketch a bar chart for this relationship. Remember to put the categories of the independent variable on the horizontal axis. On the vertical axis, show the percentage of cases falling into the "approve" response of the dependent variable.

C. Would you describe this relationship as linear? Or would you describe it as nonlinear? Think about the pattern of this relationship. Why do you suppose it has this shape? Explain.

6. Do people who frequently read a newspaper know more about politics than do people who read a newspaper less frequently? Consider this hypothesis: In comparing individuals, people who read a newspaper less often will have a lower level of political knowledge than will people who read a newspaper more often.

A. Suppose you have information on two variables for a large number of individuals: The number of days per week that they read a newspaper (independent variable) and their level of political knowledge, from low to high (dependent variable). Does this hypothesis suggest a positive relationship between the independent and dependent variables? Or does the hypothesis suggest a negative relationship between the variables? Explain your reasoning.

B. The 2000 National Election Study provides data that can be used to address the hypothesis. The independent variable divides people into four groups according to the number of days per week that they read a newspaper: zero or one day per week, two or three days, four or five days, and six or seven days. The dependent variable, political knowledge, is a scale that ranges from 0 on the low-knowledge end to 6 on the high-knowledge end. The mean political knowledge scores for each value of the independent variable: For people who read the newspaper zero or one day, 2.2; two or three days, 2.5; four or five days, 2.8; six or seven days, 3.2. Construct a mean comparison table from these data.

C. Sketch a line graph from the mean comparison table you have constructed. Remember to put the values of the independent variable on the horizontal axis. Record the mean of the dependent variable on the vertical axis.

D. Interpret the results. Are the data consistent or inconsistent with the hypothesis? Explain.

7. You are probably familiar with (and may have used) back belts, which are widely used by workers to protect their lower backs from injuries caused by lifting. A study was conducted to determine the usefulness of this protective gear. Here is a partial description of the study, published in the *Journal of the American Medical Association* and reported by the Associated Press (December 5, 2000):

> New research suggests that back belts, which are widely used in industry to prevent lifting injuries, do not work. The findings by the National Institute for Occupational Safety and Health stem from a study of 160 Wal-Mart stores in 30 states. Researchers [based their findings on] workers' compensation data from 1996 to 1998.

Although you probably are not aware of the study's particulars, think about how you would go about investigating the effect of back belt usage on back injuries among a large group of employees. Assume that you have data on each of the 160 retail stores in your study. For each store, you know whether back belt usage was low, moderate, or high. You classify 50 stores as having low belt usage by employees, 50 stores as having moderate usage, and 60 stores as high usage. You also know the number of back-injury workers' compensation claims from each store. This information permits you to calculate the mean number of claims for low-usage, moderate-usage, and high-usage stores.

A. The following hypothesis suggests that back belt usage helps prevent injury: In comparing stores, stores with low back belt usage by employees will have more worker injuries than will stores with high back belt usage. What is the independent variable? What is the dependent variable? Does this hypothesis suggest a positive or negative relationship between the independent and dependent variables? Explain.

B. Fabricate a mean comparison table showing a linear pattern that is consistent with the hypothesis. Sketch a line graph from the data you have fabricated. (Note: Because you do not have sufficient information to fabricate a plausible mean for all of the cases, you do not need to include a "Total" row in your mean comparison table.)

C. Use your imagination. Suppose the data showed little difference in the worker injury claims for low-usage and moderate-usage stores, but a large effect in the hypothesized direction for high-usage stores. What would this relationship look like? Sketch a line graph for this relationship.

4

The "How Else?" Question: Making Controlled Comparisons

LEARNING OBJECTIVES

In this chapter you will learn:
- Three possible scenarios for the relationship between an independent variable and a dependent variable, controlling for a rival cause
- How to set up controlled comparisons using cross-tabulation analysis and mean comparison analysis
- How to use the three possible scenarios to interpret the results of controlled comparison analysis

Describing explanations, stating hypotheses, making comparisons, looking for interesting patterns in the data—these are all genuinely creative activities, and sometimes they are even accompanied by the joy of discovering something new. But as we have seen in the preceding chapters, discovery is an ongoing process. For every explanation we describe, a plausible alternative explanation exists for the same phenomenon. Each time we test the relationship between an independent variable and a dependent variable, we must ask, "How else, besides the independent variable, are the subjects not the same?" Is the dependent variable being caused by the independent variable, or is some other cause, some other independent variable, affecting the dependent variable?

Chapter 2 introduced the controlled comparison research design, the most common method for dealing with the "How else?" question in political research. In this chapter we look closely at both the logic and the practice of controlled comparison. In the first part of the chapter we emphasize the logic behind the method. After controlling for a rival cause of the dependent variable, what *can happen* to the relationship between the independent variable and the dependent variable? Hypothetical data and relationships illustrate three logical possibilities, three "possible scenarios" for what can happen. In the second part of the chapter we use empirical data to illustrate the practice of controlled comparison in the real world of political research. After controlling for a rival cause of the dependent variable, what *does happen* to the relationship between the independent variable and the dependent variable?

You will find that the procedures for setting up controlled comparisons are natural extensions of procedures you learned in Chapter 3 for setting up cross-tabulations and mean comparisons. You also will find that the three possible scenarios illustrated in the first part of this chapter are valuable interpretive tools in helping you to understand and describe complex empirical relationships.

To keep the presentation consistent, we focus on one familiar example: the hypothetical relationship between partisanship (independent variable) and gun control opinions (dependent variable), controlling for gender (rival cause). Thus the logical question becomes: After controlling for gender, what *can happen* to the relationship between partisanship and gun control opinions? In the first scenario, the partisanship–gun control relationship could be a **spurious relationship**. A spurious relationship is a "false" relationship, a relationship that does not survive when a rival cause is taken into consideration. For example, you may believe that the independent variable is causally linked to the dependent variable. However, after you control for a rival cause, the causal connection turns out to be completely coincidental—not causal at all. Thus it could be that, before you control for gender, party identification has a strong relationship with gun control opinions: Democrats are more likely than Republicans to favor a gun ban. However, after you control for gender, party identification no longer shows a causal link with gun control attitudes: Democrats and Republicans have similar attitudes on gun control. In a spurious relationship, for reasons we discuss, the rival cause accounts for the observed relationship between the independent and dependent variables.

In the second possible scenario, the partisanship–gun control relationship could be an **additive relationship**. In an additive relationship, the independent variable and the rival cause *both* help to explain the dependent variable. Both the independent variable and the rival variable expand or "add to" our understanding of the phenomenon we wish to explain. It could be that, after we control for gender, partisanship retains its explanatory relationship with gun opinions: Regardless of gender, Democrats are more likely to favor a ban. Yet gender, too, might contribute to the explanation of the dependent variable: Regardless of party, women are more likely to favor a ban than are men. In additive relationships, each variable is an independent cause of the dependent variable. And both variables, taken together, enhance our causal understanding of the dependent variable.

A third possible scenario is characterized by a complex set of relationships that can result when a rival cause is controlled. In an **interaction relationship**, the relationship between the independent variable and the dependent variable depends on the *value* of the control variable. Suppose that, among women, partisanship has no effect on gun control attitudes: Democratic women and Republican women are equally likely to favor a ban on handguns. So for one value of the control variable, female, the independent variable, party, bears no relationship to the dependent variable. But suppose that, among men, partisanship plays a big explanatory role: Democratic men are much more likely to favor a ban than are Republican men. So for another value of the control variable, male, party is strongly related to the dependent variable. Thus the question "Does partisanship cause gun control opinions?," does not admit to a simple yes or no response. Instead one must offer a qualified answer: "For women, no, but for men, yes." In interaction relationships, the control variable is said to specify or define the conditions under which the independent variable affects the dependent variable.

It needs to be reemphasized that spurious relationships, additive relationships, and interaction relationships are logical possibilities. All three possibilities are illustrated here with hypothetical data and using the gun control example. But because these possibilities tell us what *can happen* to the relationship between partisanship and gun control opinions, controlling for gender, they give us the interpretive tools we need for describing what *does happen* when we perform the analysis using real data. Empirical data analysis rarely yields results that perfectly fit one of the possibilities. However, most empirical relationships closely approximate one of the three possible scenarios.

THREE SCENARIOS: X→Y, CONTROLLING FOR Z

Let's begin by reviewing some familiar basics and by introducing some new terminology. As you know, a hypothesis is a testable statement about the relationship between an independent variable and a dependent variable. The explanation on which the hypothesis is based tells us how the independent variable is causally linked to the dependent variable. By convention, the independent variable is represented by the letter X and the dependent variable by the letter Y. The causal connection between an independent variable and a dependent variable is symbolized by the expression X→Y, which can be read, "X causes Y." For example, one may offer an explanation that proposes a causal connection between party identification (X) and opinions on gun control (Y). The explanation would support this testable hypothesis: In comparing individuals, Democrats will be more likely to favor a gun ban than will Republicans. We have seen, however, that one might offer an alternative or rival explanation proposing that gender is a cause of gun control attitudes. The independent variable that represents an alternative cause is represented by the letter Z, and its relationship to the dependent variable is symbolized by the expression Z→Y, meaning "Z causes Y." So one might offer the alternative hypothesis that gender (Z) is the main driver of opinions about gun control (Y): In comparing individuals, women will be more likely to favor a gun ban than will men. This is familiar terrain.

Since we usually must study people and things as we find them in their natural settings, it may be that the two independent variables, Z and X, are related in some way. Suppose, for example, that gender (Z) is causally linked to partisanship (X), that women are more likely to be Democrats than are men. This relationship is symbolized by the expression, Z→X, "Z causes X." So, when we measure partisanship (X), gauging the difference between Democrats and Republicans, we (perhaps unwittingly) also would be measuring gender (Z), gauging the difference between females and males. If so, then by comparing the gun opinions (Y) of Democrats and Republicans we would also be comparing the gun opinions of women and men. Furthermore, if the alternative hypothesis has merit—if women are more likely to favor a ban than are men—then some part of the observed relationship between X and Y is really the unobserved relationship between Z and Y. The only way to sort all of this out is to hold Z constant, to isolate the effect of X on Y while controlling for Z. This is accomplished by examining the X→Y relationship *within* the values of Z, by comparing, for example, the gun opinions of Democrats and Republicans only among women and the gun opinions of Democrats and Republicans only among men.

Spurious Relationships
The true relationship between X and Y, then, will depend on the relationship between Z and X and the relationship between Z and Y. Suppose that gender (Z) has a big effect on partisanship (X). Women become Democrats and men become Republicans. Suppose further that gender (Z) causes gun control attitudes (Y), with women developing pro-gun control opinions and men anti-gun control opinions. Obviously, if we were unaware that Z was such a

Figure 4-1 Spurious Relationship Between X and Y (arrow diagram)

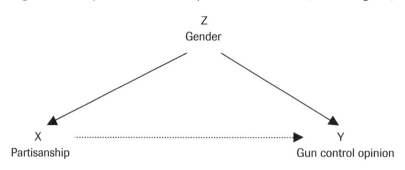

primal cause, and we were to forge ahead with an analysis of the relationship between X and Y, we would mistakenly attribute differences in gun control attitudes to differences in partisanship. In this classic situation, X has a spurious relationship with Y.

There are two useful ways to represent a spurious relationship. Figure 4-1 shows an **arrow diagram**. An arrow diagram is a schematic representation that depicts the causal relationships between the variables. The solid arrow between Z and X says, "Z causes X." The solid arrow between Z and Y says, "Z causes Y." The dotted arrow between X and Y says, "controlling for Z, X has no effect on Y." Applied to the gun control example, the arrow diagram in Figure 4-1 tells us that gender affects partisanship *and* gun control opinions, with women becoming Democrats and developing pro–gun control opinions and men becoming Republicans and developing anti–gun control opinions. Thus the relationship between partisanship and gun control opinions is not causal. It is being artificially created or "manufactured" by gender.[1] As gender varies, partisanship varies and gun control opinions vary, but no causal link exists between party and opinions.

Figure 4-2 presents an idealized line graph of a spurious relationship between party (X) and gun opinions (Y), controlling for gender (Z). The categories of X are represented along the horizontal axis, Democrats on the left and Republicans on the right. The vertical axis reports the percentage of subjects falling into one value of the dependent variable (Y), the percentage favoring a gun ban. Two lines inside the graph, the solid line for women and the dashed line for men, represent values of Z. By reading along each line, from one value of X (Democrat) to the other value of X (Republican), you get a visual feel for the effect of X on Y. As you can see, tracing the line for women, nothing happens to the line. It remains flat. Ditto for men: A comparison of Democrats and Republicans reveals no difference. By looking at the distance between the lines, you can gauge the effect of Z on Y. For Democrats and Republicans alike, gender is the main determinant of gun control opinions. This is the visual signature of a spurious relationship. If the empirical data were to produce a line graph such as the graphic depicted in Figure 4-2, one would have to conclude that partisanship bears a spurious relationship with gun control opinions.

Mundane examples are sometimes used to illustrate spuriousness. The age-old legend that storks "cause" babies to appear may have been based on the abundance of storks in geographic areas with a high number of births and their rarity in areas where births were fewer. So the independent variable, the number of storks (X), is linked to the dependent variable, the number of births (Y). But of course storks prefer to roost in the nooks and crannies of buildings, so as the numbers of buildings and people (Z) increase, so too will the number

Figure 4-2 Spurious Relationship Between Partisanship and Gun Control Opinion, Controlling for Gender (line graph)

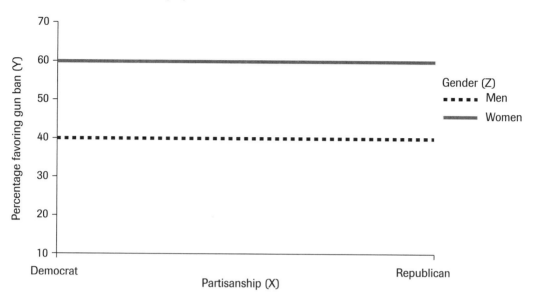

of storks and the number of babies. The storks-babies relationship is purely an artifact of the number of people.[2] In serious research, however, spurious relationships are not always so easily identified. We might find, for example, that adolescents who play violent video games (X) are more prone to antisocial behavior (Y) than adolescents who do not play violent video games. But can we say that the game playing *causes* the behavior? Or, to consider another hypothetical example, a policy researcher may discover dramatically lower recidivism rates for mental patients treated at community-based facilities than for patients treated at state hospitals. Is the type of facility (X) causing the difference in recidivism rates (Y)? It could be that patients with more severe illness, and who thus are more prone to recidivism, are also more likely to be treated at state hospitals. The policy researcher would need to hold severity (Z) constant, comparing the recidivism rates of each type of hospital only among severe cases and only among less severe cases.

The specter of an unknown Z making spurious mischief with an X→Y relationship is a constant worry for the political researcher. The good news is that, in controlling for potentially troublesome variables, we almost always learn something new about the phenomenon being studied. For example, the relationship between smoking and lung cancer, for years vulnerable to skeptics touting an array of uncontrolled variables, is now more firmly established. This enhanced understanding has occurred in large measure because of—not despite—the suggestion that the relationship could be spurious.

Additive Relationships

These examples edge us closer to the second possible scenario for the interrelationships of X, Y, and Z. Consider the arrow diagram of Figure 4-3. A key difference exists between Figure 4-1, which diagrammed a spurious relationship, and Figure 4-3. In a spurious relationship, a strong causal link exists between Z and X. But in Figure 4-3, which diagrams a set of additive relationships, Z and X have no causal connection. Changes in the values of Z do not produce

Figure 4-3 Additive Relationships Between X, Y, and Z (arrow diagram)

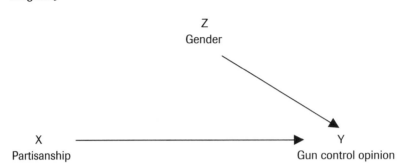

changes in the values of X. To return to the gun control example, suppose that gender (Z) affects gun opinions (Y) in that women are more likely to favor a ban than are men. Suppose further that partisanship (X) shapes attitudes (Y) such that Democrats are more supportive of a ban than Republicans. To the extent that gender and party are not related in some way—women and men do not differ in partisanship—both X and Z make independent contributions to the explanation of Y.

The term *additive* describes this situation, in that knowledge of both sets of relationships, X→Y and Z→Y, adds to or strengthens the explanation of the dependent variable. Suppose the researcher finds that partisanship "works"—a larger percentage of Democrats than Republicans favor a ban. Thus, by knowing partisanship, the researcher can explain some differences in gun control opinions between people. But suppose that the gun control opinions of some subjects cannot be explained by party differences. Some Democrats are anti-ban and some Republicans are pro-ban. What might account for these "unexplained" subjects? If gender also explains gun control opinions, then women will be more likely than men to fall into the pro-ban camps of both parties, Democrats *and* Republicans. Similarly, men will be more likely than women to be anti-ban, regardless of party. Thus, by adding gender to the explanation, the researcher can account for additional differences in gun opinions, over and above differences explained by partisanship alone.

Figure 4-4 provides an idealized line graph of additive relationships. Again, by reading along each line, from Democrat to Republican, you can see what happens to gun control attitudes separately for women (solid line) and for men (dashed line). Each line, considered by itself, drops predictably: Democrats are more supportive of a ban than are Republicans. And notice that the effect of party is the same for both genders. In the hypothetical depiction of Figure 4-4, 60 percent of Democratic women favor restrictions, compared with 40 percent for Republican women—a 20-percentage-point partisan difference. Similarly, 40 percent of male Democrats are pro-ban, compared with only 20 percent of male Republicans—also a 20-percentage-point partisan difference. So, after controlling for gender, party has an effect. By knowing party, we can explain some of the differences between subjects on the dependent variable. But there is a gap between the lines, as well, with the line for women consistently higher than the line for men. Again note that the effect of gender is the same for both Democrats and Republicans. Among Democrats there is a 20-point gender difference (60 percent of women support a ban versus 40 percent of men), and among Republicans there is a 20-point gender difference (40 percent of women and 20 percent of men).

Figure 4-4 Additive Relationships Between Partisanship, Gender, and Gun Control Opinion (line graph)

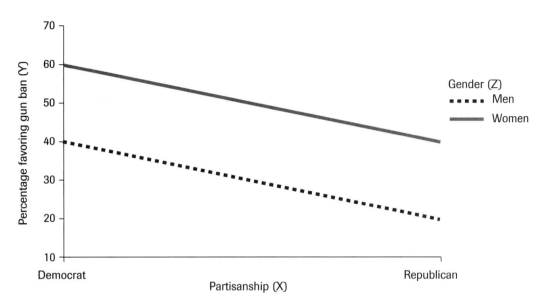

So, controlling for party, gender has an effect. By knowing gender, we can account for additional differences between subjects on the dependent variable. Knowledge of both variables, party and gender, allows an enhanced explanation of gun control attitudes.[3]

Interaction Relationships

The two possible scenarios of spurious relationships and additive relationships would seem to be polar opposites. In the case of spuriousness, controlling for Z has a devastating effect on the relationship between X and Y, reducing it to zero. In the case of additive relationships, controlling for Z has little impact on the relationship between X and Y, leaving it as strong as it was before Z was controlled. As incompatible as these two options seem, the third possibility can be understood by combining what you have learned thus far.

Try to imagine the following set of relationships between partisanship, gender, and attitudes toward gun control. Suppose that, for women, there is no difference between Democrats and Republicans. When we control for gender (Z) and look at the relationship between partisanship (X) and gun opinions (Y), we find no difference among women between the categories of X: Democratic women and Republican women are equally supportive of a gun ban. For women, therefore, the effect of X on Y is zero. But suppose that, for men, there is a huge difference between Democrats and Republicans. That is, when we control for gender and look at the relationship between partisanship and gun opinions, we find, among men, a large difference between categories of X: Democratic men are much more supportive of a ban than are Republican men. Thus, for men, the effect of X on Y is large. Now, if someone were to ask you, "What is the relationship between partisanship and gun opinions, controlling for gender?," you might reply: "It depends on whether you're talking about the opinions of women or men. To be specific, for women partisanship has no effect on gun control attitudes, but for men partisanship has a big effect."

Figure 4-5 Interaction Relationships Between X, Y, and Z (arrow diagram)

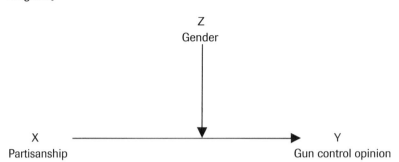

Political researchers use two interchangeable terms, *interaction relationships* or *specification relationships*, to describe this situation. As depicted in Figure 4-5, the arrow from X to Y says that, yes, a relationship exists. But notice that the arrow from Z is not pointed directly at X or at Y. Rather, it is pointed at the *relationship* between X and Y. This says that the specific relationship between X and Y will depend on the value of Z. For one value of Z, when gender takes on the value "women," the relationship between partisanship (X) and gun opinion (Y) is not the same as it is for a different value of Z, when gender takes on the value "men." [4]

Figure 4-6 illustrates an idealized line graph of interaction for the gun control example. The visual profile of interaction is in the tracks of the lines, which are different for each gender. Fill a room with women—Democrats and Republicans—and most of them would favor a gun ban. Their party allegiances would not matter. But fill a room with men, and their partisanship would make a great deal of difference. A proposal to ban guns would be widely supported by the male Democrats and widely rejected by the male Republicans. And notice,

Figure 4-6 Interaction Relationship Between Partisanship and Gun Control Opinion, Controlling for Gender (line graph)

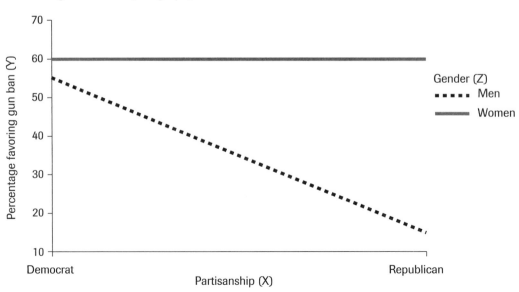

Figure 4-7 Relationship Between Partisanship and Gun Control Opinion, Controlling for Gender (empirical findings)

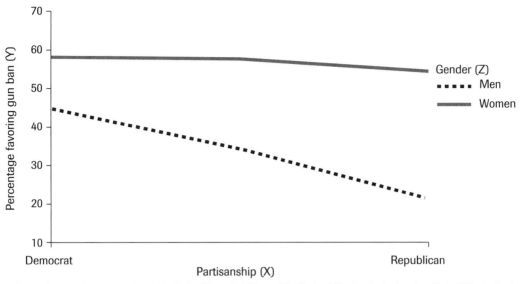

Source: Steven J. Rosenstone, Donald R. Kinder, Warren E. Miller, and the National Election Study, *American National Election Study, 1996: Pre- and Post-election Survey,* 4th version (Ann Arbor: University of Michigan, Center for Political Studies [producer], 1999; Inter-university Consortium for Political and Social Research [distributor], 2000).

Note: Based on the following percentages and numbers of Democrats, independents, and Republicans favoring a gun ban: (men) 44.3 percent of the Democrats (101 of 228); 34.2 percent of independents (77 of 225); and 21.5 percent of Republicans (46 of 214); (women) 58.2 percent of the Democrats (213 of 366); 57.5 percent of independents (146 of 254); and 57.0 percent of Republicans (116 of 213).

too, the varied distance between the lines. Although there is virtually no gender gap among Democrats—gender has a small effect—a big gender gap is seen among Republicans.

When you begin to analyze and interpret actual data, you will find interaction to be a very common pattern. In fact, the empirical relationship between party identification and gun control opinion, controlling for gender, closely approximates the hypothetical representation of interaction depicted in Figure 4-6. Figure 4-7 was constructed using data from the 1996 National Election Study. For women, party identification has no effect on this issue. For men, support drops sharply as the line moves across the values of X, from Democrat to Republican. One can see why campaign consultants consider gun control a "wedge issue"—an issue capable of attracting the votes of a large bloc of supporters from the opposing party. To be sure, a Democratic candidate who advocates stricter gun laws would run some risk of losing support from male Democrats, since the data show about a 14-percentage-point gender gap among Democrats. But this risk might be outweighed by the prospect of attracting large numbers of females from the opposing party, given that a 35-percentage-point "gender chasm" is seen among Republicans on the gun control issue.

These examples of interaction, both hypothetical and actual, have shown one particular profile: For one value of Z, the effect of X on Y is zero, but for another value of Z, the effect of X on Y is large. This is a common pattern of interaction. However, this is not the only way that interaction can work. The idea behind interaction is that the relationship between X and Y depends on the value of Z, and this can take several forms. Consider Figure 4-8, which uses hypothetical relationships to depict three basic patterns of interaction. (Two possible variants of each basic pattern, labeled A and B, are shown.) By now, pattern 1A is familiar to you.

Figure 4-8 Patterns of Interaction

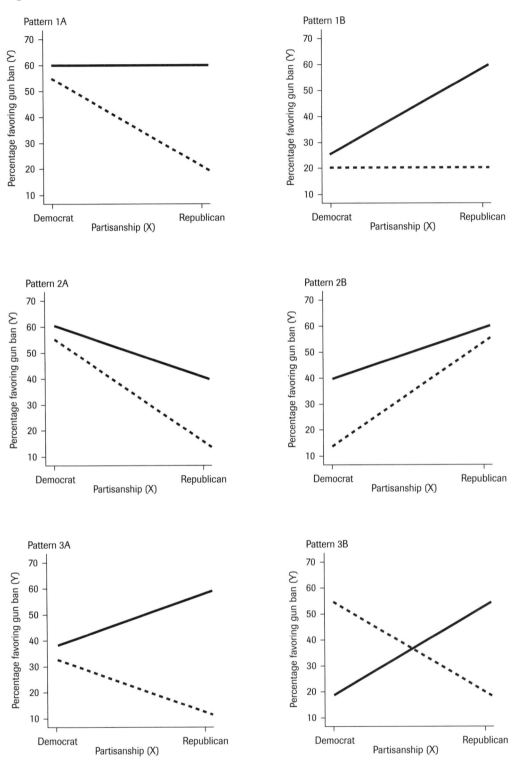

Note: Hypothetical data. For illustrative purposes, women's opinions are represented by the solid line in each graph, and men's opinions are represented by the dashed line.

This is the pattern that best fits the actual relationship between partisanship and gun opinions, controlling for gender: For women, the relationship is essentially zero; for men, the percentage of Democrats favoring a ban is much higher than the percentage of Republicans favoring a ban, resulting in a downward-sloping line as one moves from left to right along the horizontal axis. Of course, in your own analyses you may encounter one of several upward-sloping variants of this same pattern (as in 1B). But profiles 1A and 1B share a basic similarity: For one value of the control variable, the X-Y relationship is zero; for another value of the control variable, the relationship is strongly positive or negative.

Often the relationship between X and Y has the same tendency for all values of Z, but the tendency is stronger for some values of Z. For example, tracing along the solid line in pattern 2A, we see that female Democrats (60 percent in favor) are more likely than female Republicans (40 percent in favor) to support a ban—a 20-point difference. So, among women, partisanship works as expected, with Republicans less supportive than Democrats. Yet the relationship is clearly stronger for men, with 55 percent of Democrats in favor, compared with only 15 percent of Republicans—a 40-point difference. Again, pattern 2B displays the same thing with tendencies reversed. For patterns 2A and 2B, the relationship between X and Y has the same tendency for both values of the control variable, but it is quite a bit stronger for one value of Z than for the other value of Z.

Occasionally you will find the interesting profile depicted in patterns 3A and 3B, in which the relationship between X and Y has a different tendency for each value of Z. According to the 3A profile, for example, Republican women are more supportive of a ban than are Democratic women, producing an upward-sloping line, as partisanship shades from Democrat to Republican. For men, however, party identification has just the opposite effect, resulting in lower levels of support among Republican males than among Democratic males. An extreme variant of this form of interaction is depicted in pattern 3B. Consider this pattern for a moment. Notice that, just as in 3A, the effect of X on Y is strongly positive for one value of Z and strongly negative for the other value of Z. Unlike 3A, however, Z also has large and very different effects on Y, controlling for X. So, in pattern 3B's mocked-up scenario, Democrats are deeply divided on gender, with this qualification: Men are much more pro-ban than women. The Republicans show a large gender gap, too—with women much more supportive than men. Should you encounter pattern 3B in your research, you can label it with one of these commonly used descriptors: crossover interaction or disordinal interaction.

MAKING CONTROLLED COMPARISONS

You now have an idea of what can happen to the relationship between an independent variable and a dependent variable, controlling for a rival cause. The three scenarios provide the tools you will need to interpret the relationships you will find when performing controlled comparison analysis. In this section we first consider how to set up and interpret controlled comparisons for relationships between nominal-level or ordinal-level independent and dependent variables. We then turn to situations in which the independent variables are nominal or ordinal and the dependent variable is measured at the interval level.

Cross-tabulation Analysis

Chapter 3 laid out some ground rules for setting up a cross-tabulation analysis of the relationship between an independent variable and a dependent variable. Let's begin with a simple tabular analysis of the following hypothesis: In comparing individuals, whites will be more

Table 4-1   Relationship Between Race (X) and Turnout (Y)

Voted? (Y)	Race (X)		Total
	White	*Black*	
No	22.0%	32.2%	23.2%
	(290)	(55)	(345)
Yes	78.0	67.8	76.8
	(1,027)	(116)	(1,143)
Total	100.0%	100.0%	100.0%
	(1,317)	(171)	(1,488)

Source: Steven J. Rosenstone, Donald R. Kinder, Warren E. Miller, and the National Election Studies, *American National Election Study, 1996: Pre- and Post-election Survey*, 4th version (Ann Arbor: University of Michigan, Center for Political Studies [producer], 1999; Inter-university Consortium for Political and Social Research [distributor], 2000).

likely to vote than will blacks. Table 4-1, based on data from the 1996 National Election Study, presents a cross-tabulation that addresses the hypothesis. The values of the independent variable, race, define the columns of the table, and the values of the dependent variable, whether or not respondents reported voting, define the rows. Reading across the columns of the "Yes" category of the dependent variable, we see a noticeable racial difference. Whereas 78.0 percent of whites reported voting in the 1996 election, about 10 percent fewer blacks (67.8%) voted. A difference obtained from a simple comparison—by dividing subjects on X and comparing on Y—is called a **zero-order relationship**. A zero-order relationship is an overall relationship between two variables, a relationship that does not take into account other possible differences between subjects.

Zero-order relationships always invite the "How else?" question. How else do whites and blacks differ that may account for the observed difference in turnout? We know that education (Z) and race (X) are related. Whites, on average, have more education than blacks. It is also the case that education is related to turnout (Y). Could the zero-order relationship between race and turnout be a spurious artifact of these educational differences? What is the relationship between race (X) and turnout (Y), controlling for education (Z)?

The answer is provided by Table 4-2, which sets up a **controlled comparison table**. A controlled comparison table, or "control table" for short, presents a cross-tabulation between an independent variable and a dependent variable for each value of the control variable. Subjects are first divided into groups according to their values on the control variable. So, in constructing Table 4-2, respondents were separated into two groups on the basis of education (Z): 660 subjects having "High school or less" and 825 subjects with "More than high school." A separate cross-tabulation analysis between X and Y is then performed for each value of Z. Thus the left-hand cross-tab of Table 4-2 shows the relationship between race (X) and turnout (Y) for respondents sharing the same value of Z, a high school education or less. The right-hand cross-tab shows the race-turnout relationship for respondents sharing the other value of Z, more than high school. Now we have two comparisons to evaluate—the voting rates of whites and blacks with low education and the voting rates of whites and blacks with high education.[5]

How would you describe the relationship between race and voting among the less educated? Among people with more education? Clearly, racial differences still exist, though

Table 4-2   Relationship Between Race (X) and Turnout (Y), Controlling for Education (Z)

Voted? (Y)	Level of education (Z)					
	High school or less			More than high school		
	Race (X)			Race (X)		
	White	Black	Total	White	Black	Total
No	32.8%	40.4%	33.9%	14.1%	20.8%	14.7%
	(184)	(40)	(224)	(106)	(15)	(121)
Yes	67.2%	59.6%	66.1%	85.9%	79.2%	85.3%
	(377)	(59)	(436)	(647)	(57)	(704)
Total	100.0%	100.0%	100.0%	100.0%	100.0%	100.0%
	(561)	(99)	(660)	(753)	(72)	(825)

Source: 1996 National Election Study.

they are not as pronounced as in the zero-order relationship. About 67 percent of the less-educated whites reported voting, compared with about 60 percent of less-educated blacks, a 7-percentage-point difference. Among subjects with more education, we find virtually the same 7-percentage-point difference—nearly 86 percent for whites and about 79 percent for blacks. Thus, controlling for education, we find that whites still are more likely to vote than are blacks. A difference obtained from a controlled comparison—by first separating subjects on Z and then comparing Y for different values of X—is called a **partial relationship**. A partial relationship is a relationship between two variables that takes into account other possible differences between subjects.[6] By setting up a control table in this way, you can isolate the partial relationship between an independent variable and a dependent variable, controlling for a rival cause.

Notice, too, that Table 4-2 permits us to isolate the effect of the control variable, education (Z), on turnout (Y), controlling for race (X). What is the relationship between education and turnout *among whites*? To make this comparison, we would jump between the cross-tabulations, comparing the percentage of less-educated whites who voted (67%) with the percentage of more-educated whites who voted (86%). This comparison yields a large difference, 19 percentage points. What about the effect of education on turnout among blacks? Again holding race constant, we would compare the percentage of less-educated blacks who reported voting (60%) with the percentage of more-educated blacks who voted (79%)—a difference of 19 percentage points. Thus the partial effect of education on turnout—the effect of Z on Y, controlling for X—is 19 percent.[7]

Is the relationship between race and turnout a spurious artifact of educational differences? Is this a set of additive relationships? Or is interaction in play? It is here that the three possible scenarios can be put to good use. If the race-voting relationship were spurious, then controlling for education would rob race of its explanatory power. There would be very little difference in the voting turnouts of less-educated whites and blacks, and little difference between the turnouts of more-educated whites and blacks. Spuriousness does not describe the data, because racial differences persist, controlling for education. If interaction were at work, then the strength or tendency of the race-turnout relationship would be different for less-educated individuals than for more-educated individuals. Is this the case? Are racial differences more (or less) pronounced among people with a lower level of education than for

Figure 4-9 Relationship Between Race and Turnout, Controlling for Education (line graph)

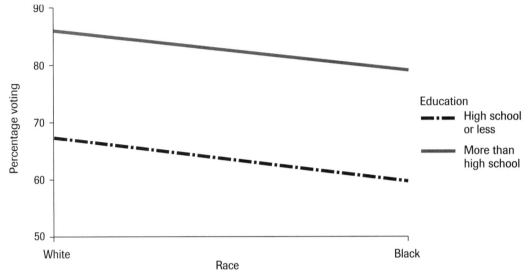

Source: 1996 National Election Study.

people with a higher level of education? No, the effect of race on turnout is about the same for both values of the control. So interaction does not describe the pattern.

Table 4-2 reveals a set of additive relationships between race, education, and turnout. The independent variable, race, helps to explain differences in turnout between individuals. Regardless of education, whites are more likely to vote than blacks. Race alone accounts for a 7-percentage-point difference on the dependent variable. The control variable, education, adds to the explanation. Regardless of race, people with more education are more likely to vote than are people with less education. Education alone accounts for a 19-percentage-point difference on the dependent variable. Now consider the explanatory power of race and education combined. If the racial difference is 7 percent and the education difference is 19 percent, what is the difference in turnout between individuals having various combinations of race and education? Suppose we wanted to compare turnouts for individuals having different values on both independent variables: less-educated blacks compared with more-educated whites. Both variables are at work in this comparison. Because we know that the racial difference is 7 percent and the education difference is 19 percent, then the combined effect is 26 percent. As Table 4-2 reveals, the percentage-point difference between less-educated blacks (60%) and more-educated whites (86%) is 26 percent. What about less-educated whites compared with more-educated blacks? Well, the percentage of more-educated blacks who voted will be 19 percentage points higher than for less-educated whites—that's the education "part" of the comparison—minus 7 percentage-points—the race "part" of the comparison: a 12 percent difference. All additive relationships have this straightforward quality. Each independent variable, considered separately, helps to explain the dependent variable. Both independent variables, considered together, enhance the power of the explanation.

Chapter 3 described how to construct a line graph based on the cross-tabulation of an independent variable and a dependent variable. Line graphs are especially useful for lending clarity and simplicity to controlled comparison relationships. How would one construct a line graph for the relationships in Table 4-2? Consider Figure 4-9. Just like the line graphs you constructed for simple comparisons, the values of the independent variable (X) appear on the horizontal axis—whites on the left and blacks on the right. And, as before, the percentage of subjects falling into one value of the dependent variable—the percentage who reported voting—are represented on the vertical axis. For controlled comparisons, the lines inside the graph depict the X→Y relationship for each value of the control. The "High school or less" line (dashed line) connects two percentages from Table 4-2: 67 percent (the percentage of less-educated whites who voted) and 60 percent (the percentage of less-educated blacks who voted). The "More than high school" line (solid line) connects 86 percent (the percentage of more-educated whites who voted) with 79 percent (the percentage of more-educated blacks who voted). Whereas control tables can be tedious to contemplate, graphic depictions often assist interpretation. It is plain from Figure 4-9 that the independent variable, race, continues to do some explanatory work within each education category, since each line drops 7 percentage points across the values of race. And the distance between the lines, 19 percentage points for whites and 19 percentage points for blacks, records the large contribution of Z. Figure 4-9 closely approximates the visual profile of an additive relationship.

The Rule of Direction for Nominal Variables

One aspect of controlled comparisons sometimes causes confusion. This has to do with how one indicates the direction of a percentage difference for the relationship between variables. For ordinal-level variables, such as education, the answer is intuitive: If higher values of the independent variable are associated with higher values of the dependent variable, then the percentage-point difference is positive. If higher values of the independent variable are associated with lower values of the dependent variable, then the difference is negative. Since, for whites and blacks alike, more education leads to higher turnout, the percentage-point difference between education categories is positive, +19 percentage points.

For relationships involving nominal variables, such as race, one ordinarily does not talk about direction, because it is perfectly reasonable to arrange the categories of nominal variables in any order. So the 7 percentage-point difference can be either positive, +7 percent, by subtracting the percentage of blacks who voted from the percentage of whites who voted, or negative, –7 percent, by subtracting the percentage of whites who voted from the percentage of blacks who voted. If it makes sense to do it either way, why bring it up? Because confusion can arise when describing patterns of interaction for nominal-level relationships. Suppose that, among less-educated people, whites were more likely to vote than blacks. Among more-educated individuals, however, suppose that the relationship were reversed, with whites being less likely to vote than blacks. How would one succinctly summarize the fact that the race-turnout relationship "runs in different directions" for less-educated and more-educated individuals?

In this book we use the following **rule of direction for nominal variables**: The value of the independent variable that defines the left-most column of a cross-tabulation is the base category. A relationship is positive if the percentage in the base category is higher than the percentage in the category to which it is being compared, and negative if the percentage in the base category is lower than the category to which it is being compared. Since the racial category "White" defines the left-most column of Table 4-2, then, by this rule, the relationship between race and the percentage who voted is positive in both categories of Z. For less-educated individuals the race-turnout relationship is +7 percentage points, and for more-educated individuals it is +7 percentage points.

Let's apply the rule of direction to an example of interaction using actual data. Table 4-3, based on data from the 2000 National Election Study, presents a controlled comparison table

Table 4-3 Relationship Between Gender (X) and Support for the Death Penalty (Y), Controlling for Race (Z)

Favor death penalty? (Y)	Race (Z)					
	White			Black		
	Gender (X)			Gender (X)		
	Male	Female	Total	Male	Female	Total
Favor	89.8%	86.3%	87.9%	75.5%	84.3%	80.5%
	(474)	(528)	(1,002)	(40)	(59)	(99)
Oppose	10.2%	13.7%	12.1%	24.5%	15.7%	19.5%
	(54)	(84)	(138)	(13)	(11)	(24)
Total	100.0%	100.0%	100.0%	100.0%	100.0%	100.0%
	(528)	(612)	(1,140)	(53)	(70)	(123)

Source: Nancy Burns, Donald R. Kinder, Steven J. Rosenstone, Virginia Sapiro, and the National Election Studies, *American National Election Study, 2000: Pre- and Post-election Survey*, 2nd version (Ann Arbor: University of Michigan, Center for Political Studies [producer], 2001; Inter-university Consortium for Political and Social Research [distributor], 2002).

Note: Question: "Do you favor or oppose the death penalty for persons convicted of murder?"

for the relationship between gender (X) and support for the death penalty (Y), controlling for race (Z). Table 4-3 was constructed according to protocol. Subjects first were divided into two groups on the basis of the control variable, race. Separate cross-tabulation analyses for the relationship between gender and death penalty opinions were then performed for whites (the left-hand cross-tab) and blacks (the right-hand cross-tab). An examination of Table 4-3 reveals unmistakable signs of interaction. The X→Y relationship is different in strength and tendency for each value of Z. Consider the relationship between gender and death penalty opinions among whites. Reading across the "Favor" value of the dependent variable, one can see that men are somewhat more likely to favor the death penalty, although this tendency is not especially robust. Applying the rule of direction, the left-most value of gender, "Male," defines the base category. To describe the gender–death penalty relationship for whites, then, we would begin with the percentage of men in favor (89.8%) and subtract the percentage for women (86.3%), a +3.5-percentage-point difference. For blacks, by contrast, men are less likely than women to fall into the "Favor" category of the dependent variable. This tendency is stronger than for whites, and it "runs in a different direction." Again applying the rule of direction for nominal variables, we would begin with the percentage of men in favor (75.5%) and subtract the percentage for women (84.3%), yielding a −8.8-percentage-point difference. Thus the two percentage-point differences—a +3.5-point-difference for whites and a −8.8-point difference for blacks—summarize the tendencies and magnitudes of the partial effects of gender on death penalty opinions, controlling for race. One would have to say that interaction is at work here. Both the strength and the tendency of the relationship between gender and opinions about the death penalty are different for whites and blacks.

Figure 4-10, constructed from the data in Table 4-3, provides a clear visual summary of the interaction relationships between gender, race, and death penalty opinions. The values of the independent variable, "Male" and "Female," appear along the horizontal axis. One value of the dependent variable, the percentage favoring the death penalty, is represented on the vertical axis. There are two lines inside the graph, one for whites (dashed line) and one for

Figure 4-10 Relationship Between Gender and Support for the Death Penalty, Controlling for Race (line graph)

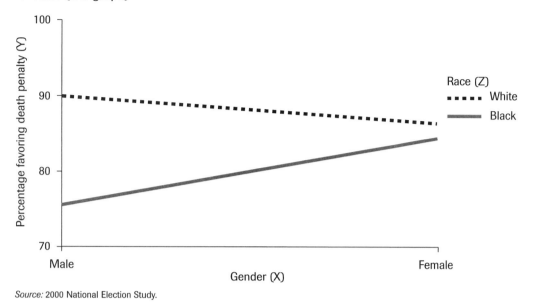

Source: 2000 National Election Study.

blacks (solid line). The tracks of the lines clearly communicate interaction. The relationship between gender and opinion is not at all the same for both races. And note, too, that the effect of race is much greater for males than for females. Since "White" is the left-most category of Table 4-3, then by the rule of direction the race–death penalty opinion relationship for males would be 89.8 percent minus 75.5 percent, or +14.3 percentage points. This sizable racial difference is reflected in the large gap between the lines in Figure 4-10 when X is equal to "Male." The relationship for females, by contrast, would be 86.3 percent minus 84.3 percent, or only +2.0 percentage points. This much weaker racial difference is also clearly seen in Figure 4-10. When X is equal to "Female," the "White" line and the "Black" line converge.

Mean Comparison Analysis

The same mechanics of control—and the same graphic representations—apply when the dependent variable is summarized by means. Consider, for example, this dependent variable: subjects' "feeling thermometer" ratings of Hillary Rodham Clinton. The National Election Study routinely includes a series of questions that ask individuals to rate institutions, groups, and contemporary political figures on a scale from 0 to 100. The ratings gauge the range from very unfavorable feelings (ratings close to 0) to feelings that are very favorable and "warm" (ratings close to 100).[8] What independent variable might be causally linked to ratings of Ms. Clinton? Of course, Hillary Clinton is a prominent Democrat and a highly partisan individual. So one would plausibly hypothesize that partisanship (X) would play a large role in explaining feelings toward her: In comparing individuals, Democrats will give Hillary Clinton higher thermometer ratings than will Republicans. Table 4-4, based on data from the 2000 National Election Study, presents a mean comparison table showing the relationship between party identification (X) and mean thermometer ratings of Ms. Clinton (Y). Not surprisingly, as partisanship changes in value from Democrat to independent to Republican, mean scores on the dependent variable decline—from 70.8 to 48.8 to 29.6.

Table 4-4 Mean Hillary Clinton Thermometer Ratings (Y), by Partisanship (X)

Party identification (X)	Thermometer rating (Y)
Democrat	70.8
	(612)
Independent	48.8
	(694)
Republican	29.6
	(444)
Total	51.6
	(1,750)

Source: 2000 National Election Study.
Note: Numbers of cases are in parentheses.

How else, besides partisanship, are the individuals in Table 4-4 not the same? Might some other, uncontrolled variable be at work in the data, affecting the X→Y relationship? In addition to her status as a Democratic icon, Ms. Clinton, the only former first lady to be elected to the U.S. Senate, may be a powerful symbol of achievement for women, regardless of party. It would seem plausible to hypothesize that gender (Z) plays a role in explaining the dependent variable: In comparing individuals, women will give Hillary Clinton higher ratings than will men. What is the relationship between partisanship (X) and thermometer ratings (Y), controlling for gender (Z)?

Table 4-5 introduces the format for a mean comparison control table. The categories of gender (Z) appear across the top of the table and define the columns. The values of party identification (X) appear along the side of the table and define the rows. So, by reading down each column, we can see what happens to the partisanship-thermometer relationship separately for males (left-hand column) and females (right-hand column). For example, among the 769 males, we find that ratings of Hillary Clinton are still related to party identification:

Table 4-5 Mean Hillary Clinton Thermometer Ratings (Y), by Partisanship (X), Controlling for Gender (Z)

| Party Identification (X) | Gender (Z) | | Total |
	Male	*Female*	
Democrat	68.3	72.4	70.8
	(231)	(381)	(612)
Independent	44.4	52.4	48.8
	(316)	(378)	(694)
Republican	26.4	32.8	29.6
	(222)	(222)	(444)
Totals	46.4	55.7	51.6
	(769)	(981)	(1,750)

Source: 2000 National Election Study.
Note: Numbers of cases are in parentheses.

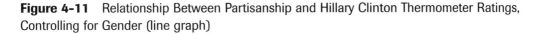

Figure 4-11   Relationship Between Partisanship and Hillary Clinton Thermometer Ratings, Controlling for Gender (line graph)

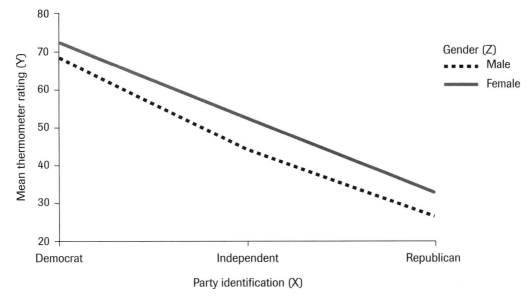

Source: 2000 National Election Study.

Democrats, at 68.3 "degrees," are more favorable than independents (44.4), who in turn are more favorable than Republicans (26.4). For males, the mean difference between Democrats and independents is 23.9 (68.3 minus 44.4), and the mean difference between independents and Republicans is 18.0 (44.4 minus 26.4). Indeed, the same X→Y pattern applies to the 981 females: 72.4 degrees for Democrats, 52.4 for independents, and 32.8 for Republicans. Female independents are 20 degrees chillier toward Ms. Clinton than are female Democrats, and average ratings drops another 19.6 degrees between independents and Republicans. Thus, controlling for gender, party retains its hypothesized relationship to the dependent variable. And notice that, controlling for party, men are less favorably disposed toward Ms. Clinton than are women. Democratic males (at 68.3) register a lower mean than Democratic females (72.4), as do independent males compared with independent females (44.4 versus 52.4) and Republican males compared with Republican females (26.4 and 32.8). Thus, controlling for party, gender retains its hypothesized relationship with the dependent variable.

Now let's obtain a line graph of the relationships and interpret these patterns. Figure 4-11, based on Table 4-5, was constructed just as the earlier line graphs. The values of the independent variable, party identification, are along the horizontal axis, and the mean values of the dependent variable, Hillary Clinton thermometer ratings, are recorded on the vertical axis. There are two lines inside the graph, one for each value of the control variable, gender. Examine Table 4-5 and consider the visual profile of Figure 4-11. Apply the three scenarios. Which scenario best describes the relationships between party, gender, and thermometer ratings? Clearly, the relationship between partisanship and feelings toward Hillary Clinton is not spurious, since the X→Y relationship "survives" after gender is controlled. Is this a set of interaction relationships? Or is this a straightforward example of an additive relationship?

Think about this for a moment. If interaction were at work, then the relationship between party and thermometer ratings would differ in tendency or magnitude for men and women. If this were an additive pattern, then both party and gender would independently contribute to the explanation of thermometer ratings. Party would explain some differences between subjects on the thermometer scale, and gender would add to the explanation, accounting for additional differences between subjects' thermometer ratings of Hillary Clinton. Which of these two possible scenarios best describes the empirical relationships?

Clearly the direction of the relationship between the independent variable and the dependent variable is the same for both values of the control. And the magnitude of the relationship is approximately the same, too. For males and females alike, each change in party identification occasions about a 20-point drop in mean thermometer ratings of Hillary Clinton. To be sure, the relationship between party and thermometer ratings is not exactly the same for men and women. Real data rarely correspond perfectly to one of the possible scenarios. But one would say that the relationships depicted in Table 4-5 and Figure 4-11 are best described as additive. Partisanship "works," accounting for differences between subjects' thermometer ratings. And gender "works," allowing us to account for additional differences, regardless of party.

So that you can become more comfortable setting up and interpreting controlled comparisons, particularly those involving interaction relationships, we will work through two more examples. For the first example, we will look more closely at the dramatic outcome of the 2000 presidential election. As you know, the election's eventual conclusion was highly controversial. Vice President Al Gore conceded the election to George W. Bush one day after a pivotal decision by the U.S. Supreme Court that effectively ended Gore's request for a recount of disputed ballots in Florida. Ordinarily above the political fray, the Supreme Court generally has enjoyed high approval ratings from the American public. But it seems plausible to entertain the idea that the Court's controversial decision engendered negative feelings toward the Supreme Court, particularly among people who had voted for Gore.

Imagine a set of relationships among three variables: a dependent variable (Y) measuring thermometer ratings of the U.S. Supreme Court, an independent variable (X) measuring whether subjects voted for Gore or Bush, and a control variable (Z) measuring the timing of the interview—whether subjects were interviewed before or after Gore conceded the election. Think about the X→Y relationship among respondents who were interviewed before Gore had conceded. Would you expect the Gore voters in this "pre-concession" group to have different evaluations of the Supreme Court than would the Bush voters in this group? Probably not, since all of these people, Gore voters and Bush voters alike, were interviewed during the time before the Court had made its momentous decision. Now think about the X→Y relationship among respondents who were interviewed after Gore had conceded. Would you expect Gore voters and Bush voters in this "post-concession" group to have different evaluations of the Supreme Court? Indeed, you might plausibly expect post-concession Gore voters to give the Court lower thermometer ratings than would post-concession Bush voters.

This idea suggests a set of interaction relationships among vote choice (X), Supreme Court thermometer ratings (Y), and the timing of the interview (Z). For one value of the timing variable, pre-concession, there should be no relationship between vote choice (X) and Supreme Court ratings (Y): Gore voters and Bush voters should have similar mean ratings of the Court. But for the other value of the timing variable, post-concession, a relationship should be found to exist: Gore voters should have lower mean ratings than Bush voters. Plausible enough. But what do the actual data have to say about these expectations?

Table 4-6, based on information from the 2000 National Election Study, presents a mean comparison control table for the relationships. Figure 4-12 presents the line graph. Consider the relationship between the independent variable and the dependent variable for

Table 4-6 Mean Supreme Court Thermometer Ratings (Y), by Vote Choice (X), Controlling for Timing of Interview (Z)

Vote choice (X)	Timing of interview (Z)		Total
	Pre-concession	*Post-concession*[a]	Total
Gore	67.7	57.7	67.1
	(541)	(32)	(573)
Bush	65.6	66.1	65.6
	(488)	(27)	(515)
Totals	66.7	61.5	66.4
	(1,029)	(59)	(1,088)

Source: 2000 National Election Study.

Note: Numbers of cases are in parentheses. Compares Gore voters and Bush voters only. Respondents casting ballots for other candidates are not included in the analysis.

[a] Includes all respondents interviewed on the day of or after Gore's concession.

pre-concession respondents. Reading down this column and comparing mean values of the dependent variable, one finds only a modest difference between Gore voters (67.7) and Bush voters (65.6). As expected, changes in the value of X do not occasion noticeable changes in the mean values of Y. But the situation is markedly different for post-concession respondents. The Gore-voter mean, at 57.7, is more than 8 degrees lower than Bush-voter mean (66.1). Interestingly, people who voted for Bush appear to have been largely unaffected by the Court's decision. Their post-concession mean is much the same as their pre-concession mean. People who voted for Gore, by contrast, registered a 10-point drop—from 67.7 to 57.7 on the dependent variable. This is a clear instance of interaction. The relationship between vote choice and thermometer ratings depends on the timing of the interview.

Figure 4-12 Relationship Between Vote Choice and Supreme Court Thermometer Ratings, Controlling for Timing of Interview (line graph)

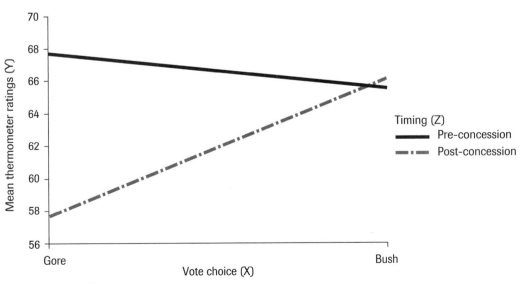

Source: 2000 National Election Study.

Table 4-7 Mean Turnout in Legislative Elections[a] (Y), by Electoral System (X), Controlling for Literacy Rate (Z)

| PR electoral system? (X) | Literacy rate[b] (Z) | | Total |
	Low	*High*	
No	59.4%	68.8%	64.7%
	(11)	(14)	(25)
Yes	71.6	74.9	73.2
	(17)	(15)	(32)
Total	66.8%	72.0%	69.4%
	(28)	(29)	(57)

Source: Shared Global Database (Revised Fall 2004), Pippa Norris, John F. Kennedy School of Government, Harvard University, Cambridge, Mass.

Note: Numbers of cases are in parentheses. Displayed data are for 57 of the 58 democracies analyzed in *Comparing Democracies 2: New Challenges in the Study of Elections and Voting,* Lawrence LeDuc, Richard G. Niemi, and Pippa Norris, eds. (London: Sage Publications, 2002). Complete data not available for Taiwan.

[a] For each country, turnout is the average of all national legislative elections held during the 1990s.

[b] Based on 1998 data. Countries with literacy rates below 97.5 are classified as "Low;" those with literacy rates above 97.5 are classified as "High."

For another example of interaction, we return to a hypothesis about comparative electoral systems proposed in Chapter 2: In comparing countries, those having proportional representation electoral systems will be more likely to have higher voter turnout than will those having plurality electoral systems. As you may recall, this hypothesis was based on the idea that, because they permit smaller parties to win legislative seats, proportional representation (PR) systems provide voters a wider array of choices at election time. Seeing a reasonable chance that a party with an agreeable—if narrow—issue agenda will gain legislative representation, voters might be more motivated to show up at the polls. By contrast, a plurality system, like that used in U.S. elections, encourages broad-based parties having general and sometimes vague agendas—agendas designed to attract large, heterogeneous groups of voters. Seeing favored issue positions only bluntly represented by one of the competing parties, voters would entertain lower expectations of having their views translated into legislative outcomes. Thus turnouts will be lower in plurality systems than in PR systems. Or so the argument goes. A skeptic might point out that, quite apart from their electoral systems, countries differ on many institutional and social factors that may affect turnout in elections: Whether voting is voluntary or required by law, whether elections are held on workdays or weekends, whether citizens are well educated or poorly educated, whether legislative power is wielded by a dominant party or by a coalition of smaller parties, and so on. Do PR systems have higher turnouts than non-PR systems, controlling for these other variables?

Table 4-7 presents a mean comparison control table for the relationship between turnout (Y) and electoral system (X), controlling for literacy rate (Z), an important social characteristic known to affect turnout. Does proportional representation have the hypothesized effect on turnout? Yes, it does. Comparing mean values of the dependent variable for non-PR and PR systems among "Low" literacy countries, we see about a 12-percentage-point difference—from 59.4 percent for non-PR to 71.6 percent for PR systems. Performing the same comparison for countries with "High" literacy, we also find the expected relationship. Those without

Figure 4-13 Relationship Between Electoral System and Turnout, Controlling for Literacy Rate (line graph)

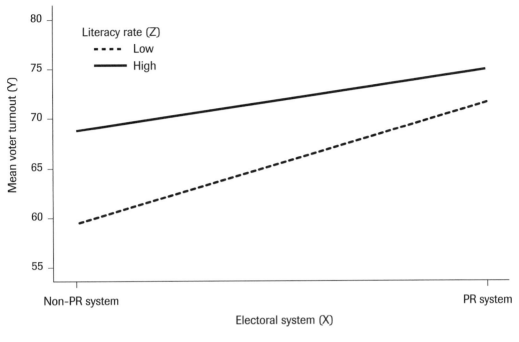

Source: Shared Global Database.

proportional representation averaged 68.8 percent, whereas those with proportional representation averaged 74.9 percent—a turnout boost of about 6 percentage points. So the relationship between the independent variable and the dependent variable has the same tendency for both values of the control variable: PR systems have higher turnouts than do non-PR systems. Why, then, would one say that interaction is at work in this set of relationships? Because the relationship is much stronger for countries with lower literacy rates, in which the comparison of non-PR and PR systems shows a 12-point effect, than for countries with higher literacy rates, in which the same comparison yields a 6-point effect. This difference in strength is evident in Figure 4-13, which shows a line graph of the relationship. The low-literacy line rises sharply across the values of the independent variable. The high-literacy line shows a milder increase. And note this interesting twist, which perhaps reveals the potential power of electoral institutions: Although literacy plays a large role in explaining turnout differences between non-PR countries, low-literacy countries with proportional representation enjoy turnouts that approach parity with their high-literacy counterparts.

SUMMARY

In this chapter we explored the logic and the practice of controlled comparisons in political research. What can happen to the relationship between an independent variable (X) and a dependent variable (Y), controlling for a rival cause (Z)? You have learned to identify and apply three possible scenarios when you perform controlled comparison analysis. In the first possible scenario, the X→Y relationship is spurious. In a spurious relationship, the rival cause is doing all of the explanatory work—causing changes in X and causing changes in Y. After Z is controlled, the relationship between X and Y greatly weakens or completely disappears. In the second possible scenario, additive relationships, both the independent variable and the control variable contribute to the explanation. After Z is controlled, the independent variable retains its hypothesized relationship to the dependent variable. And when X is controlled, the control variable also is found to affect the dependent variable. In additive relationships, the X→Y relationship has the same tendency and similar magnitude for each value of the control variable. Both variables, taken together, enhance the researcher's ability to account for differences between subjects on the dependent variable. In the third possible scenario, interaction relationships, the relationship between the independent variable and the dependent variable is not the same for all values of the control variable. The X→Y relationship may differ in direction. It may be positive for one value of Z and negative for another value of Z. Or the X→Y relationship may differ in magnitude—noticeably stronger for one value of the control variable.

In this chapter we presented several examples of actual empirical analysis. These examples, by and large, have closely approximated one of the three possible scenarios. You will often find this to be the case in your own analyses. After setting up a control table and constructing a line graph of the relationships, you will find that your results come pretty close to one of the scenarios. Yet you often will need additional assistance in figuring out what is going on in the data. The distinction between additive relationships and interaction relationships, in particular, can be a tough call to make. Is the X→Y relationship "similar enough" for all values of Z to call it additive? Or is the X→Y relationship "really different" for each value of Z? It is here that statistical inference enters the picture. Inferential statistics is a key resource for the political researcher and an important interpretive tool for evaluating relationships between variables. In the chapters that follow, you will come to appreciate the central importance of statistical inference in political analysis.

KEY TERMS

additive relationship (p. 78)	partial relationship (p. 89)
arrow diagram (p. 80)	rule of direction for nominal variables (p. 91)
controlled comparison table (p. 88)	spurious relationship (p. 78)
interaction relationship (p. 78)	zero-order relationship (p. 88)

EXERCISES

1. Does a relationship exist between parents' levels of education and the level of education attained by their children? We would assume that parents who have less education might be less inclined—or less able—to further the education of their offspring, whereas parents with higher levels of education would be more inclined and able to do so. But which parent makes more of a difference, the father or the mother? Below are data from the 1998 General Social Survey. The independent variable (X) is father's level of education, measured in three ordinal values: less than high school, high school, and more than high school. The control variable (Z) is mother's level of education, measured by the same three ordinal values. Table entries are the values of the dependent variable (Y), the mean number of years of schooling completed by respondents. For example, respondents whose fathers had less than high school (X) and whose mothers had less than high school (Z) averaged 12.1 years of schooling (Y).

Father's education (X)	Mother's education (Z)		
	Less than high school	*High school*	*More than high school*
Less than high school	12.1	12.9	13.9
High school	13.1	13.9	14.2
More than high school	13.9	14.7	15.6

Note: Entries are mean values of Y, respondents' years of education.

A. Sketch a line graph from this information.
B. Write a paragraph describing the relationship between X and Y, controlling for Z. Which of the following best describes what is going on here: spurious relationship, additive relationship, or interaction relationship? Explain.
C. Consider this statement: "The father's level of education is of primary importance in the educational attainment of children. Unless the father has more than a high school education, the mother's education makes little difference." Based on the data, is this statement accurate? Why or why not?

2. Each of the following conclusions is based on a relationship between X and Y that could be spurious. For each one (i) identify a plausible control variable, Z, and (ii) briefly describe how Z might be affecting the relationship between X and Y.
   A. Ice cream sales (X) and crime rate (Y) are strongly related: As sales go up, so does the crime rate. Conclusion: To reduce the crime rate, ice cream sales should be prohibited.
   B. Adolescents who watch a lot of TV (X) receive lower grades in school (Y) than do adolescents who watch less TV. Conclusion: TV watching lowers school performance.

3. Who favors legalizing marijuana? Pundits frequently cast this issue in generational terms. Older generations, so the explanation goes, are less likely to favor legalization than are younger generations. A more sophisticated version of this generational idea would take the so-called baby boom generation—people born between 1950 and 1965—into account: In comparing individuals, baby boomers will be more likely to favor legalization than will older cohorts or younger cohorts. A variable often forgotten, however, is whether or not people have children. It may be that, reasonably enough, having and raising kids would lead people toward more "conservative" views on legalizing an illegal substance. What is the relationship between generational cohort (X) and opinions on legalizing marijuana (Y), controlling for children (Z)? The 1998 General Social Survey supplies the data:

Year of birth (X)	Have children? (Z)	
	Yes	*No*
1949 or before	22%	24%
1950–1965	28	48
After 1965	26	42

Note: Entries are the percentages of respondents favoring the legalization of marijuana (Y).

A. Sketch a line graph based on this information.
B. Consider the graphic closely. Does the relationship between X and Y fit the generational hypothesis? How would you characterize the interrelationships of X, Y, and Z—spurious relationships, additive relationships, or interaction relationships? Explain.

5

Sampling
and Inference

LEARNING OBJECTIVES

In this chapter you will learn:
- Why random sampling is of cardinal importance in political research
- Why samples that seem small can yield accurate information about much larger groups
- How to figure out the margin of error for the information in a sample
- How to use the normal curve to make inferences about the information in a sample

There is power in numbers. This, at least, would seem a logical conclusion to draw from the steady flow of predictions and speculations based on opinion polls from media of all kinds—television, radio, newspapers, even the Internet. Virtually every broadcast or cable network has its own in-house polling organization or public opinion expert, as do most major journalistic outlets. And it is an uncommon day when you can load your favorite Web site and not be asked to register your opinion on a current issue with some online organization that has an agenda to promote. Indeed, opinion polling reached a dubious zenith during the 2000 presidential election contest. A lack of day-to-day agreement between the large number of tracking polls—and an embarrassing early call for Al Gore that was based, as it turned out, on faulty exit poll numbers—focused renewed attention on the methodology (and partisan sympathies) of the various polling enterprises.[1] Exit polls again created confusion late into the evening on Election Day 2004, as they continued to show Democrat John Kerry leading incumbent Republican George W. Bush in pivotal states, even though actual voting returns showed that Bush was ahead.[2] Yet we continue to hunger for numbers and for the certainty they seem to convey. Which candidate *is* the likely choice among voting age adults? By how large a margin? For which candidate were young people more likely to vote, the Democrat or Republican? What about different racial, gender, and income groups? Was there a sharpening of these dimensions of partisan polarization among the more than 120 million voters in the 2004 election?

Anyone who is interested in politics, society, or the economy wants to understand the attitudes, beliefs, or behavior of very large groups. These large aggregations of units are populations. A **population** may be generically defined as the universe of subjects the researcher wants to describe. If I were studying the financial activity of political action committees in the 2004 election, for example, my population would include all PAC contributions in 2004. Students analyzing the choices made by voters in the 2004 election, by contrast, would define their population as all voting age adults. A characteristic of a population—the dollar amount of the average PAC contribution, the percentage of voting age adults who are Republicans—is called a **population parameter**. Identifying a population's characteristics, its parameters, is a main goal of the social science investigator. Researchers who enjoy complete access to their populations of interest—they can observe and measure every PAC, eligible voter, every member of Congress, Supreme Court decision, or whatever—are working with a **census**. A census allows the researcher to obtain measurements for all members of a population. Thus the researcher does not need to infer or estimate any population parameters when describing the units of analysis.[3]

More often, however, researchers are unable to examine a population directly and must rely, instead, on a **sample**. A sample is a number of cases or observations drawn from a population. Samples, like death and taxes, are fixtures of life for the political researcher. Because population characteristics are frequently hidden from direct view, we turn to samples, which yield observable sample statistics. A **sample statistic** is an estimate of a population parameter, based on a sample drawn from the population. Public opinion polls, for example, never survey every person in the population of interest (for example, all voting-age adults). The pollster takes a sample, elicits an opinion, and then infers or estimates a population characteristic from this sample statistic. Sometimes such samples—a sample size of 1,500 would be typical—seem perilously small. Your natural skepticism is warranted at this point. How can one confidently describe an entire population of voting-age adults with such a minuscule number of observations? Put another way: Just how accurately does a sample statistic estimate a population parameter?

In this chapter we will discuss three factors that determine how closely a sample statistic reflects a population parameter. The first two factors have to do with the sample itself: the procedure that we use to choose the sample and the sample's size, the number of cases in the sample. The third factor has to do with the population parameter we want to estimate: the amount of variation in the population characteristic. First we turn to a discussion of the nature and central importance of random sampling in political research. We then consider how a sample statistic, computed from a random sample, is affected by the size of the sample and the amount of variation in the population. Finally, we show how the normal distribution comes into play in helping researchers determine the margin of error of a sample estimate and how this information is used for making inferences.

RANDOM SAMPLING

The procedure we use in picking the sample is of cardinal importance. For a sample statistic to yield an accurate estimate of a population parameter, the researcher must use a **random sample**, that is, a sample that has been randomly drawn from the population. In taking a random sample, the researcher ensures that every member of the population has an equal chance of being chosen for the sample. To appreciate the importance of random sampling, consider a famous (or infamous) sample that was taken during the 1936 presidential election campaign. Then-president Franklin Roosevelt, a Democrat whose policies were widely viewed as benefiting the lower and working classes, was seeking reelection against Republican candidate

Alf Landon, who represented policies more to the liking of higher-income individuals and business interests. In a well-intentioned effort to predict the outcome (and boost circulation), the magazine *Literary Digest* conducted perhaps the largest poll ever undertaken in the history of electoral politics. Using lists of names and addresses obtained from phone records, automobile registrations, and the ranks of its own subscribers, the *Digest* mailed out a staggering 10 million sample ballots, over 2.4 million of which were filled out and returned. Basing its inferences on responses from this enormous sample, the *Digest* predicted a Landon landslide. The *Digest* estimated that 57 percent of the two-party vote would go to Landon and 43 percent to Roosevelt. History, as you know, reached a somewhat different verdict. The election indeed produced a landslide—but not for Landon. Roosevelt ended up with over 60 percent of the vote. (And the *Literary Digest* ended up going out of business.)

What went wrong? In what ways did the magazine's sampling procedure doom its predictions? As you have no doubt surmised, people who owned cars and had telephones (and could afford magazine subscriptions) during the Great Depression may have been representative of Landon supporters, but they decidedly were not a valid reflection of the electorate at large. In the parlance of social science, the *Digest* used the wrong **sampling frame**, the wrong method for defining the population it wanted to study. Poor sampling frames invariably give life to the insidious "evil twins" of sampling. **Selection bias**, or sampling bias, occurs when some members of the population are more likely to be included in the sample than are other members of the population. **Response bias** occurs when some cases in the sample are more likely than others to be measured. The *Digest*'s poll suffered from selection bias from the get-go, since only people with phones, automobiles, or magazine subscriptions were sent sample ballots. Furthermore, because only a portion of the sample returned their ballots, response bias was also at work. "Sound off" polls, familiar staples of daily newspapers and radio talk shows, suffer from selection bias and response bias. Consider a newspaper poll in which readers are invited to call a toll-free number to register their opinions on a current political controversy. Since only those who read the newspaper are sampled, selection bias is at work. And because only those newspaper readers who are sufficiently self-motivated to call the toll-free number are measured, response bias is at work as well. Samples drawn in this manner are guaranteed to produce sample statistics that are meaningless. Garbage in. Garbage out.

Fortunately, thanks in part to lessons learned from legendary mistakes like the *Literary Digest* poll, social science has figured out how to construct sampling frames that virtually eliminate selection bias, and we have devised sampling procedures that minimize response bias. A valid sample is based on **random selection**. Random selection occurs when every member of the population has an equal chance of being included in the sample. So, if there are 100 members of the population, then the probability that any one member would be chosen is 1 out of 100. Thus the *Literary Digest* should have defined the population they wanted to make inferences about—the entire voting-age population in 1936—and then taken a random sample from this population. By using random selection, every eligible voter, not just those who owned cars or had telephones, would have had an equal chance of being included. But of course the *Digest*, probably believing that a huge sample size would do the trick, ignored the essential principle of random selection. If a sample is not randomly selected, then the size of the sample simply does not matter.

Let's explore these points, using a hypothetical example. Suppose that a student organization wants to gauge a variety of student characteristics—grade point averages, the percentage of students who own a computer, student opinions on campus-related issues, and so on. As a practical matter, the campus group cannot survey all 20,000 students enrolled at the university, so they decide to take a sample of 100 students. The group would first define the sampling frame by assigning a unique sequential number to each student in the population, from 00001 for the first student listed in administration records to 20000 for the last-listed. No problem so far. But how do the pollsters guarantee that each student has exactly one chance in 20,000 of being sampled? A systematic approach, such as picking every two-hundredth student, would result in the desired sample size (since 20,000/200 = 100), but it would not produce a truly random sample. Why not? Because two students appearing next to each other in the sampling frame would not have an equal chance of being selected.

To obtain a random sample, the pollsters would need a list of five-digit random numbers, available in most statistics books or created by many computer programs. A random number has a certain chaotic beauty. The first digit is randomly generated from the numbers 0–9. The second is randomly generated from 0–9 as well, and so its value is not connected in any way to the first digit. The third digit is completely independent of the first two, and so on, for each of the five digits. Since there is no rhyme or reason to these numbers, the pollsters can begin anywhere on the list, adding to their sample the student having the same number as the first random number, using the second random number to identify the second student, and continuing until a sample of 100 students is reached. (Any random number over 20,000 can be safely skipped, since the list has no systematic pattern.) Variants of this basic procedure are used regularly by big-time polling firms, like Gallup or the CBS/New York Times Poll, and academically oriented survey centers, such as the University of Michigan's Institute for Social Research.[4]

Random sampling is the only way to guard against the sort of error we have been discussing: selection bias or sampling bias. Selection bias introduces systematic sampling error. In Chapter 1 we saw how systematic measurement error affects the validity of the measurement of a concept. Recall that, in evaluating the validity of a measurement, we can sometimes figure out how a measurement is being affected by systematic error, but we almost never know the magnitude of the effect. An instructor who administers a math exam to a group of students might know that verbal ability or test anxiety are affecting the measurement of students' test scores, but it is hard to know by how much the scores are being affected. The same logic applies to systematic sampling error. Suppose the hypothetical student organization wants to estimate the mean grade point average (GPA) of the student population. Suppose further that they obtain their sample by setting up a table outside the library entrance and sampling students who enter or leave. Now, the student pollsters might plausibly assume that the statistic obtained from such a sample, mean GPA of the sampled students, would depart from the mean GPA of all students at the school. And they would know how their estimate is being affected: The mean obtained from their sample would be higher than for students who do not frequent the library. But they would have no way of estimating the size of this error. The estimate contains systematic sampling error and thus is biased, to be sure, but by how much? The only way to eliminate systematic sampling error, to get rid of sampling bias, is to take a random sample. Period.

It is important to point out, however, that in eliminating bias we do not eliminate error. In fact, in drawing a random sample, we are consciously introducing **random sampling error**. Random sampling error is defined as the extent to which a sample statistic differs, *by chance*, from a population parameter. Trading one kind of error for another kind of error may seem like a bad bargain. But random sampling error is vastly better, because we know how it affects a sample statistic, and we fully understand how to estimate its magnitude. Assuming sampling bias to be 0, the population parameter will be equal to the sample statistic, plus any random error that was introduced by taking the sample:

Population parameter = Sample statistic + Random sampling error.

Again notice the similarity between random sampling error and random measurement error, covered in Chapter 1. A math instructor may devise a test instrument that eliminates systematic measurement error, such as the systematic error associated with verbal ability or test anxiety. Yet his test measure may still be affected by haphazard "noise," such as disturbance outside the classroom, late-arriving students, broken pencils, or inadvertent mistakes in grading the exam. This random noise may or may not be present if the instructor readministers the test at a later time, and it may or may not affect the same students in the same way. The instructor's measurement of students' exam scores, then, will be equal to their true scores plus the error introduced by haphazard or random occurrences.

Random sampling error affects a sample statistic in much the same way. The hypothetical student group wants a sample statistic that provides an unbiased estimate of a true population parameter, a characteristic of all students at the university. They eliminate selection bias—they eliminate systematic sampling error—by taking a random sample. But they know that random sampling error is affecting their estimate of the population parameter. If the campus organization computes, say, the mean GPA of the students in its sample, it knows that the sample GPA is the same as the population GPA, plus the random error it introduced by taking the sample. Now, what makes random sampling error a "better" kind of error is that we have the statistical tools for figuring out by how much a sample statistic is affected by random sampling error.

The magnitude of random sampling error depends on two components: (1) the size of the sample and (2) the amount of variation in the population characteristic being measured. Sample size has an inverse relationship with random sampling error: As the sample size goes up, random sampling error goes down. Variation in the population characteristic has a direct relationship with random sampling error: As variation goes up, random sampling error goes up. These two components, the variation component and the sample size component, are not separate and independent. Rather, they work together, in a partnership of sorts, in determining the size of random sampling error. We can introduce this partnership by using ideas and terminology that we have already discussed:

Random sampling error = (Variation component) / (Sample size component).

Before exploring the exact properties of this "formula" for random sampling error, consider its intuitive appeal. Notice that "Variation component" is the numerator. This reflects its direct relationship with random sampling error. "Sample size component" is the denominator, depicting its inverse relationship with random sampling error. Return to the student organization example and consider an illustration of how these two components work together. Suppose that there is a great deal of variation in GPAs among students—the student population is widely dispersed across the values of GPA—*and* that the campus group is working with a small-sized random sample. Thus the variation component is a "big" number and the sample size component is a "small" number. Dividing the large variation component by the small sample size component would yield a large amount of random sampling error. Under these circumstances, the organization could not be very confident that their sample statistic provides an accurate picture of the true population mean, because their estimate contains so much random sampling error. But notice that, if the campus group were to take a larger sample, or if student GPAs were not so spread out, random sampling error would diminish, and the student pollsters would gain confidence in their sample statistic.

Of course, determining the size of random sampling error is not an interpretive exercise of declaring its two components to be "big" or "small." Both components have known properties that give the researcher a good idea of just how much random sampling error is contained in a sample statistic. We consider these properties in turn, beginning with the sample size component.

How Sample Size Affects Random Sampling Error
We have noted the basic effect of sample size on random sampling error: As the sample size increases, error decreases. Adopting conventional notation—in which sample size is denoted by a lowercase *n*—we would have to say that a sample of n = 400 is preferable to a sample of n = 100, since the larger sample would provide a more accurate picture of what we are after. But there is a catch. Even though the larger sample is four times the size of the smaller one, it does not deliver a fourfold reduction in random sampling error. Why not? Because the inverse relationship between sample size and sampling error is curvilinear. For smaller sample sizes, for smaller values of n, an increase in sample size decreases error a lot. For larger sample sizes, for larger values of n, an increase in sample size has a more modest effect on error reduction. It is not unlike learning a new skill, in which the boost in competence between the first and second lessons is greater than the gain between the ninth and tenth. For sampling (and perhaps for piano lessons), the shape of the curve fits this pattern: As sampling size increases, random sampling error is reduced by the square root of the sample size. That is, the sample size component of random sampling error is equal to the square root of the sample size, n:

$$\text{Sample size component of random sampling error} = \sqrt{n}.$$

Plugging this into our conceptual formula for random sampling error:

$$\text{Random sampling error} = (\text{Variation component}) / \sqrt{n}.$$

The curvilinear relationship between sample size and random sampling error is not easily grasped, so let's illustrate the principle involved. Consider three samples: n = 400, n = 1,600, and n = 2,800. The sample size component of the smallest sample size is the square root of 400, which is equal to 20. So, for a sample of this size, we would calculate random sampling error by dividing the variation component by 20. Now add 1,200 cases, bringing us to the second sample, n = 1,600. Random sampling error for this sample would be the variation component divided by the square root of 1,600, equal to 40. So by going from a sample size of 400 to a sample size of 1,600, we can increase the sample size component of random sampling error from 20 to 40. Notice that by increasing the sample size component from 20 to 40, we double the denominator, "$\sqrt{n}$." This has a beneficial effect on random sampling error, effectively cutting it by half. But let's add another 1,200 cases and see what happens to error reduction. For the largest sample, n = 2,800, we would calculate the denominator of random sampling error by taking the square root of 2,800, which is equal to 53. Does the second 1,200-unit increase in sample size, from 1,600 to 2,800, have the same effect on the sample size component as the first 1,200-unit increase, from 400 to 1,600? No, it doesn't. The first jump in sample size, from 400 to 1,600, delivered a big boost in the sample size component, from 20 to 40. But the next jump, from 1,600 to 2,800, gave us a more modest increase, from 40 to 53. Thus, the same 1,200-case increase in sample size produces a bigger reduction in sampling error for smaller values of n than for larger values of n. In the practical world of political research, sophisticated sampling is an expensive undertaking, and pollsters must balance the cost of drawing larger samples against the payoff in precision. For this reason, most of the surveys you see and read about have sample sizes in the 1,500 to 2,000 range, an acceptable comfort range for estimating a population parameter.

Sample size is an important part of the story behind the accuracy of a sample statistic. And you now have a better idea of how random sampling error is affected by n. Suppose the campus organization successfully collects its sample (n = 100) and computes a sample statistic, a sample mean GPA equal to 2.80. The group wants to know how much random sampling error is contained in this estimate. As we have just seen, part of the sampling error will depend on the sample size. In this case, the sample size component is equal to $\sqrt{100} = 10$. Now what? What does a sample size error component of 10 have to do with the accuracy of the sample mean of 2.80, the campus group's estimate of the true GPA of the student population?

The answer depends on the second component of random sampling error, the amount of variation in the population characteristic being measured. As we have seen, this connection is direct: As variation in the population characteristic goes up, random sampling error goes up. To better appreciate how variation in the population parameter affects random sampling error, consider Figure 5-1, which depicts two possible ways that student GPAs might be distributed within the student population. First suppose the mean GPA of all 20,000 students in the population is 2.80 and that all students' GPAs are clustered closely around the population mean, as in Panel A of Figure 5-1. Since variation in the population characteristic is low, the variation component of random sampling error is low. A random sample taken from the population would produce a sample mean that is close to the population mean. What is more, repeated sampling from the same population would produce sample mean after sample mean that are close to the population mean—and close to each other. Now suppose that the mean GPA of all 20,000 students in the population is 2.80 but that students are more widely dispersed around the population mean, as in Panel B of Figure 5-1. There are large numbers of students in each value of GPA, from lower to higher, with only a slight amount of clustering around the population mean of 2.80. Since variation in the population characteristic is high, the variation component of random sampling error is high. A random sample taken from the population would produce a sample mean that may or may not be close to the population mean—it all depends on which cases were randomly selected. Because each student has an equal chance of being chosen for the sample, one sample might pick up a few more students who reside above the population mean and would produce a sample mean of, say, 2.90. Another sample from the same population may randomly choose a few more students from below the population mean and yield a sample mean closer to 2.70. In fact, one might draw a very large number of random samples, each one producing a different sample estimate of the population mean.

Hypothetical scenarios demonstrate basic principles. But how does one go about determining the amount of variation in a population characteristic? The answer to that question requires a more detailed look at the statistical meaning and measurement of variation. We look first at a key measure of variation, one that you may have encountered before: the stan-

Figure 5-1 Low Variation and High Variation in a Population Parameter

A. Low Variation in GPAs in the Student Population

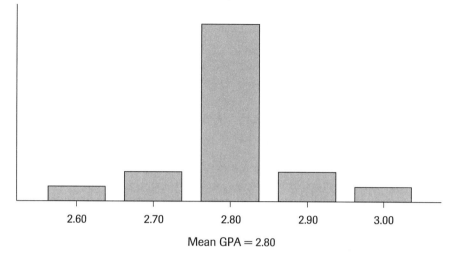

Mean GPA = 2.80

B. High Variation in GPAs in the Student Population

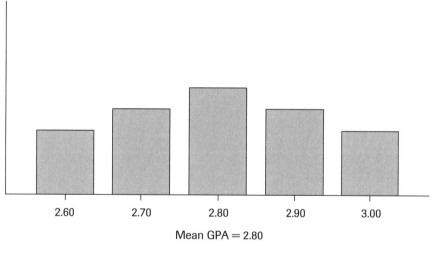

Mean GPA = 2.80

Note: Hypothetical data.

dard deviation. We then return to the question of how the standard deviation affects random sampling error.

Variation Revisited: The Standard Deviation

The amount of variation in a variable is determined by the dispersion of cases across the values of the variable. For nominal and ordinal variables, as discussed in Chapter 3, this often requires a judgment call. The researcher finds the modal or median value of the variable and then observes the extent to which the cases fall into, or cluster around, the distribution's central tendency. If the cases tend to fall in or close to the modal or median value, the researcher would say that the variable has a low amount of variation. If the cases are more dispersed—perhaps the distribution is bimodal or the mode and median are different values—the researcher might say that the variable has a high amount of variation.

For interval-level variables, a more precise measure of variation is used. The **standard deviation** summarizes the extent to which the cases in an interval-level distribution fall on or close to the mean of the distribution. Though more precise, the standard deviation is based on the same intuition as the less precise judgment calls applied to nominal and ordinal variables. If, on the whole, the individual cases in the distribution do not deviate very much from the distribution's mean, then the standard deviation is a small number. If, by contrast, the individual cases tend to deviate a great deal from the mean—that is, large differences exist between the values of individual cases and the mean of the distribution—then the standard deviation is a large number.

To illustrate the calculation of the standard deviation—and to introduce necessary symbols and notation—we will work through an example. Consider Table 5-1, which presents raw data on the wages earned by eleven members of a fictional population. As discussed earlier, a sample size is denoted by a lowercase n. In contrast, a population size is denoted by an uppercase N. In Table 5-1, then, N = 11. The wages for each member of the population are in the "Wages" column, from $2.00 for the lowest paid to $18.00 for the highest paid. What is the population mean in Table 5-1? By dividing the summation of all wages ($2.00 + $5.00 + $7.00 + . . .), $110.00, by the population size, 11, we arrive at the mean wage rate, or central tendency, for the population, $10.00. Unlike sample statistics, which (as we will see) are represented by ordinary letters, population parameters are always symbolized by Greek letters. A population mean is symbolized by the Greek letter μ (pronounced "mew"). Thus, in Table 5-1, μ = $10.00. This is a familiar measure of central tendency for interval-level variables.

How might we summarize variation in wages among members of this population? A rough-and-ready measure is provided by the range, defined as the maximum actual value minus the minimum actual value. So, in this example, the range would be the highest wage, $18.00, minus the lowest wage, $2.00, a range of $16.00. In gauging variation in interval-level variables, however, the measure of choice is the standard deviation. The standard deviation of a population is symbolized by the Greek letter σ ("sigma"). As its name implies, the standard deviation measures variation as a function of deviations from the mean of a distribution. The first step in finding the standard deviation, then, is to express each value as a deviation from the mean or, more specifically, to subtract the mean from each value:

$$(\text{Individual value} - \mu) = \text{Deviation from the mean.}$$

An individual whose wage is below the population mean will have a "negative" deviation, and a member of the population whose wage is above the mean will have a "positive" deviation. An individual with wages equal to the population mean will have a deviation of 0. In Table 5-1, the deviations for each member of the population are shown in the column labeled "Deviations from the mean." These deviations, which are expressed in interval-level units of measurement (dollars), tell us the locations of each population member relative to the population mean. So, for example, Wage earner 1, who's making a paltry $2.00 per hour, has a deviation of –$8.00, eight dollars below the population mean of $10.00. Wage earner 7, at $10.50 an hour, is slightly above the population mean, earning 50 cents more than the population mean of $10.00. Deviations from the population mean provide the starting point for figuring out the standard deviation.

Table 5-1   Central Tendency and Variation in Hourly Wage Rates for a Fictional Population

Wage earner	Wages ($)	Deviation from the mean ($)	Squared deviation from the mean ($)	Z score
1	2.00	−8.00	64.00	−1.86
2	5.00	−5.00	25.00	−1.16
3	7.00	−3.00	9.00	−.70
4	8.00	−2.00	4.00	−.46
5	9.50	−.50	.25	−.12
6	10.00	.00	.00	.00
7	10.50	.50	.25	+ .12
8	12.00	2.00	4.00	+ .46
9	13.00	3.00	9.00	+ .70
10	15.00	5.00	25.00	+1.16
11	18.00	8.00	64.00	+1.86

Summary information:

Central tendency
Summation of wages = $110.00

N = 11

μ = $10.00

Dispersion
Summation of squared deviations = $204.50
Average of the squared deviations (variance) = $18.59

σ = $4.31

To obtain the population mean (μ), sum the individual values and divide by the number of values (N).	To obtain the standard deviation (σ): First, add up all the squared deviations. Second, find the average of this number by dividing it by N. Third, find the square root of this average.	To obtain Z scores, divide each deviation from the mean by the standard deviation.

All measures of variation in interval-level variables, including the standard deviation, are based on the square of the deviations from the mean of the distribution. In Table 5-1, these calculations for each wage earner in the population appear in the column labeled "Squared deviations from the mean." Squaring each individual deviation, of course, removes the minus signs on the "negative" deviations, those members of the population whose wages fall below the population mean. Notice, for example, that the square of Wage earner 1's deviation, −$8.00, is the same as the square of Wage earner 11's deviation, $8.00. Both square to $64.00. Why perform a calculation that treats Wage earner 1 and Wage earner 11 as equal, when they clearly are not equal at all? Because, in the logic of the standard deviation, both of these wage earners make equal contributions to the *variation* in wages. Both lie an equal distance from the population mean of $10.00, and so both deviations figure equally in determining the dispersion of wages around the mean. Rest assured that, when all is said and done, the standard deviation will provide the information we need to distinguish between wage earners who fall below the population mean and those who fall above the population mean. Notice, too, that wages close to the mean—Wage earner 5 or Wage earner 7, for instance—have smaller deviations and thus make smaller contributions to the variation in wages.

If we add up all the squared deviations in the "Squared deviations from the mean" column, we arrive at the sum $204.50. The summation of the squared deviations, often called the total sum of squares, can be thought of as an overall summary of the variation in a distribution. When calculated on real-world data with many units of analysis, the total sum of squares is always a large and seemingly meaningless number. However, the summation of the squared deviations becomes important in its own right when we discuss correlation and regression analysis (see Chapter 7).

For present purposes, we will focus on an important derivative of the summation of the squared deviations: the average of the squared deviations. The average of the squared deviations is known by a statistical name, the **variance**. The variance "looks at" the overall summary of variation in the distribution and then computes the mean of this amount by dividing by N. For the population depicted in Table 5-1, the variance is the summation of the squared deviations ($204.50) divided by the population size (N = 11), which yields an average of $18.59. So the contribution each individual wage earner makes to the overall variation in wages is, *on average*, $18.59. Notice that, as with any mean, the size of the average of the squared deviations is sensitive to values that lie far away from the mean. Wage earners toward the tails of the distribution—Wage earners 1 and 2 on the low end and Wage earners 10 and 11 on the high end—make greater contributions to the variance than do wage earners who lie closer to the population mean. That's the beauty of the variance. If a population's values cluster close to the mean, then the average of the squared deviations will record the closer clustering. Clearly, if Wage earners 1 and 2 had higher wages and Wage earners 10 and 11 had lower wages, then the average of the squared deviations would shrink in size. The variance would be a smaller number. As deviations from the mean increase, then the variance increases, too. The variance plays a recurring role in many statistical techniques. What is more, the population parameter of current concern, the standard deviation, is based on the variance. In fact, the standard deviation is the square root of the variance. The standard deviation (σ) for the population of wage earners, then, is the square root of $18.59, or $\sqrt{18.59}$ = $4.31.[5]

The standard deviation has two important applications. First, when combined with some workable assumptions about a variable's distribution, knowledge of σ permits useful inferences about a single case drawn at random from a population. Second, when combined with knowledge of the sample-size component of random sampling error, the standard deviation allows the researcher to estimate the accuracy of a statistic from a random sample drawn from a population. In both applications, this inferential leverage is rooted in the known properties of the normal distribution.

The Normal Distribution

The **normal distribution** is a bell-shaped distribution used to describe interval-level variables. You probably recognize the normal distribution's bell-like shape, depicted in Figure 5-2. You may not recognize some of the notation. The mean of the normal distribution is marked by 0. Any member of a population having the population's mean value on some characteristic, such as wage rates, would fall under the tallest part of the curve above the zero-point of the normal distribution. The hash marks along the horizontal axis represent the number of standard deviations relative to the mean, +1 for the point one standard deviation above the

Figure 5-2 The Normal Distribution

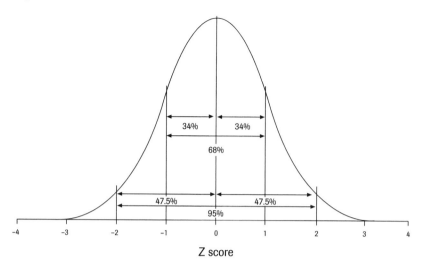

Z score

mean, −1 for the point one standard deviation below and mean, and so on. If, for example, a member of a population has a value on some characteristic that puts that member one standard deviation above the population mean, then the member would fall under the somewhat shorter part of the curve, above the +1 point on the normal distribution.

The numbers along the horizontal axis are known as standardized scores, or Z scores. A **Z score** is obtained for any value in a population by finding the value's deviation from the mean and dividing by the standard deviation of the distribution. A Z score, then, converts a "raw" deviation from the mean into a "standardized" deviation from the mean. A Z score tells us how many standard deviations a case lies above the mean (a positive sign on Z) or below the mean (a negative sign on Z). If a case has a value equal to the mean, its Z score is 0. So, for any value in a population,

$$Z = (\text{Deviation from the mean}) / \sigma.$$

Return to the fictional population of wage earners depicted in Table 5-1. The column labeled "Z scores" reports the value of Z for each of the 11 members of the population. These scores convert the values in the "Deviations from the mean" column, which are expressed in units of measurement (dollars), into standardized scores, which are expressed in units of standard deviation above (positive Z scores) or below (negative Z scores) the population mean. Thus Wage earner 1, with a raw deviation from the mean of −$8.00, gets a standardized Z score of −$8.00 / $4.31 = −1.86. Wage earner 1's $2.00 wage situates him 1.86 standard deviations *below* the mean. And the Z score for Wage earner 11, at +1.86, affirms his highly paid status relative to everyone else in the population. His hourly wage of $18.00 places him 1.86 standard units *above* the population mean. Clearly enough, by knowing the mean (μ) and the standard deviation (σ) we can locate any value in a distribution relative to the mean of the distribution.

But there is substantially more to it than this. Again consider the bell-shaped curve of Figure 5-2. Notice the percentages inside the curve. The arrow stretching between Z = −1 and Z = +1 bears the label "68%." What does this mean? It means this: If a distribution is normally distributed, then 68 percent of the cases in the distribution will have Z scores between −1 (one standard deviation below the mean) and +1 (one standard deviation above the mean). Moreover, since the curve is perfectly symmetrical, half of that 68 percent—34 percent of the cases—will fall between the mean (Z equal to 0) and a Z score of +1, and the other 34 percent will fall between the mean and a Z score of −1. So the range between Z = −1 and Z = +1 is the fattest and tallest part of the curve, containing over two-thirds of the cases. Notice the arrow labeled "95%," the one stretching between Z = −1.96 and Z = +1.96. These numbers tell us that, in a normal distribution, 95 percent of the cases will have Z scores in the long interval between 1.96 standard deviations below the mean and 1.96 standard deviations above the mean. This long interval, in other words, will contain just about all the cases. But of course 5 percent of the cases—those with Z scores of less than −1.96 or greater than +1.96— will lie outside this interval, in the sparsely populated tails of the distribution. Again, since the curve is symmetrical, half of this 5 percent, or 2.5 percent, will fall in the region below Z = −1.96, and the other 2.5 percent will fall in the region above Z = +1.96.

Now consider the normal distribution's essential role in making probabilistic inferences about the individuals in a population. A **probability** is defined as the likelihood of the occurrence of a single event. If we know the mean and the standard deviation of a distribution, then we can calculate the Z score for any individual in the population. Furthermore, if we assume that the distribution is normally distributed, we can make reasonable inferences about the Z score of any single case drawn at random from the distribution. Imagine being blindfolded and randomly picking a single case from Figure 5-2. What is the probability that your randomly chosen case will have a Z score between −1 and +1? Thanks to the inferential leverage of the normal distribution, you know that 68 percent of all the cases fall in this interval. Thus there is a 68-percent probability that a single case drawn at random will have a Z score in the interval between Z = −1 and Z = +1. That is, you could be fairly confident, "68 percent confident" anyway, that the case will have a Z score in this interval. But because random processes are at work, there is a chance that the case you choose will have a Z score outside the −1 to +1 region. How much of a chance? Well, since 68 percent of the cases are in the Z = ± 1 area, then the rest of the cases, 32 percent, must lie in the area above Z = +1 or below Z = −1. Thus there is a 32-percent probability—about one chance in three—that a randomly chosen case will have a Z score outside the fat and tall part of the curve. Suppose you were to bet on the probability of picking a case with a Z score of greater than +1.96. Are the odds with you? Hardly. Since, according to the normal distribution, 95 percent of all the cases fall in the long interval between Z = −1.96 and Z = +1.96, only 5 percent will fall outside these boundaries: 2.5 percent falling below Z = −1.96 and 2.5 percent falling above Z = +1.96. Thus you would be betting on an unlikely event, an occurrence that would happen, by chance, fewer than 3 times out of 100. Not impossible, to be sure. Just highly unlikely.

As you can see, the percentages of cases that fall within given intervals of the normal distribution are directly analogous to probabilities. By knowing the mean and the standard deviation of a distribution, we can use the normal curve to estimate the probability that a randomly chosen case will have a Z score within any given interval. Of course, political researchers are not ordinarily engaged in making inferences about single cases chosen at random from a population. Rather, we are mostly concerned with making inferences about population parameters based on samples chosen at random from a population. Yet again, your knowledge of the standard deviation and the normal distribution can be directly applied when making inferences about an unseen population based on samples randomly drawn from that population.

How the Standard Deviation Affects Random Sampling Error

We now can put a finer point on the question of how a sample statistic is affected by variation in the population from which the sample is drawn. Let's begin by reacquainting ourselves with the hypothetical student group that has served as illustration. Recall that the student pollsters took a random sample of n = 100 from a student population of N = 20,000. They calculated a sample statistic, the mean GPA of the students in their sample, equal to 2.80. As we have seen, a population mean is symbolized by the Greek letter μ. To distinguish this population parameter from an estimate based on a sample, the mean of a sample is represented by the symbol $\bar{x}$ (pronounced "x bar"), the ordinary letter *x* with a bar across the top. So in this example, $\bar{x}$ = 2.80, or "x bar" equals 2.80. Now, the group knows that their sample estimate ($\bar{x}$) will be equal to the true population mean (μ) plus the random sampling error they introduced by taking the sample. They also know the magnitude of the sample size component of random sampling error. As sample size increases, the sample size error component decreases as a function of the square root of n. As calculated earlier, for a sample size of 100, this component is √100, or 10.

We can now supply the missing ingredient, the variation component of random sampling error. We already know that the connection is direct: As variation in a population characteristic increases, so does random sampling error. The variation component of random sampling error is determined by a now-familiar measure, the standard deviation (σ). For any given sample size of n, as the population standard deviation increases, random sampling error increases (and vice versa). When we combine this principle with the sample size error component, we again can represent the partnership between the two components of random sampling error:

Random sampling error = Standard deviation / Square root of the sample size.

Or, using symbols that have been discussed:

Random sampling error = σ / √n.

Reflect for a moment on how this sterile formula captures the effects of the variation component and the sample size component. If we were to use a very large sample to estimate a population parameter that had a very small standard deviation, our sample statistic would be quite accurate. If, however, the population standard deviation was large and the sample was small, our estimate would have a bigger dose of random error and thus would less accurately mirror the population parameter we are measuring.

Assuming that the population standard deviation is known, the procedure for figuring out the size of random sampling error is straightforward. The student organization has a sample of 100 and a sample mean of 2.80. Let's assume that the standard deviation of GPAs in the student population is .40. In this case, the size of random sampling error would be

$$
\begin{aligned}
\text{Random sampling error} \quad &= \quad \sigma / \sqrt{n} \\
&= \quad .40 / \sqrt{100} \\
&= \quad .40 / 10 \\
&= \quad .04.
\end{aligned}
$$

At last, a denouement of sorts! The student group can now say that their sample mean ($\bar{x}$ = 2.80) is equal to the true population GPA (μ), with random sampling error equal to .04. Let's look now at how this information can be used to draw inferences about the population.

INFERENCE USING THE NORMAL DISTRIBUTION

Thus far in this chapter we have been using the generic term *random sampling error* to describe the error introduced when a random sample is drawn. The size of this error, as we have just seen, is determined by dividing the variation component by the sample size component. Confusingly, when researchers are describing the random sampling error associated with a sample mean ($\bar{x}$), they do not ordinarily use the term *random sampling error*. Rather, they refer to the **standard error** of the mean. Computer analysis programs routinely calculate standard errors for mean estimates, and political researchers always report the standard errors for the sample estimates they publish in quantitative research articles. Let's be clear. The terms *standard error of a sample mean* and *random sampling error of a sample mean* are synonymous. Both terms refer to the bedrock foundation of inferential statistics. But because you will often encounter the term *standard error*, this book will use the term, too.

Before going on, pause for a checkpoint. We have just introduced a new term, *standard error*, which has the same adjective as another term, *standard deviation*. Understandably, students sometimes confuse these terms, so we need to be clear about the differences between them. The standard deviation (σ) is a measure of dispersion around a single mean. Again, by knowing the mean and the standard deviation, we can calculate a Z score for any case in the distribution. Also, we can figure out the probability of randomly drawing any single case from the distribution. The standard error is a measure of how closely a sample mean estimates a population mean. We take a random sample—not a single case—from the population. We then calculate a sample mean. By knowing the size of the sample (n) and the amount of dispersion in the population (σ), we can estimate how closely the sample mean reflects the population mean. In both applications, whether we are drawing a single case from a distribution or drawing a sample from a distribution, the normal curve comes into play.

Informally, we can always say that the statistic we have computed from a sample is equal to the population parameter, give or take a standard error or so. If our student group obtains a sample mean GPA of 2.80 from a sample of 100, and the population standard deviation is .40, then the standard error of the sample mean is .04. So the student group can safely infer that the true population GPA is 2.80, plus or minus .04 or so. That is, the true mean probably lies in the interval of about 2.76, a standard error below the sample estimate, to 2.84, a standard error above the sample estimate. More formally—and here is where the normal distribution applies—there is a 68-percent chance that the population mean lies within ± 1 standard error of the sample mean, and there is a 95-percent chance that it lies within ± 1.96 standard errors of the sample mean. Or, put another way, there is only a 5 percent probability that the true population mean will lie more than 1.96 standard errors above or below the sample mean, in the region defined by the sample mean minus 1.96 standard errors at the low end, or in the region defined by the sample mean plus 1.96 standard errors at the high end.

How do we know this? The **central limit theorem** is an established statistical rule that tells us that, if we were to take an infinite number of samples of size n from a population of N subjects, the means of these samples would be normally distributed. This distribution of sample means, furthermore, would be centered on the true population mean and have a standard deviation equal to σ divided by the square root of n. So, if we took a sample of size 100 from the student population, wrote down the sample's mean GPA, returned these cases to the population, then took a second sample of size 100, recorded the second sample's mean GPA, replaced these cases, then took a third sample, a fourth, and so on into infinity, we would find that the mean of all those sample means is equal to the population mean, that most (68%) of the sample means in this infinite group cluster within one standard error of the population mean, and that just about all (95%) fall within 1.96 standard errors. But because we are dealing with random processes, weird outcomes still can occur by chance. About 5 out of every 100 sample means will be bona fide flukes, having values out in the rarified regions of the curve, beyond 1.96 standard errors in either direction.

Because of the "fluke effect"—the random probability of obtaining a sample statistic that departs dramatically from the population parameter—researchers never talk about certainty. They talk, instead, about confidence and probability. The most common standard is the **95 percent confidence interval**, defined as the interval within which 95 percent of all possible sample estimates will fall by chance. The boundaries of the 95 percent confidence interval are defined by the sample mean minus 1.96 standard errors at the lower end, and the sample mean plus 1.96 standard errors at the upper end. Let's use this knowledge to find the 95 percent confidence interval for student GPAs:

$$
\begin{aligned}
\text{Lower confidence boundary} \quad &= \quad \text{sample mean} - 1.96 \text{ standard errors} \\
&= \quad 2.80 - 1.96 \,(.04) \\
&= \quad 2.7216 \\
\text{Upper confidence boundary} \quad &= \quad \text{sample mean} + 1.96 \text{ standard errors} \\
&= \quad 2.80 + 1.96 \,(.04) \\
&= \quad 2.8784.
\end{aligned}
$$

Conclusion: Ninety-five percent of all possible random samples of n = 100 will yield sample means between 2.7216 and 2.8784.

The 95 percent standard of confidence is widely applied, but its precise boundaries can be a bit tedious to calculate quickly. Therefore, it is customary to round off 1.96 to 2.0, resulting in a useful rule of thumb. To find the 95 percent confidence interval for a sample mean, multiply the standard error by 2. Subtract this number from the sample mean to find the lower confidence boundary. Add this number to the sample mean to find the upper confidence boundary.[6] Applying this rule of thumb, the student organization can be confident, 95 percent confident at least, that the unobserved population mean (μ) has a value between $2.80 \pm 2(.04)$, that is, between 2.72 and 2.88.

Now suppose for the sake of argument (and to demonstrate inference) that the dean of students, upon reading the results of the student survey, decrees the sample mean to be "a bit off." "There must be some mistake," the dean intones. "I would hypothesize that the mean grade point average for students at the university is at least 2.92." Now, the dean's hypothetical number *seems* reasonable, perhaps even likely, and since the fluke effect is always a possibility with random samples, the dean's impression could be right. In fact, let's begin by assuming that the dean is correct, that the true population mean (μ) really is 2.92. Now ask this question: If, as the dean claims, the population mean really is 2.92, how often, by chance, would a random sample yield a sample mean of 2.80 with a standard error of .04? Since the dean's hypothetical mean falls outside the 95 percent confidence interval, you know that such an event would occur less than 5 percent of the time. The normal distribution, however, allows for even greater precision. First, assemble all the numbers:

$$
\begin{aligned}
\text{Dean's hypothetical population mean } (\mu) &= 2.92 \\
\text{Observed sample mean } (\bar{x}) &= 2.80 \\
\text{Standard error of the sample mean} &= .04
\end{aligned}
$$

Just how far apart are the dean's hypothetical population mean, 2.92, and the observed sample mean, 2.80? To find this difference, we subtract the sample mean ($\bar{x}$) from the hypothetical population mean (μ):

$$
\begin{aligned}
\text{Hypothetical mean minus sample mean} &= \mu - \bar{x} \\
&= 2.92 - 2.80 \\
&= .12
\end{aligned}
$$

Now the question becomes: How many standard errors lie between the hypothetical mean and the observed sample mean? Thus we convert the disputed difference (.12) to a familiar standard unit, Z:

$$
\begin{aligned}
Z &= (\text{Hypothetical mean minus sample mean}) / \text{standard error} \\
&= (2.92 - 2.80) / .04 \\
&= .12 / .04 \\
&= 3.0
\end{aligned}
$$

The number of standard errors separating the hypothetical population mean and the observed sample mean—the value of Z—is 3 units. This is a large Z score, an entire standard error above the upper boundary of the 95 percent confidence interval. If the dean is right, what are the chances that the student group's random sample produced a mean that is so far off the mark?

Take a moment and once again consider Figure 5-2, which depicts the normal distribution. The hash mark at Z = 0 represents the student group's estimate of the true population GPA, a sample estimate equal to 2.80. The hash marks at Z = −1.96 and Z = +1.96 represent the 95 percent confidence boundaries of this sample estimate. The unseen population mean could very likely be somewhere within these boundaries. If the group were to calculate sample means for an infinite number of random samples of n = 100, 95 percent of the means would fall within this region, from about 2.72 on the low end to 2.88 on the high end. Now find the hash mark for Z = +3 on the horizontal axis. The hash mark at Z = +3 represents the dean's hypothetical mean, three units of Z above the sample estimate. Now ask yourself: If the dean is correct—the true population mean really is way out there at Z = +3—how often will the student pollsters get a sample mean of 2.80? What percentage of possible samples would produce such result?

The answer is contained in a normal distribution probability table, such as that presented in Table 5-2. Examine Table 5-2 for a moment. Each entry in Table 5-2 reports the proportion of the normal distribution that lies *above* the absolute value of Z. Before we test the "dean's mean" using Table 5-2, let's look up the probability for a value of Z with which you are already conversant, Z = +1.96. Read down the left-hand column until the integer value and first decimal of Z is reached (1.9), and then read across until you find the cell associated with the second decimal place of Z (.06). The cell's entry is .0250. This number confirms what we already knew: 2.5 percent, or .025, of the curve lies above a Z score of +1.96. Notice that,

Table 5-2 Proportions of the Normal Curve above the Absolute Value of Z

First digit and first decimal of Z	Second decimal of Z									
	.00	.01	.02	.03	.04	.05	.06	.07	.08	.09
0.0	.5000	.4960	.4920	.4880	.4840	.4801	.4761	.4721	.4681	.4641
0.1	.4602	.4562	.4522	.4483	.4443	.4404	.4364	.4325	.4286	.4247
0.2	.4207	.4168	.4129	.4090	.4052	.4013	.3974	.3936	.3897	.3859
0.3	.3821	.3783	.3745	.3707	.3669	.3632	.3594	.3557	.3520	.3483
0.4	.3446	.3409	.3372	.3336	.3300	.3264	.3228	.3192	.3156	.3121
0.5	.3085	.3050	.3015	.2981	.2946	.2912	.2877	.2843	.2810	.2776
0.6	.2743	.2709	.2676	.2643	.2611	.2578	.2546	.2514	.2483	.2451
0.7	.2420	.2389	.2358	.2327	.2296	.2266	.2236	.2206	.2177	.2148
0.8	.2119	.2090	.2061	.2033	.2005	.1977	.1949	.1922	.1894	.1867
0.9	.1841	.1814	.1788	.1762	.1736	.1711	.1685	.1660	.1635	.1611
1.0	.1587	.1562	.1539	.1515	.1492	.1469	.1446	.1423	.1401	.1379
1.1	.1357	.1335	.1314	.1292	.1271	.1251	.1230	.1210	.1190	.1170
1.2	.1151	.1131	.1112	.1093	.1075	.1056	.1038	.1020	.1003	.0985
1.3	.0968	.0951	.0934	.0918	.0901	.0885	.0869	.0853	.0838	.0823
1.4	.0808	.0793	.0778	.0764	.0749	.0735	.0721	.0708	.0694	.0681
1.5	.0668	.0655	.0643	.0630	.0618	.0606	.0594	.0582	.0571	.0559
1.6	.0548	.0537	.0526	.0516	.0505	.0495	.0485	.0475	.0465	.0455
1.7	.0446	.0436	.0427	.0418	.0409	.0401	.0392	.0384	.0375	.0367
1.8	.0359	.0351	.0344	.0336	.0329	.0322	.0314	.0307	.0301	.0294
1.9	.0287	.0281	.0274	.0268	.0262	.0256	**.0250**	.0244	.0239	.0233
2.0	.0228	.0222	.0217	.0212	.0207	.0202	.0197	.0192	.0188	.0183
2.1	.0179	.0174	.0170	.0166	.0162	.0158	.0154	.0150	.0146	.0143
2.2	.0139	.0136	.0132	.0129	.0125	.0122	.0119	.0116	.0113	.0110
2.3	.0107	.0104	.0102	.0099	.0096	.0094	.0091	.0089	.0087	.0084
2.4	.0082	.0080	.0078	.0075	.0073	.0071	.0069	.0068	.0066	.0064
2.5	.0062	.0060	.0059	.0057	.0055	.0054	.0052	.0051	.0049	.0048
2.6	.0047	.0045	.0044	.0043	.0041	.0040	.0039	.0038	.0037	.0036
2.7	.0035	.0034	.0033	.0032	.0031	.0030	.0029	.0028	.0027	.0026
2.8	.0026	.0025	.0024	.0023	.0023	.0022	.0021	.0021	.0020	.0019
2.9	.0019	.0018	.0018	.0017	.0016	.0016	.0015	.0015	.0014	.0014
3.0	.0013	.0013	.0013	.0012	.0012	.0011	.0011	.0011	.0010	.0010

because the normal distribution is symmetrical, Table 5-2 can be used to find probabilities associated with negative values of Z as well. For example, since .025 of the curve lies above Z = +1.96, then .025 must lie below Z = −1.96. Thus, in using Table 5-2, you can safely ignore the sign on Z and look up its absolute value. Remember, though, that for negative values of Z, the entries in Table 5-2 will tell you the proportion of the curve that lies *below* the value of Z.

Now apply Table 5-2 to the task of finding the proportion of the curve above Z = 3.0. Again, read down the left-hand column until you find the integer and first digit of Z (3.0), then read across to find the proportion corresponding to the second decimal place of Z (.00). The entry in this cell is .0013. This number may be interpreted this way: The dean is (very) probably wrong. Why can we say this? Because only .0013, or .13 percent, of all possible sample means lie above the Z score associated with the dean's hypothetical population mean. If, as the dean claims, the population mean really is 2.92, we would observe a sample mean of 2.80, by chance, only 13 times out of 10,000. An impossible event? No. An extremely unlikely event? Yes.

This example demonstrates how inference using the normal distribution, often called normal estimation for short, is used for testing hypothetical claims about a population mean. This inferential process has a definite logic. Perverse as it may seem, the researcher begins by assuming that the hypothetical claim is correct. Thus when the dean suggests that the mean GPA in the student population is "at least 2.92," the student pollsters say, "All right, let's assume that the population mean is at least 2.92." The researcher then sees how well this assumption holds up, given the observed results obtained from the sample: "If the population mean really is 2.92, how often, by chance, will we obtain a sample mean of 2.80?" The answer, which is always a probability, determines the inferential decision: "If the population mean is at least 2.92, we would obtain a sample mean of 2.80 about 13 times out of 10,000 by chance. Therefore, we infer that the population mean is *not* 2.92 or higher." These steps—assuming the hypothetical claim to be correct, testing the claim using normal estimation, and then making an inference based on probabilities—define the logic of hypothesis testing using inferential statistics. In most research situations you will encounter, normal estimation will serve you well.

There is, however, one important way in which the student pollster example has been unrealistic—and this point must now be addressed. The student group took a random sample (realistic enough) and calculated a sample mean (again, realistic). You may have noticed, however, that in figuring out the variation component of random sampling error, the standard deviation, it was assumed that the population standard deviation (σ) was a known quantity. This is not realistic. As a practical matter, of course, a researcher rarely knows any of the population's parameters. If the population's parameters were known, there would be no need to take a sample to begin with! Fortunately, a lack of knowledge about the population's standard deviation is not as serious a problem as it may seem. A different distribution—one that, under many circumstances, is very similar to the normal distribution—can be applied to problems of inference when the population standard deviation is not a known quantity. This distribution is our next topic of discussion.

INFERENCE USING THE STUDENT'S T-DISTRIBUTION

As was just noted, in most realistic sampling situations the researcher has a random sample—and that's it. The researcher uses this sample to calculate a sample mean, just as the student pollsters calculated a mean GPA from their sample. But to determine the standard error of the mean—the degree to which the sample mean varies, by chance, from the population mean—the researcher needs to know the population standard deviation. If that parameter is unavailable, as it usually is, then the researcher at least needs an estimate of the population standard deviation. A reasonable estimate is available. Why not simply calculate the standard deviation of the sample? One could then use the sample standard deviation as a stand-in for σ in calculating the standard error. So, easily enough, the standard error of the sample mean would become

Sample standard deviation / Square root of the sample size.

Or, using the ordinary letter *s* to denote the sample standard deviation, the standard error is

$$s/\sqrt{n}.$$

Now, for fair-sized samples—samples in the n = 1,000 range or larger—substituting s for σ will work fine, and normal estimation can be used. But when the researcher is using smaller samples, or if the researcher has divided up a large sample into smaller subsamples for separate analyses, the exact properties of the normal distribution may no longer be applied in making inferences. Fortunately, a similar distribution, the **Student's t-distribution**, can be applied.

The normal distribution always has the same shape. The Z scores of –1.96 and +1.96 always mark the boundary lines of the 95 percent confidence interval. The shape of the Student's t-distribution, by contrast, depends on the sample size. The boundaries of the 95 percent confidence interval are not fixed. Rather, they vary, depending on how large a sample is being used for making inferences. There is an undeniable logic here. When the population standard deviation is not known and the sample size is small, the t-distribution sets wider boundaries on random sampling error and permits less confidence in the accuracy of a sample statistic. When the sample size is large, the t-distribution adjusts these boundaries accordingly, narrowing the limits of random sampling error and allowing more confidence in the measurements made from the sample. Although the terminology used to describe the t-distribution is different from that used to describe the normal distribution, the procedures for drawing inferences about a population parameter are essentially the same.

Again we use the imaginary campus organization's sample mean to illustrate the similarities—and the differences—between the inferential properties of the Student's t-distribution and the normal curve. Let's keep most elements of the example the same as before. The pollsters' sample size is n = 100, and their sample mean GPA, the value of $\bar{x}$, is 2.80. This time, however, we will make the example reflect a practical reality: The student group does not know the population standard deviation. They must rely, instead, on the standard deviation of their sample, which their computer calculates to be .50. So s = .50. In just the manner described above, the standard error of the sample mean now becomes:

$$s/\sqrt{n} = .50/\sqrt{100}$$
$$= .50/10$$
$$= .05$$

This is the same methodology used before. The campus group just substitutes the sample standard deviation for the population standard deviation, does the math, and arrives at the standard error of the sample mean, .05. And, just as with normal estimation, the pollsters know that their sample mean is equal to the population mean, within acceptable boundaries of random sampling error. What are those boundaries? What is the 95 percent confidence interval for the sample mean? The answer is contained in a Student's t-distribution table, such as the one shown in Table 5-3.

Before following through on the example, let's become familiar with Table 5-3. Because the specific shape of the Student's t-distribution depends on the sample size, Table 5-3 looks different from Table 5-2, which showed the area under the normal curve for different values of Z. In normal estimation, we do not have to worry about the size of the sample, so we

e 5-3 The Student's t-Distribution

Degrees of freedom	80% .10	Area under the curve .05 90%	.025 95%	.01 96%
1	3.078	6.314	12.706	31.821
2	1.886	2.920	4.303	6.965
3	1.638	2.353	3.182	4.541
4	1.533	2.132	2.776	3.747
5	1.476	2.015	2.571	3.365
6	1.440	1.943	2.447	3.143
7	1.415	1.895	2.365	2.998
8	1.397	1.860	2.306	2.896
9	1.383	1.833	2.262	2.821
10	1.372	1.812	2.228	2.764
11	1.363	1.796	2.201	2.718
12	1.356	1.782	2.179	2.681
13	1.350	1.771	2.160	2.650
14	1.345	1.761	2.145	2.624
15	1.341	1.753	2.131	2.602
16	1.337	1.746	2.120	2.583
17	1.333	1.740	2.110	2.567
18	1.330	1.734	2.101	2.552
19	1.328	1.729	2.093	2.539
20	1.325	1.725	2.086	2.528
21	1.323	1.721	2.080	2.518
22	1.321	1.717	2.074	2.508
23	1.319	1.714	2.069	2.500
24	1.318	1.711	2.064	2.492
25	1.316	1.708	2.060	2.485
26	1.315	1.706	2.056	2.479
27	1.314	1.703	2.052	2.473
28	1.313	1.701	2.048	2.467
29	1.311	1.699	2.045	2.462
30	1.310	1.697	2.042	2.457
40	1.303	1.684	2.021	2.423
60	1.296	1.671	2.000	2.390
90	1.291	1.662	**1.987**	2.368
100	1.290	1.660	1.984	2.364
120	1.289	1.658	1.980	2.358
1,000	1.282	1.646	1.962	2.330
Normal (Z)	1.282	1.645	1.960	2.326

calculate a value of Z and then find the area of the curve above that value. In estimation using Student's t, however, the sample size determines the shape of the distribution.

First consider the left-hand column of Table 5-3, labeled "Degrees of freedom." What are degrees of freedom? **Degrees of freedom** refers to a statistical property of a large family of distributions, including the Student's-t distribution. The number of degrees of freedom is tied to the sample size. In the sort of estimation we are performing here, the number of degrees of freedom is equal to the sample size minus 1, or $n - 1$.

Now examine the columns of Table 5-3, under the heading "Area under the curve." The columns are labeled with different proportions: .10, .05, .025, and .01. The entries in each column are values of t. Each cell tells you the value of t above which that proportion of the curve lies. For example, the top-most cell in the .025 column says that, with one degree of freedom, .025, or 2.5 percent, of the distribution falls above a t-value of 12.706. That sets a very wide boundary for random sampling error. Imagine starting at the mean of the normal curve and having to progress over 12 units of Z above the mean before hitting the .025 boundary! The signature of the Student's t-distribution is that it adjusts the confidence interval, depending on the size of the sample. Indeed, notice what happens to the t-values in the .025 column as the sample size (and thus degrees of freedom) increases. As sample size increases, the value of t that marks the .025 boundary begins to decrease. More degrees of freedom mean less random sampling error and, thus, more confidence in the sample statistic. For illustrative purposes, the value of Z that is associated with the .025 benchmark, $Z = 1.96$, appears in the bottom cell of the .025 column of Table 5-3. Notice that the value of t for a large sample (degrees of freedom = 1,000) is $t = 1.962$. So, for large samples with many degrees of freedom, the Student's t-distribution closely approximates the normal distribution.

We can now return to the example and use Table 5-3 to find the 95 percent confidence interval of the student pollsters' sample mean. We first determine the number of degrees of freedom, which is tied to the sample size (degrees of freedom = $n - 1$.) Since the student organization's sample has $n = 100$, it has degrees of freedom equal to 99. There is no row in Table 5-3 that corresponds exactly to 99 degrees of freedom, so we will use the closest lower number, 90 degrees of freedom. Now read across to the column labeled ".025." This number, 1.987, tells us that .025, or 2.5 percent, of the curve falls above $t = 1.987$. The Student's t-distribution, like the normal distribution, is perfectly symmetrical. Thus, 2.5 percent of the curve must lie below $t = -1.987$. These t-values give us the information we need to define the 95 percent confidence interval of the sample mean:

$$
\begin{aligned}
\text{Lower confidence boundary} \;&=\; \text{sample mean} - 1.987 \text{ standard errors} \\
&=\; 2.80 - 1.987\,(.05) \\
&=\; 2.70 \\
\text{Upper confidence boundary} \;&=\; \text{sample mean} + 1.987 \text{ standard errors} \\
&=\; 2.80 + 1.987\,(.05) \\
&=\; 2.90.
\end{aligned}
$$

Thus the pollsters can be 95-percent confident that the true population mean lies between 2.70 on the low end and 2.90 on the high end. There is a 5-percent chance that the population mean falls outside these boundaries—lower than 2.70 or higher than 2.90.

There are two bits of comforting news about the Student's t-distribution. One of these features has already been pointed out: As sample size grows, the t-distribution increasingly resembles the normal curve. Again note the numbers along the bottom row of Table 5-3, which report the values of Z for each probability. You can see that, for samples with 100 degrees of freedom, the t-distribution looks just about "normalized." And for samples with 1,000 or more degrees of freedom, the two distributions become virtually identical. A second, related point has to do with the rule of thumb that you learned for normal estimation. Recall that the 95 percent confidence interval can be quickly determined by multiplying the standard error by 2, then subtracting this number from the sample mean to find the lower confidence boundary, and adding this number to the sample mean to find the upper confidence boundary. This is a good rule of thumb, because it works well in most situations. As you can see from Table 5-3, even for fairly small samples—those having 60 degrees of freedom—the rule of thumb will provide an adequate estimate of the 95 percent confidence interval.

WHAT ABOUT SAMPLE PROPORTIONS?

One attractive feature of inferential statistics is its methodological versatility. If certain preconditions are met, the rules of inference apply. We have reviewed the logic of random sampling, and we have seen that the rule of thumb for estimating the standard error of a sample mean generally applies, even when the population standard deviation is not known—provided, of course, that the sample is fair-sized. However, many of the variables of interest to political researchers are not measured at the interval level. Rather, they are measured at the nominal or ordinal level of measurement. Thus we may take a sample and compute the percentage of respondents who "favor" increased military spending or the percentage who "oppose" gun control. In this case, we are not using an interval-level sample mean ($\bar{x}$) to estimate a population mean (μ). Instead we would be working with a **sample proportion**, the number of cases falling into one category of the variable divided by the number of cases in the sample. But again the rules of inference are robust. Within reasonable limits, the same procedures apply. You already know these procedures, so only a brief exposition is required.

Let's say that the campus organization asked the students in its sample (n = 100) whether or not they own a personal computer. Suppose that 72 students answered, "Yes, own a computer," and the remaining 28 students answered, "No, do not own a computer." What is the sample proportion of computer owners?

$$\text{Sample proportion of computer owners} = \text{(Number answering "Yes")} / \text{Sample size}$$
$$= 72 / 100$$
$$= .72$$

Similarly, the sample proportion of nonowners is

$$\text{Sample proportion of nonowners} = \text{(Number answering "No")} / \text{Sample size}$$
$$= 28 / 100$$
$$= .28.$$

So the sample proportion of computer owners is .72, and the proportion of nonowners is .28. How closely does the sample proportion, .72, estimate the proportion of computer owners in the student population? What is the standard error of the observed sample statistic, .72?

The mean of a sample, as you know, is denoted by the symbol $\bar{x}$. The proportion of a sample falling into one category of a nominal or ordinal variable is denoted by the ordinary letter p. In this case, the proportion of students falling into the "Yes, own a computer" category is .72, so p = .72. The proportion of a sample falling into all other categories of a nominal or ordinal variable is denoted by the letter q. This proportion, q, is equal to one minus p, or q = 1 − p. In this example, then, q would be equal to 1 − .72, or .28, the proportion of students who responded "No, do not own a computer." Let's assemble the numbers we have so far:

Sample proportion of computer owners (p)   =   .72
Sample proportion of nonowners (q)   =   .28
Sample size (n)   =   100.

This information—the value of p, the value of q, and the sample size—permits us to estimate the standard error of the sample proportion, p. First recall that the general formula for random sampling error is the variation component divided by the sample size component:

Random sampling error = (Variation component) / (Sample size component).

In figuring out the random sampling error associated with a sample proportion, the sample size error component is the same as before, the square root of n. For sample proportions, however, the variation component of random sampling error is different. For a sample proportion, p, the variation component is equal to the square root of the product p times q. That is:

Variation component or random sampling error = Square root (pq), or $\sqrt{pq}$.

Therefore, the standard error of a sample proportion, p, is equal to:

(Variation component) / (Sample size component)
= $\sqrt{pq}$ / $\sqrt{n}$.

Now let's plug in the numbers from the example and see what we have:

pq   =   (.72) (.28) = .20
$\sqrt{pq}$ = $\sqrt{.20}$ = .45
$\sqrt{n}$ = $\sqrt{100}$ = 10
$\sqrt{pq}$ / $\sqrt{n}$ = .45/10 = .045.

Thus the proportion of computer owners in the student population is equal to the sample proportion, .72, with a standard error of .045. So the student pollsters know that the true population proportion is equal to .72, give or take .045 or so. Indeed, just as with normal estimation, there is a 68-percent chance that the population parameter falls within one standard error of the sample proportion, between .72 minus .045 (which is equal to .675) and .72 plus .045 (which is equal to .765). And the 95 percent confidence interval would be defined by:

Lower confidence boundary   =   sample proportion − 1.96 standard errors
  =   .72 − 1.96 (.045)
  ≈   .63
Upper confidence boundary   =   sample proportion + 1.96 standard errors
  =   .72 + 1.96 (.045)
  ≈   .81.

Voilà! The student pollsters can be 95 percent confident that the true percentage of computer owners in the student population is between 63 percent and 81 percent.

A final statistical caveat. We have just demonstrated how normal estimation can be applied in determining the standard error of a sample proportion. Under most circumstances, this method works quite well. However, we know that normal estimation works best for sample proportions closer to .50, and it begins to lose its applicability as p approaches .00 or 1.00. How can one know if normal estimation may be used? Here is a general procedure. Multiply p by the sample size, and multiply q by the sample size. If both numbers are 10 or higher, then normal estimation will work fine. (Actually, if both numbers are 5 or more, normal estimation will still work okay.) The student pollsters are on solid inferential ground, since $(100)(.72) = 72$ and $(100)(.28) = 28$. Trouble could begin to brew, however, if the pollsters were to subset their sample into smaller groups—subdividing, say, on the basis of gender or class rank—and were then to make inferences from these smaller subsamples.

As consumers of popular media, we are much more likely to encounter percentages or proportions than arithmetic means. Sometimes, of course, the sampling procedures used by media-based organizations are questionable, and their reported results should be consumed with a large grain of salt. Reputable pollsters always report some measure of random sampling error (normally following the form "margin of error ± . . ."), which typically defines the boundaries of the 95 percent confidence interval. You are now well equipped to interpret such percentages on your own. You are also armed with all the inferential statistics you will (probably) ever need in order to make sense of more advanced topics in political analysis.

SUMMARY

Just how accurately does a sample statistic estimate a population parameter? You now know that the answer is a resounding "It depends on three factors." It depends, first, on whether the sample was randomly selected from the population. By ensuring that each member of the population has an equal chance of being included in the sample, the researcher eliminates "bad" error, systematic error, from the sample statistic. A random sample permits the researcher to estimate the amount of "good" error, random error, contained in the sample statistic. It depends, second, on the size of the random sample. Larger samples yield better estimates than smaller samples. But you now understand why samples that seem small can nonetheless provide a solid basis for inference. It depends, third, on the amount of variation in the population. You are now familiar with a key measure of variation for interval-level variables, the standard deviation. And you know how the standard deviation works together with sample size in bracketing the confidence interval for a sample mean.

Many symbols and terms were discussed in this chapter. Table 5-4 provides a list, arranged in roughly the order in which these terms and symbols were introduced. Let's review them. The population mean (μ) is the parameter of chief concern—the measure of central tendency that the researcher is most interested in estimating. Variation around the population mean is determined by the standard deviation (σ), the measure of dispersion that summarizes how much clustering or spread exists in the population. The relative position of any member of a population is expressed as a Z score, the number of standard deviations a case falls above or below the mean. So, by knowing Z and applying the inferential properties of the normal distribution, the researcher can estimate the probability associated with drawing a single case at random from a normally distributed population.

The enterprise of inference, of course, usually centers on the accuracy of the sample mean, symbolized by $\bar{x}$. However, the same inferential logic that applies to drawing a single case from a population also applies to $\bar{x}$. The researcher knows that the sample mean will be equal to the population mean, plus any random sampling error that was introduced in drawing the sample. The size of this error, termed the standard error of the sample mean, is determined by σ and the sample size (n). Again applying the normal distribution, the researcher

Table 5-4 Terms and Symbols and the Roles They Play in Inference

Term or symbol (pronunciation)	What it is or what it does	What role it plays in sampling and inference
μ ("mew")	Population mean	Usually μ is unknown and is estimated by $\bar{x}$.
N	Population size	
σ ("sigma")	Population standard deviation	Measures variation in a population characteristic. The variation component of random sampling error.
Z score	Converts raw deviations from μ into units of σ	Defines the hash marks of the normal distribution; 68 percent of the distribution lies between $Z = -1$ and $Z = +1$, and 95 percent of the distribution lies between $Z = -1.96$ and $Z = +1.96$.
$\bar{x}$ ("x bar")	Sample mean	Sample statistic that estimates μ.
n	Sample size	The sample size component of random sampling error is $\sqrt{n}$.
s	Sample standard deviation	Substitutes for σ as the variation component of random sampling error when σ is unknown.
Standard error of the sample mean	Measures how much $\bar{x}$ departs, by chance, from μ	Random sampling error. Equal to $\sigma/\sqrt{n}$, if σ is known. Equal to $s/\sqrt{n}$, if σ is unknown.
95 percent confidence interval	The interval in which 95 percent of all possible values of $\bar{x}$ will fall by chance	Defined by $\bar{x} \pm 1.96$ standard errors in normal estimation. Can usually be determined by rule of thumb: $\bar{x} \pm 2$ standard errors in all estimation.
p	Proportion of a sample falling into one value of a nominal or ordinal variable	Sample estimate of a population proportion.
q	Proportion of a sample falling into all other values of a nominal or ordinal variable	Equal to $1 - p$.
Standard error of a sample proportion	Measures how much p departs, by chance, from a population proportion	Defined by $\sqrt{pq}/\sqrt{n}$. Ordinarily can be applied in finding the 95 percent confidence interval of p, using normal estimation.

can estimate the 95 percent confidence interval for $\bar{x}$, the boundaries within which 95 percent of all possible sample means will fall by chance. Z scores are directly applied here. By multiplying the standard error by Z = 1.96—or rounding up to 2 by rule of thumb—the researcher can figure the probable boundaries of the true population mean. In practice, the population standard deviation is rarely known, so the researcher uses the sample standard deviation, denoted by s, as a stand-in for σ, and then applies the Student's t-distribution. As you know, much political research, especially survey research, involves nominal and ordinal variables. Thus in this chapter we also discussed how normal estimation may be usefully applied in estimating the 95 confidence interval for a sample proportion.

KEY TERMS

census (p. 103)
central limit theorem (p. 116)
degrees of freedom (p. 122)
95 percent confidence interval (p. 117)
normal distribution (p. 112)
population (p. 102)
population parameter (p. 103)
probability (p. 114)
random sample (p. 103)
random sampling error (p. 105)
random selection (p. 104)

response bias (p. 104)
sample (p. 103)
sample proportion (p. 124)
sample statistic (p. 103)
sampling frame (p. 104)
selection bias (p. 104)
standard deviation (p. 110)
standard error (p. 116)
Student's t-distribution (p. 121)
variance (p. 112)
Z score (p. 113)

EXERCISES

1. A polling firm wants to know which candidate is likely to win the presidential election. The major party candidates are Republican Dewey Cheatum and Democrat Andy Howe. The pollsters set up an Internet site and ask site visitors to indicate their preferred choice. The results: After months of polling and a sample of hundreds of thousands of individuals, Republican Cheatum held a huge edge. The only problem: On election day, Howe won handily.

   A. There was obviously a big difference between the preference of the population about which the polling firm wanted to draw inferences and the preference of the sample they obtained. What was the population the firm was interested in? What was the firm's sampling frame? Describe two reasons why the sampling technique was a poor one.

   B. Internet polls like the one described here almost always find a preference for the Republican candidate over the Democratic candidate. Why do you suppose this is?

2. The leadership of a large interest group is trying to decide whether to raise its membership dues. The average income of the group's members is an important consideration. Though the group lacks current information on member incomes, they do have data from a previous census of the membership. According to this census, mean income is $45,000 with a standard deviation of $15,000.

   A. Assuming a normal distribution of incomes, what percentage of the members make between $30,000 and $60,000? What percentage make more than $75,000?

   B. A statistician hired by the group picks three members at random from the census data. The first has a Z score of +1.5. The second has a Z score of −.6. The third has a Z score of 0. What are the incomes of each of these three members?

C. The group decides that the census is too old, so they discard it. Since they lack the resources to conduct a new census, they ask the statistician to take a sample. Assuming that the statistician has access to the membership rolls, describe how the statistician would go about obtaining a random sample of n = 400.

3. The sheriff is concerned about speeders on a certain stretch of county road. The sheriff sets up a radar device and, over a long period of time, obtains data on all vehicles using the road. The parameters of this population: mean vehicle speed, 52 miles per hour; standard deviation, 4 miles per hour. (Assume that speeds are normally distributed.)
   A. If the speed limit is 45 miles per hour, what percentage of vehicles exceed the speed limit? (Hint: Find the Z score associated with 45 mph, then use Table 5-2 to determine the percentage of the normal curve that lies above this value of Z.)
   B. The sheriff decides to crack down on speeders. He instructs his deputies to ignore any vehicles traveling less than 48 mph, to issue warnings to vehicles traveling between 48 and 51 mph, and to issue tickets to vehicles traveling more than 51 mph. What percentage of vehicles will be issued warnings? What percentage will get tickets?
   C. Following the crackdown, the sheriff takes a random sample (n = 144) of vehicle speeds on the roadway. The sample data: sample mean, 47 mph, sample standard deviation, 6 mph. Using the sample standard deviation as a substitute for the population standard deviation, calculate the standard error of the sample mean. Using the ± 2 rule of thumb, calculate the 95 percent confidence interval of the sample mean.
   D. A skeptical county commissioner claims that the crackdown had no effect and that average speed on the roadway is still 52 mph. Is the skeptic on solid statistical ground? Explain how you know.

4. Sociologists have conducted much interesting research on gender stereotypes in American society. A curious aspect of stereotypes is that people tend to perceive differences between groups to be greater than they actually are. This suggests, for example, that when asked about the heights of men and women, survey respondents would tend to perceive men to be taller than women. Suppose you wanted to test this idea, the notion that individuals perceive a greater height difference between men and women than exists in the population. Let's say that, in the population, men, on average, are 4 inches taller than women. So the true population difference between men and women is 4 inches.

   You obtain a random sample of 400 individuals. For each respondent you record his or her perceptions of the difference between male and female heights. In your sample, you find that the mean difference in perceived heights is 5 inches. So respondents perceive that men are 5 inches taller than women. The sample standard deviation is 4 inches. Figure out the standard error of the sample mean. Using the ± 2 rule of thumb, calculate the 95 percent confidence interval. If the true gender difference is 4 inches, can you infer from your sample that individuals perceive a greater difference than actually exists? Explain.

5. The following proportions are from the 1998 General Social Survey. How closely does each sample proportion estimate the true population proportion? For each proportion, use the ± 2 rule of thumb to determine the 95% confidence interval.
   A. When asked if they believe in life after death, .59 said they "definitely believe" (n = 1,127).
   B. How much confidence do people have in the U.S. Congress? According to the survey (n = 1,208), .34 have "little or none."
   C. In the sample (n = 1,860), .45 say their life is "exciting."

6

Tests of Significance and Measures of Association

LEARNING OBJECTIVES

In this chapter you will learn:
- How the empirical relationship between two variables is affected by random sampling error
- How to use an informal test in making inferences about relationships
- How to use formal statistical tests in making inferences about relationships
- How measures of association gauge the strength of an empirical relationship
- Which measure of association to use in performing and interpreting political analysis

The first four chapters of this book—which covered thinking about concepts, writing hypotheses, comparing percentages and means, making controlled comparisons—had much to do with systematic thinking but dealt very little with statistics. In Chapter 5, however, we got a glimpse of the role of statistics in political analysis. When using information from a random sample to estimate an attribute of a population, the political researcher must know the boundaries of random sampling error, the likelihood that the observed statistic departs from the population parameter. As a practical matter, of course, researchers are much more interested in making inferences and testing hypotheses about an observed relationship between two variables than in making inferences about a single mean or a proportion that has been computed from sample data. In most situations, we are in the business of comparing two sample statistics—the percentage of women favoring a gun ban compared with the percentage of men, for example, or the mean number of years of schooling of whites compared with the mean for blacks—and then asking inferential questions about the observed difference. Is the difference large or small? Could the difference we observe in the sample have occurred because of random sampling error, or is the difference too large to have occurred by chance? In this chapter we look at how to answer such questions—how to make inferences about empirical relationships and how to assess their strength.

Suppose, for example, that we wish to test this hypothesis: In comparing individuals, women will give Hillary Clinton higher feeling thermometer ratings than will men. Working with a random sample, we set up the analysis by dividing subjects on gender, the independent variable, and then comparing values of the dependent variable, mean thermometer ratings of Ms. Clinton. Suppose we find this: The mean thermometer rating among women is 55 degrees, while the mean for men is 46 degrees. So we observe a mean difference of 9 degrees between female respondents and male respondents. In any event, that is the difference we observe in our random sample. But just how closely does this difference between women and men in the sample reflect the true difference between women and men in the population from which the sample was drawn? Think about this question for a moment. Do you notice an analogy to the problems of sampling and inference discussed in Chapter 5?

Indeed, in addressing inferential questions about the relationship between an independent variable and a dependent variable, the logic you learned in Chapter 5 can be applied directly. You already know about the standard error of a single sample mean—the extent to which the sample mean departs, by chance, from the population mean. In this chapter you will learn that, just as a single mean contains random sampling error, the difference between two sample means contains random error as well. Just as the researcher uses the standard error to estimate the likely boundaries of an unseen population mean, so too the researcher uses the standard error of the difference between two sample statistics to estimate an unseen difference in the population. And, just as the researcher can use the normal curve or the Student's t-distribution to test a hypothetical claim about a population mean, so too the researcher can use those techniques to test a hypothetical claim about a relationship between two variables in the population. In all of these ways, this chapter builds on the skills that you already have.

There are two ways, however, in which this chapter focuses and expands your skills. First, we concentrate more directly on how inferential statistics can help you decide whether an observed relationship between an independent variable and a dependent variable really exists in the population or whether it could have happened by chance. Thus, in the first part of this chapter, we enter the realm of the **test of statistical significance**. Then we discuss how to gauge the strength of the relationship between an independent variable and a dependent variable. In the latter part of the chapter, then, we consider some of the more widely used measures of association. A **measure of association** tells the researcher how well the independent variable works in explaining the dependent variable.

STATISTICAL SIGNIFICANCE

By way of illustrating the role of inferential statistics in evaluating relationships, let's follow through on the gender–Hillary Clinton hypothesis: In comparing individuals, women will give Hillary Clinton higher feeling thermometer ratings than will men. The first two columns of Table 6-1, based on data from the 2000 National Election Study, address this hypothesis. The female mean, 55.7, appears along the top row, and the male mean, 46.4, appears below it. The value 9.3, the male mean subtracted from the female mean, appears in the row labeled "Mean difference." So, on average, women are 9.3 degrees warmer toward Ms. Clinton than are men. Thus it would appear that the hypothesis has merit, that the independent and dependent variables are related in the hypothesized way.

But adopt a skeptic's stance. Suppose that, in the population from which the sample was drawn, there is really no relationship between gender and ratings of Hillary Clinton. Assume that the mean difference we found in the sample is nonexistent, is equal to 0, in the population.

Table 6-1   Mean Hillary Clinton Thermometer Ratings, by Gender

Gender	Sample Mean	Standard Error of Sample Mean	Squared Standard Error (Mean Variance)
Female	55.7	.96	.92
	(994)		
Male	46.4	1.10	1.21
	(784)		
Total	51.2		
	(1,778)		
Mean difference	9.3		
Variance of the mean difference			2.13
Standard error of the mean difference			1.46

Source: Nancy Burns, Donald R. Kinder, Steven J. Rosenstone, Virginia Sapiro, and the National Election Studies, *American National Election Study, 2000: Pre- and Post-election Survey,* 2nd version (Ann Arbor: University of Michigan, Center for Political Studies [producer], 2001; Inter-university Consortium for Political and Social Research [distributor], 2002).

Notes: Numbers of cases are in parentheses. The standard deviation of the female sample is 30.2. The standard deviation of the male sample is 30.7.

This skeptical assumption, called the **null hypothesis**, plays a vital role in hypothesis testing. As its name implies, the null hypothesis states that, in the population, there is no relationship between the independent and dependent variables. Any relationship observed in a sample, furthermore, was produced by random sampling error.

The null hypothesis, which is labeled H_0 (pronounced "H-Oh"), could just as easily be called the "fluke effect hypothesis," since it reminds us that observed sample results could have been produced by random sampling error. The hypothesis that we have formulated, the hypothesis suggesting that there *is* a relationship between gender and thermometer ratings, is considered the "alternative hypothesis," and is labeled H_A ("H-A"). Therefore, if we are to have confidence in the alternative hypothesis, then it must be shown that H_0 represents a sufficiently remote event. Figure 6-1 displays this inferential tension.

The large circles in Figure 6-1 reflect what is really going on in the unseen population. The null hypothesis could, in fact, be true or it could, in fact, be false. The arrows coming out of each of the population circles depict two possible inferential decisions, made on the basis of results observed in a sample. Based on the sample, the researcher might decide to reject the null hypothesis, or the researcher might decide not to reject the null hypothesis. Obviously, every researcher wishes to make the correct inference about the data, rejecting the null hypothesis when it is false and not rejecting it when it is true. But there are two ways to get it wrong. **Type I error** occurs when the researcher takes too big of a chance on the sample results, concluding that there is a relationship in the population when, in fact, there is none. **Type II error** occurs when the researcher plays it safe, inferring that there is no relationship in the population when, in fact, there is. In testing a hypothesis, it is important to be cautious, to allow random chance every plausible opportunity to account for the observed results. So Type II error is considered acceptable error, because it gives the null hypothesis the benefit of the doubt. Type I error, however, is not acceptable error, so we need to adopt a decision rule that minimizes the probability that it will occur.

Figure 6-1 Type I and Type II Errors

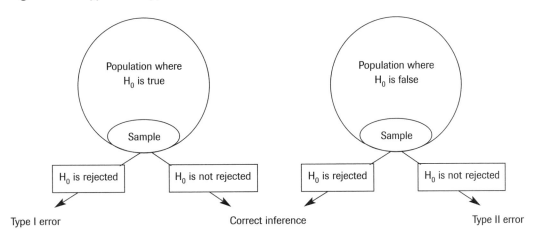

Accordingly, we always begin by assuming that the null hypothesis is true, and we proceed by setting a fairly high threshold for rejecting it. The minimum standard is the **.05 level of significance**. If we decide to reject H_0, we want to commit Type I error fewer than 5 times out of 100. The .05 threshold frames the inferential fate of H_0 and H_A: If H_0 is true, how often, by chance, will we obtain the relationship observed in the sample? If the answer is "more than 5 times out of 100," we do not reject the null hypothesis. If the answer is "5 times out of 100 or less," we reject the null hypothesis. For the relationship between gender and Hillary Clinton thermometer ratings, the null hypothesis says that the mean difference in the population is equal to 0. If the observed difference, 9.3 degrees, could have occurred more than 5 times out of 100, by chance, then the probability of Type I error is too high, and we cannot reject H_0. If, by contrast, the observed mean difference is likely to have occurred fewer than 5 times out of 100, then we are on safer ground and can reject the null hypothesis. How do we test for the .05 threshold? The answer depends on a familiar factor, the amount of random sampling error.

Comparing Two Sample Means

Even though we are now dealing with two sample means, one based on female respondents and one based on male respondents, the idea behind sampling error is the same as before. In Chapter 5 we saw that a single sample mean ($\bar{x}$) is equal to the population mean, give or take some random sampling error. The size of this error depends on two components, the size of the sample (n) and the magnitude of the population standard deviation (σ). When the population standard deviation is unknown—and it almost never is known—the standard deviation of the sample, s, substitutes for σ. The standard error of the mean is equal to the standard deviation divided by the square root of n, or $s/\sqrt{n}$. The same logic applies, as well, to the difference between two sample means. The difference between two sample means is equal to the real but unobserved difference in the population, give or take some random sampling error. How large is this error?

Turn your attention back to Table 6-1. The sample means appear in the second column, 55.7 for women and 46.4 for men. The standard errors for these means, which appear in the third column, were derived in the now-familiar way—by dividing the standard deviation of each sample by the square root of each sample's size. Thus the female mean has a standard error of .96, and the male mean has a standard error of 1.10. So far we are on familiar terrain. Now consider the numbers in the last column, labeled "Squared standard error (mean variance)." These values were calculated by squaring each standard error: Squaring .96 (the standard error of the female mean) yields .92, and squaring 1.10 (the standard error of the male mean) yields 1.21. These values, more commonly called mean variances, are the main building blocks for finding the **standard error of the difference** between two means. By adding these two numbers together, the mean variance of the female mean plus the mean variance of the male mean, we obtain a statistic called variance of the mean difference. Thus summing .92 and 1.21 gives us 2.13, the variance of the mean difference. The standard error of the difference between two sample means is derived from this statistic. In fact, it is the square root of the mean variance. The square root of 2.13 is 1.46, so the standard error of the difference between the female mean and the male mean is 1.46.

Now let's take a step back from these calculations and assemble our inferential resources. We obtained a mean difference on the dependent variable of 9.3 degrees. We know that the true difference in the population is equal to 9.3, give or take 1.46, the standard error of the difference. The null hypothesis claims that, in the population, women and men do not differ on the thermometer scale, that the true mean difference is 0. If the null hypothesis is correct, how likely is it that we would obtain a sample difference of 9.3? How do we find the .05 threshold? There are two correct ways to answer this question, one based on an informal practice and one based on a more formal statistical procedure.

The informal practice follows your first instinct—apply the rule of thumb for the 95 percent confidence interval. As you know, given a sample mean and standard error, 95 percent of all possible sample means will fall within ± 2 standard errors in either direction. The same rule holds for mean differences. So, if the sample difference is 9.3 and has a standard error of 1.46, we can be 95-percent confident that the true population difference lies in the interval between 9.3 minus 2(1.46) at the low end and 9.3 plus 2(1.46) at the high end. Thus the true population difference probably falls in the interval between 6.4 and 12.2. What about the null hypothesis? Since the difference asserted by H_0, a population difference equal to 0, lies in the region outside these boundaries, the probability of Type I error is acceptably low, and the null hypothesis can be safely rejected.

In practice, many researchers, upon obtaining a sample statistic and standard error, apply a rough-and-ready "eyeball test" of statistical significance. According to this informal test, if the sample statistic is at least twice as large as its standard error, then the result surpasses the .05 threshold and H_0 can be rejected. So, for example, the sample difference of 9.3 passes the eyeball test, given that 9.3 is (a lot) more than twice 1.46. This is the correct logic, and it would not steer you in the wrong direction. However, this informal rule has a wrinkle.

When we perform the informal eyeball test using the ± 2 rule of thumb, we are finding the upper *and* lower limits of random sampling error. There is a .025 probability that the true population difference falls below the lower limit of 6.4, and there is a .025 chance that it falls above the upper limit of 12.2. The informal test applies what is termed a **two-tailed test of significance**. In finding the upper and lower limits of random sampling error, it divides the .05 "rejection region" in half, reporting the value above which .025 of the curve falls and the value below which .025 of the curve falls. Note, however, that the upper boundary is not relevant to the alternative hypothesis, the hypothesis being tested against the null hypothesis. We do not want to know whether the population difference could be greater than 12.2. We want to know only if it is greater than 0, as claimed by the null hypothesis. Accordingly, instead of finding upper and lower limits and dividing the .05 rejection region in half, we need find only a lower limit, the lowest plausible difference between the female mean and the male mean in the population. If this limit is greater than 0, we reject H_0 and gain confidence in the idea that, in the population, the independent and dependent variables are related.

In most of the research situations you will encounter, the .05 threshold will be the standard and a **one-tailed test of significance** will be the order of the day. In performing a one-tailed test of statistical significance, we do not divide .05 in two and find upper and lower confidence boundaries. Rather, we place the entire rejection region in null hypothesis territory, the region of the curve containing a population difference equal to 0. With a sample difference of 9.3 and a standard error of 1.46, we would ask: "What is the probability that the population difference could be as low as 0? Is this probability less than .05?" In normal estimation, which can reasonably be used with fair-sized samples, the absolute value of Z that marks the boundary between .95 of the curve and .05 in one tail is 1.645. Therefore, the lowest plausible difference is defined by the sample statistic minus 1.645 standard errors. If this value is greater than 0, then we can reject the null hypothesis. In our example, this lower limit would be 9.3 minus 1.645(1.46), which is equal to 9.3 minus 2.4, or 6.9. Because this value is greater than 0, we can reject H_0.

It is worth pointing out that the $\pm$ 2 eyeball test provides a more stringent .025 one-tailed significance test. Why? Because by dividing the .05 threshold in half, the rule of thumb extends the lower limit closer to H_0's territory. In the example, the $\pm$ 2 rule gave us a lower boundary of 6.4, which is closer to 0 than the lower boundary provided by the 1.645 rule, 6.9. Either way, H_0 is rejected.

Sometimes when you calculate the difference between two sample statistics, you will obtain a positive number, as we did in the current example. Other times, the calculated difference will be a negative number. Students are sometimes confused about how to apply the one-tail, 1.645 rule when the difference between two sample statistics is negative. Remember that the normal curve is perfectly symmetrical. At Z = −1.645, .05 of the curve lies below Z and .95 of the curve lies above Z. At Z = +1.645, the symmetry is reversed, with .95 lying below Z and .05 lying above Z. Therefore, for the sole purpose of determining statistical significance, you can safely ignore the sign of the sample difference and deal, instead, with its absolute value. Multiply the standard error by 1.645, and then subtract this number from the absolute value of the sample difference. If the result is greater than 0, then reject H_0. If the result is not greater than 0, do not reject H_0.

So far we have been discussing confidence-interval approaches to inference. For the informal rule of thumb test, see if the sample difference is at least twice its standard error. For the more formal 1.645 test, see if the sample difference lies at least 1.645 standard errors from zero. These approaches work fine and involve a bare minimum of calculation. But they are blunt. A more precise way of doing it is to find out how many standard errors lie between the sample statistic and the population parameter hypothesized by H_0, and then figure out the likelihood of obtaining this difference if H_0 is true. This is how all computer programs do it, so we need at least to understand the principle involved.

To determine the exact probability of obtaining a given sample difference if the true population difference is 0, we need to know three things: the difference associated with the alternative hypothesis, H_A, the difference claimed by the null hypothesis, H_0, and the standard error of the difference. This information permits us to calculate a **test statistic**. A test statistic tells us exactly how many standard errors separate the sample difference from zero, the difference claimed by H_0. The general formula for any test statistic is

$$\text{Test statistic} = (H_A - H_0) / \text{Standard error of the difference.}$$

H_A is the observed sample difference, H_0 is the assumed difference in the population (which equals 0), and the standard error is the same as before. Now, the particular test statistic that the researcher uses will depend on the type of estimation being performed. If we use normal estimation, then the test statistic is expressed in units of Z:

$$Z = (H_A - H_0) / \text{Standard error of the difference.}$$

If we use the Student's t-distribution, then the test statistic is expressed in units of t:

$$t = (H_A - H_0) / \text{Standard error of the difference.}$$

Which test statistic is appropriate? Strictly speaking, the Student's t-distribution should be applied in the Hillary Clinton example. After all, in determining the standard errors of the female mean and the male mean, we used their sample standard deviations, not their population standard deviations, which are unknown. But let's use the example to demonstrate both sorts of estimation, beginning with Z. Under normal estimation,

$$
\begin{aligned}
Z &= (H_A - H_0) / \text{Standard error of the difference} \\
&= (9.3 - 0) / 1.46 \\
&= 6.37.
\end{aligned}
$$

So the observed difference, 9.3, and the difference asserted by the null hypothesis, 0, are 6.37 standard errors apart. Yet again, things look bad for the null hypothesis. But how bad? If the population difference really is 0, how often, by chance, will we observe a sample difference of 9.3? Most computer programs answer this question by reporting a **P-value**. A P-value, or probability value, is the precise magnitude of the region of the curve above the absolute value of Z. If the P-value is greater than .05, we cannot reject H_0. If it is less than or equal to .05, we can reject H_0. A popular spreadsheet, Microsoft Excel, using scientific notation, returned a P-value of "9.49447E-11" for Z = 6.37. The number "9.49447E-11" can be read, "Start with 9.49447 and move the decimal point 11 places to the left." Doing so produces an extremely low P-value: .0000000000949447. This number is not 0, but it certainly rounds to 0. From the eyeball test we already knew that the P-value was less than .025. The computer gives us much greater precision. We now can say that, if the null hypothesis were correct, we would (almost) never observe a sample difference of 9.3. The null hypothesis represents a highly remote random event. Reject H_0.[1]

For large samples, the normal distribution and the t-distribution are virtually identical. Even so, computer programs usually return the P-values that are associated with a Student's t-distribution test statistic. This test statistic, sometimes called a **t-ratio**, is calculated just like Z:

$$
\begin{aligned}
t &= (H_A - H_0) / \text{standard error of the difference} \\
&= (9.3 - 0) / 1.46 \\
&= 6.37.
\end{aligned}
$$

Table 6-2 Opinions on Gay Adoptions, by Gender

Favor gay adoptions?	Gender		Total
	Female	*Male*	
Yes	49.7%	39.4%	45.1%
	(458)	(289)	(747)
No	50.3%	60.6%	54.9%
	(464)	(445)	(909)
	100.0%	100.0%	100.0%
Total	(922)	(734)	(1656)

Source: 2000 National Election Study.

Note: Question: "Do you think gay or lesbian couples (in other words, homosexual couples) should be legally permitted to adopt children?"

Unlike the normal curve, however, the P-value for t = 6.37 will depend on degrees of freedom. As we saw in Chapter 5, the number of degrees of freedom for a single sample mean is equal to the sample size, n, minus 1. In comparing two sample means, the number of degrees of freedom is equal to the size of the first sample plus the size of the second sample, minus 2. According to Table 6-1, there are 994 individuals in the female sample and 784 individuals in the male sample. So the test statistic, 6.37, has 994 + 784 − 2, or 1,776 degrees of freedom. Microsoft Excel reveals that, under the assumption that the null hypothesis is correct, we would observe a mean difference of 9.3 exactly 1.20088E-10 of the time. Moving the decimal point 10 places to the left again raises serious doubt about H_0: .00000000012088. Reject H_0.

Comparing Two Sample Proportions

The same principles that apply to the comparison of two sample means also apply to the comparison of two sample proportions. This is not too surprising, given that sample proportions, in a statistical sense, *are* sample means.[2] To illustrate the similarities, we consider another gender gap hypothesis: In comparing individuals, women are more likely than men to favor laws that permit homosexual couples to adopt children. Table 6-2 shows a cross-tabulation analysis of the dependent variable, whether or not respondents favor gay adoptions, by the independent variable, gender. Are the data consistent with the hypothesis? It would seem so. Reading across the columns at the "Favor" value of the dependent variable, 49.7 percent of the females are in favor, compared with 39.4 percent of the males, a difference of 10.3 percentage points. Expressed in proportions, the difference would be .497 minus .394, or .103. The always redundant null hypothesis, of course, claims that this sample difference of .103 resulted from random sampling error, that the true difference in the population is .00. Thus the inferential question becomes: Assuming that the null hypothesis is correct, how often will we observe a sample difference of .103? Again the answer depends on the size of the standard error.

Chapter 5 introduced conventional labeling for sample proportions. The ordinary letter p represents the proportion of cases falling into one value of a variable, and the letter q represents the proportion of cases falling into all other values of a variable. (The proportion q, sometimes called the complement of p, is equal to 1 − p.) For the female sample shown in Table 6-2, for example, p is equal to .497 and q is equal to .503. In Chapter 5 we also learned that the standard error of a sample proportion, the extent to which it departs from the population proportion it is estimating, is equal to the square root of pq divided by the square root

Table 6-3 Proportions Favoring Gay Adoptions, by Gender

Gender	Sample proportion	Standard error of sample proportion	Variance of sample proportion
Female	.497 (922)	.016	.00027
Male	.394 (734)	.018	.00032
Difference in proportions	.103		
Variance of the difference			.00059
Standard error of the difference			.0243

Source: 2000 National Election Study.

Notes: Numbers of cases are in parentheses. The standard deviation of the female proportion is .50. The standard deviation of the male proportion is .49. Question: "Do you think gay and lesbian couples (in other words, homosexual couples) should be legally permitted to adopt children?"

of the sample size, or $\sqrt{pq} / \sqrt{n}$. The standard error of the female proportion, then, is obtained by multiplying .497 by .503, deriving the square root, and then dividing by the square root of the sample size.

Table 6-3 presents the relevant calculations for determining the standard error of the difference between the proportions of females and males who favor gay adoptions. Table 6-3 is directly analogous to Table 6-1, which presented the relevant calculations for determining the standard error of the difference between two sample means. The female proportion, .497, and the male proportion, .394, appear in the left-hand column, with the difference, .103, appearing at the bottom. The standard errors of each proportion, .016 for women and .018 for men, which are in the next column, were calculated using the formula, $\sqrt{pq} / \sqrt{n}$. Just as with sample means, the numbers in the right-most column, labeled "Variance of sample proportion," were obtained by squaring the standard errors. Squaring .016 yields .00027, and squaring .018 yields .00032. In the case of two sample means, we found that the variance of the difference between two means is equal to the sum of their mean variances. The same rule applies to sample proportions. The variance of the difference between two sample proportions is equal to the sum of their variances. So, adding .00027 and .00032 equals .00059, the variance of the difference. And, just as with two sample means, the standard error of the difference between two proportions is the square root of the variance. The square root of .00059 is .0243, the standard error of the difference.

Does the observed difference, .103, pass muster with the informal eyeball test? Yes, it does, given that .103 is at least twice its standard error, .024. How about the more formal 1.645 test? Well, .103 minus 1.645(.024) is equal to .103 minus 0.039, or .064. Since .064 is greater than 0, we know that the sample difference would occur fewer than 5 times out of 100 by chance. What is the precise probability, the P-value, associated with the difference in sample proportions? Using normal estimation,

$$Z = (H_A - H_0) / \text{standard error of the difference}$$
$$= (.103 - 0) / .024$$
$$= 4.29.$$

The computer returned a P-value of .000009 for Z = 4.29. If the null hypothesis is correct, then the probability of obtaining a sample difference of .103 would be roughly akin to the probability of winning the Florida lottery. Reject H_0.

In both of the above illustrations—the gender–Hillary Clinton example and the gender–gay adoptions example—the null hypothesis has been rejected. It is important to note, however, that in the real world of political research the null hypothesis frequently fares much better.

The Chi-square Test of Significance

You are now versed in the most common statistical tests—the comparison of two means and the comparison of two proportions. A different but complementary test looks at how the cases are dispersed across the values of the dependent variable. The **chi-square test of significance** determines whether the observed dispersal of cases departs significantly from what we would expect to find if the null hypothesis were correct. Developed by British statistician Karl Pearson in 1900, chi-square (pronounced "ki-square" and denoted by χ^2) is the oldest statistical test still in use.[3] It is simple and versatile, two traits that probably account for its longevity.

Chi-square is perhaps the most commonly used statistical test in cross-tabulation analysis. It is especially useful for this purpose because, in determining statistical significance, it takes all the tabular data into consideration. It does not evaluate a specific difference between two percentages or proportions. This makes it easier to analyze relationships between nominal or ordinal variables that may have several categories or values. To illustrate chi-square, we will test this hypothesis: In comparing individuals, people who attend religious services more frequently will be less likely to favor abortion rights than will people who attend religious services less frequently.

Table 6-4 sets up the cross-tabulation for testing the hypothesis. The values of the independent variable, level of attendance at religious services ("low," "moderate," or "high"), are on the columns, and the values of the dependent variable, opinions about abortion rights ("never allow," "depends," or "personal choice") are on the rows. However, in acquainting yourself with Table 6-4, ignore—for the moment—the main body of the table, the distributions of cases down the "low," "moderate," and "high" columns. Focus exclusively on the right-most "Total" column, the distribution for all 1,679 individuals in the sample. This is the column that the null hypothesis hones in on. In its chi-square guise, the null hypothesis states that the distribution of cases down each column of a table should be the same as the total distribution for all cases in the sample. According to this reasoning, for example, if 11.9 percent of all respondents fall into the "never allow" category, then 11.9 percent of the 802 "low" attendance individuals will be expected to hold this view, as will 11.9 percent of the 445 "moderate" types and 11.9 percent of the 432 people with "high" attendance. The null hypothesis applies the same relentless logic to every value of a dependent variable. Since, overall, 45.7 percent of the sample falls into the "depends" category of the dependent variable, then 45.7 percent of the cases in the "low" column can be expected to hold this abortion opinion, as will 45.7 percent of the people in the "moderate" column and 45.7 percent of the cases in the "high" column. And, since 42.4 percent said "personal choice," then 42.4 percent of each column can be expected to give this response. As usual, of course, the null hypothesis hedges its bet: Any observed departures from this expected pattern are accounted for by random sampling error.

Reflect for a moment on this particular model of the null hypothesis. H_0 offers the view that, in the population, religious attendance and abortion attitudes have nothing to do with

Table 6-4 Abortion Opinions, by Level of Attendance at Religious Services

| Abortion opinion[b] | Level of attendance at religious services[a] | | | Total |
	Low	Moderate	High	
Never allow	5.5%	9.2%	26.6%	11.9%
	(44)	(41)	(115)	(200)
Depends[c]	39.0	49.0	54.9	45.7
	(313)	(218)	(237)	(768)
Personal choice	55.5	41.8	18.5	42.4
	(445)	(186)	(80)	(711)
Total	100.0%	100.0%	100.0%	100.0%
	(802)	(445)	(432)	(1,679)

Source: Steven J. Rosenstone, Donald R. Kinder, Warren E. Miller, and the National Election Studies, *American National Election Study, 1996: Pre- and Post-election Survey,* 4th version (Ann Arbor: University of Michigan, Center for Political Studies [producer], 1999; Inter-university Consortium for Political and Social Research [distributor], 2000).

Note: Numbers of cases are in parentheses.

[a] Question: "Do you go to religious services every week, almost every week, once or twice a month, a few times a year, or never?" "Low" includes respondents who never attend or who attend a few times a year; "Moderate" combines respondents who attend once or twice a month or almost every week; "High" includes respondents who attend every week.

[b] Question: "There has been some discussion about abortion during recent years. Which one of the [following] opinions best agrees with your view? (1) By law, abortion should never be permitted; (2) the law should permit abortion only in case of rape, incest, or when the woman's life is in danger; (3) the law should permit abortion for reasons other than rape, incest, or when a woman's life is in danger; (4) by law, a woman should always be able to obtain an abortion as a matter of personal choice."

[c] Combines response codes (2) and (3).

each other, that the values of one are not related to the values of the other. So any way you break down a random sample—into smaller groups of 802, 445, 432, or whatever—you can expect the same pattern, the same distribution of cases, that you see in the overall sample. The alternative hypothesis (H_A) says that, in the population, the two variables have a lot to do with each other, that the values of one variable, abortion opinions, *depend on* the values of the other variable, religious attendance. The face-off between H_0 and H_A, then, centers on the question of how well H_0's expectations are met by the observed data.

Chi-square is based on the difference between two numbers: the observed frequency, which is the actual number of cases falling into each cell of a cross-tabulation, and the expected frequency, the hypothetical number of cases that should fall into each cell, if H_0 is correct. For any given cell, an observed frequency is usually labeled f_o. For example, 44 individuals fall into the "low attendance–never allow" cell of Table 6-4. Thus, f_o for this cell is 44. An expected frequency for any given cell, the number of cases that the null hypothesis claims should fall into that cell, is labeled f_e. How would one figure out this hypothetical number? Looking at the distribution of all cases across the values of the dependent variable, the null hypothesis would see that 11.9 percent (or .119) of the sample said, "never allow." According to H_0's logic, then, 11.9 percent of the 802 low-attendance individuals should fall into the "never allow" category. Thus, .119 times 802 individuals, or about 95 people, should be in this cell, if the null hypothesis is correct. Now, the building block of the chi-square test statistic is the difference between an observed frequency and an expected frequency: f_o minus f_e. For the "low attendance–never allow" cell, this difference is 44 minus 95, or –51. So, in this cell anyway, the null hypothesis missed the mark by 51 cases. It "overestimated," by 51 individuals, the number of cases that actually fall in this cell.

The difference between f_o and f_e is the starting place for the chi-square test statistic. In calculating chi-square, however, several additional steps are required. And the chi-square test statistic looks much different from the other formulas we have discussed:

$$\chi^2 = \Sigma(f_o - f_e)^2 / f_e.$$

Before we illustrate how to apply this formula, consider the central role played by the difference between f_o and f_e. Notice that, if the null's expectations, on the whole, are more or less accurate (that is, if $f_o - f_e$ is close to 0), then χ^2 is a small number. As the real-world situation departs from H_0's model world, however, χ^2 grows in size, and we can begin to entertain the idea of rejecting the null hypothesis. How do we obtain the chi-square test statistic?

According to this formula, one obtains a chi-square test statistic for an entire cross-tabulation by following five steps:

1. Find the expected frequency for each cell. As shown above, this can be accomplished by applying the proportion falling into a given category of the dependent variable to each column total. Example: Since .119 of the total sample said "never allow," the expected frequency for the "low attendance–never allow" cell would be .119 times 802, or about 95.[4]
2. For each cell, subtract the expected frequency from the observed frequency. Example: Subtracting 95 from 44 yields –51.
3. Square this number for each cell. Example: Squaring –51 yields 2,601.
4. Divide this number by the expected frequency. Example: 2,601 divided by 95 is roughly equal to 27.
5. To arrive at the chi-square test statistic, add up all of the cell-by-cell calculations.

Table 6-5 shows the cell-by-cell building blocks of the chi-square statistic for the religious attendance–abortion opinions example. The first number in each cell, f_o, is the actual number of cases from the sample data, and the next number, f_e, is the number of cases expected by H_0. (In Table 6-5, expected frequencies have been calculated to one-decimal precision.) The remaining values show each tedious step in the calculation: The difference between f_o and f_e, the square of the difference, and the squared difference divided by f_e.

Let's use the calculated numbers in Table 6-5 to stay abreast of the duel between H_0 and H_A. Which cells of Table 6-5 depart the most from H_0's expectations? Are they the cells that support H_A, the idea that abortion attitudes depend on religious attendance? Reading across the columns for the "never allow" category of the dependent variable, you can see that the null hypothesis misses the mark just where H_A says it should. The null hypothesis "overestimates" (by 51.5 cases) the actual number of low-attendance respondents who say abortion should "never" be allowed, and H_0 "underestimates" (by 63.5) the real number of high-attendance individuals in this category. At the "personal choice" value of the dependent variable, we see the same systematic departures—more observed cases than expected among low-attendance people, and many fewer than expected among highly observant individuals. The null hypothesis says that, after squaring each departure and dividing by f_e, and then aggregating all the numbers, we should get a result that is close to 0, give or take some random sampling error. But in Table 6-5 the calculated value of chi-square is 216.20. It might be

Table 6-5 Chi-square for Abortion Opinions, by Level of Attendance at Religious Services

Abortion opinion[b]		Level of attendance at religious services[a]			Total
		Low	*Moderate*	*High*	
Never allow	f_o	44	41	115	200
	f_e	95.5	53.0	51.5	
	$f_o - f_e$	−51.5	−12.0	63.5	
	$(f_o - f_e)^2$	2,652.25	144.00	4,032.25	
	$(f_o - f_e)^2 / f_e$	*27.77*	*2.72*	*78.30*	
Depends[c]	f_o	313	218	237	768
	f_e	366.8	203.5	197.6	
	$f_o - f_e$	−53.8	14.5	39.4	
	$(f_o - f_e)^2$	2,894.44	210.25	1,552.36	
	$(f_o - f_e)^2 / f_e$	*7.89*	*1.03*	*7.86*	
Personal choice	f_o	445	186	80	711
	f_e	339.6	188.4	182.9	
	$f_o - f_e$	105.4	−2.4	−102.9	
	$(f_o - f_e)^2$	11,109.16	5.76	10,588.41	
	$(f_o - f_e)^2 / f_e$	*32.71*	*.03*	*57.89*	
$\Sigma(f_o - f_e)^2 / f_e$		*68.37*	*3.78*	*144.05*	*216.20*
Total		802	445	432	1,679

Source: 1996 National Election Study.

[a] Question: "Do you go to religious services every week, almost every week, once or twice a month, a few times a year, or never?" "Low" includes respondents who never attend or who attend a few times a year; "Moderate" combines respondents who attend once or twice a month or almost every week; "High" includes respondents who attend every week.

[b] Question: "There has been some discussion about abortion during recent years. Which one of the [following] opinions best agrees with your view? (1) By law, abortion should never be permitted; (2) the law should permit abortion only in case of rape, incest, or when the woman's life is in danger; (3) the law should permit abortion for reasons other than rape, incest, or when a woman's life is in danger; (4) by law, a woman should always be able to obtain an abortion as a matter of personal choice."

[c] Combines response codes (2) and (3).

another poor showing for H_0. What are the limits of random sampling error for a calculated value of chi-square?

A χ^2 statistic has its own distribution, but its inferential interpretation is roughly analogous to a Z score or t-statistic: The larger it gets, the lower the probability that the results were obtained by chance. However, the precise value of χ^2 that marks the boundary of the .05 threshold is not fixed. Rather, it depends, as does the Student's t-distribution, on degrees of freedom. For chi-square, the number of degrees of freedom is determined by the number of rows and columns in a cross-tabulation. Specifically, the number of degrees of freedom is equal to the number of rows in the cross-tabulation, minus one, multiplied by the number of columns, minus one:

Number of degrees of freedom = (number of rows − 1)(number of columns − 1).

So Table 6-5 has $(3 − 1)(3 − 1) = 4$ degrees of freedom.

Table 6-6 Critical Values of χ^2

Degrees of freedom	Area to the right of critical value			
	.10 (90%)	.05 (95%)	.025 (97.5%)	.01 (99%)
1	2.706	3.841	5.024	6.635
2	4.605	5.991	7.378	9.210
3	6.251	7.815	9.348	11.345
4	7.779	9.488	11.143	13.277
5	9.236	11.070	12.833	15.086
6	10.645	12.592	14.449	16.812
7	12.017	14.067	16.013	18.475
8	13.362	15.507	17.535	20.090
9	14.684	16.919	19.023	21.666
10	15.987	18.307	20.483	23.209
11	17.275	19.675	21.920	24.725
12	18.549	21.026	23.337	26.217
13	19.812	22.362	24.736	27.688
14	21.064	23.685	26.119	29.141
15	22.307	24.996	27.488	30.578
16	23.542	26.296	28.845	32.000
17	24.769	27.587	30.191	33.409
18	25.989	28.869	31.526	34.805
19	27.204	30.144	32.852	36.191
20	28.412	31.410	34.170	37.566
21	29.615	32.671	35.479	38.932
22	30.813	33.924	36.781	40.289
23	32.007	35.172	38.076	41.638
24	33.196	36.415	39.364	42.980
25	34.382	37.652	40.646	44.314
26	35.563	38.885	41.923	45.642
27	36.741	40.113	43.195	46.963
28	37.916	41.337	44.461	48.278
29	39.087	42.557	45.722	49.588
30	40.256	43.773	46.979	50.892
40	51.805	55.758	59.342	63.691
50	63.167	67.505	71.420	76.154
60	74.397	79.082	83.298	88.379
70	85.527	90.531	95.023	100.425
80	96.578	101.879	106.629	112.329
90	107.565	113.145	118.136	124.116
100	118.498	124.342	129.561	135.807

Now consider Table 6-6, a table of critical values of χ^2. A **critical value** marks the upper boundary of random error and so defines H_0's limit. A specific critical value depends on degrees of freedom (the left-hand column of Table 6-6) and level of significance chosen by the researcher. In our example we have 4 degrees of freedom, and we will apply the .05 standard. Find 4 in the degrees of freedom column and read across to the .05 column. The critical value, 9.488, tells us this: If the null hypothesis is correct that, in the population, religiosity and abortion beliefs are completely independent of each other, we would obtain a χ^2 of less than 9.488 more frequently than 5 times out of 100 by chance. So the null hypothesis claims all of the territory between 0 (chi-square cannot assume negative values) and the critical value of chi-square, 9.488. But of course our χ^2 value, 216.20, vastly exceeds this limit. Again, the computer can tell us precisely how often we would get a value this huge if H_0 were true. Microsoft Excel, using scientific notation, returned this P-value for 216.20 (and 4 degrees of freedom): 1.23194E-45. That's a decimal point followed by 44 zeros and the digits 123194. Not very likely. Reject H_0.

Chi-square is remarkably adaptable. It can be used to test for independence between any categorical variables, nominal or ordinal, in any combination, for tables of any size. Chi-square can also be used to test whether the distribution of a single variable departs from chance—or from an expected distribution devised by the researcher. George Bornstedt and David Knoke cite the (somewhat whimsical) example of the distribution of birth months.[5] Are some months more "popular" for giving birth than others? In the absence of any alternative reasoning or unforeseen events (don't think about blackouts or hurricanes!), one would expect an even distribution of cases across the 12 months of the year. In a random sample of individuals, one-twelfth should report being born in each of the 12 months, January through December. So for a random sample of, say, 120 individuals, an expected frequency of 10 should fall into each category. Chi-square, in precisely the manner we have discussed, would compare these expected frequencies with the observed data and report a calculated value of χ^2, which could be compared with the plausible limit of random error. (When examining the distribution of a single variable, the number of degrees of freedom is simply the number of categories minus one. because there are 12 months, there are 11 degrees of freedom in this example.) Bornstedt and Knoke's analysis, we should report, reveals no statistically significant departure from the expected pattern.[6]

As durable as it is, chi-square also has shortcomings. When expected frequencies are small (generally five or fewer), it does not work well. This problem can often be addressed by collapsing the categories of the offending variable, thereby repopulating the cells with higher numbers of cases. Statisticians have developed other "patches" to address this problem.[7] More generally, chi-square is quite sensitive to sample size. In fact, χ^2 is directly proportional to n. If we were to double the observed frequencies in Table 6-5, for example, the χ^2 statistic also would double, producing a P-value even more remote than the one we obtained originally. Thus sizable samples often produce statistically significant results even though, from a substantive viewpoint, the relationship between the independent and dependent variables may appear rather anemic. Remember that chi-square, like any test of significance, can reveal only the likelihood that the observed results occurred by chance. It does not interpret the data for us, and it does not give us a direct reading of the strength of the relationship. Interpretation requires thought and imagination, attributes not supplied by tests of significance. However, other statistics can help the researcher in the strength-of-relationship department.

MEASURES OF ASSOCIATION

There are literally dozens of ways to answer the question "How strong is the relationship between the independent and dependent variables?" Even a partial inventory of the many different measures of association reads like a (mainly Greek) alphabet soup: λ ("lambda"), φ ("phi"), γ ("gamma"), τ_b ("tau-b"), τ_c ("tau-c"), V (Cramer's V), C (contingency coefficient),

d_{yx} (Somer's d), r (correlation coefficient), R^2 (coefficient of determination), ρ ("rho"), Q (Yule's Q), to identify a few. In the days before desktop computing, and before the point-and-click ease of powerful data analysis software packages, students and scholars faced an arduous question: "Of all the measures of association that I could calculate by hand, which is the most appropriate measure to include in my analysis of the relationship?" For you, most likely, the question is different, if no less daunting: "Of all the measures of association that the computer will calculate in a matter of nanoseconds, which ones should I include and which should I exclude from my analysis of the relationship?" This text does not provide an exhaustive discussion of measures of association. Here we consider the conventional features of the most widely used statistics, and we introduce one family of measures that applies the same logic to the question of strength. In this chapter we look at relationships between nominal and ordinal variables. Interval-level measures are considered in Chapter 7.

Any good measure of association helps the researcher by providing a standard for judging the strength of a relationship. This standard is usually bracketed by 0, indicating that no relationship exists, and by 1, indicating a perfect relationship. When both the independent and dependent variables are ordinal level, furthermore, a measure will communicate direction. A negative value, between 0 and -1, imparts an inverse relationship: An increase in the independent variable is associated with a decrease in the dependent variable. A positive value, between 0 and $+1$, indicates a direct relationship: An increase in the independent variable is associated with an increase in the dependent variable.

All measures of association are generally tailored around these standards, but they approach them from different angles. Here we discuss one family of measures, **proportional reduction in error**, or PRE, measures of association. All PRE measures are prediction based. That is, they all frame the "how strong?" question this way: "How much better can we predict the dependent variable by knowing the independent variable than by not knowing the independent variable?" If knowledge of the independent variable does not provide any help in predicting the dependent variable, then a PRE statistic will assume a value of 0. If knowledge of the independent variable permits perfect prediction of the dependent variable, then a PRE statistic will assume a magnitude of 1. The appropriate PRE measure to use, as we will see, depends on the level of measurement of the independent and dependent variables. First we illustrate the common PRE logic.

The PRE Approach

Suppose you were presented with the upper half of Table 6-7 and asked to summarize the relationship between gender and gun control opinions. Obviously, this cross-tabulation provides no information about the independent variable. You can, however, identify the dependent variable, the distribution of oppose/favor responses for all 1,514 respondents. You can further report its mode, "oppose," the response given by 807 individuals. Assume that, based only on this knowledge, you had to guess the value of the dependent variable for each of the 1,514 subjects taken one by one from the sample. What is your best guess for each individual case, "oppose" or "favor"? The modal response, "oppose." Why? Because, by consistently guessing "oppose" for each and every case, you will get more correct "hits," 807 correct guesses, than by guessing "favor." But of course you will record a "miss" for every case that is not in the modal category, for a total of 707 errors. In the PRE logic, these errors summarize prediction error based only on knowledge of the dependent variable. Let's label this error, the 707 misses, E_1.

Now suppose that the relationship between the dependent variable and an independent variable is revealed to you, as in the lower half of Table 6-7, which shows a cross-tabulation of

Table 6-7   Gun Control Attitudes and Gender

Gun ban?	Gender		Total
	Male	*Female*	Total
	Without knowledge of the independent variable		
Oppose	?	?	807
Favor	?	?	707
Total	?	?	1,514
	With knowledge of the independent variable		
Oppose	449	358	807
Favor	226	481	707
Total	675	839	1,514

Source: 1996 National Election Study.

Note: Question: "Do you favor or oppose a ban on the sale of all handguns, except those that are issued to law enforcement officers?"

gender, the independent variable, and attitudes toward gun control. If you were to summarize the dependent variable for each category of the independent variable, you would again report the mode, but this time you would do so for each value of the independent variable. So you would say that, among males, "oppose" is the mode; among females, "favor" is the mode. Now restart the case-by-case guessing game, applying the new knowledge you have gained. Because each case is drawn from a certain known category of the independent variable, your best guess is the central tendency for that category. For each male you would guess "oppose," for each female, "favor." This is not a foolproof strategy, of course, because you will still "miss-guess" quite a few cases—the 226 males who favor gun restrictions and the 358 females who oppose them. These misses, which total 584, summarize the prediction error based on knowledge of the independent variable. Let's label this error E_2.

Though their particular computational bases vary, proportional reduction in error measures take the general form

$$\text{Proportional reduction in error (PRE)} = (E_1 - E_2) / E_1.$$

The numerator, prediction error without knowledge of the independent variable minus prediction error with knowledge of the independent variable, is the reduction-in-error part of PRE. If the independent variable does not provide much improvement, if E_2 is about the same as E_1, then $(E_1 - E_2)$ approaches 0. If E_2 is a lot smaller than E_1, if many fewer prediction errors are made by knowing the independent variable, then the numerator retains a value close to E_1. In the gun control example, there were 707 errors without knowledge of the independent variable and 584 missed guesses when the independent variable was taken into account, improving the prediction by 707 minus 584, or 123. So $E_1 - E_2 = 123$. The denominator, E_1, translates error reduction into a ratio, providing the proportional part of PRE. Of the 707 errors that were made using only the dependent variable as a guide, the independent variable helped us pick up 123, or 123 / 707, which is about .17. So the independent variable provided a 17-percent reduction in error.

Table 6-8 Campaign Interest, by Level of Education

	Level of education			
Interested in campaign?	*Less than high school*	*High school*	*More than high school*	Total
Very	17.8%	22.6%	32.4%	27.3%
	(41)	(124)	(302)	(467)
Somewhat	47.0%	48.0%	50.9%	49.4%
	(108)	(263)	(475)	(846)
Not very	35.2%	29.4%	16.7%	23.3%
	(81)	(161)	(156)	(398)
Total	100.0%	100.0%	100.0%	100.0%
	(230)	(548)	(933)	(1,711)

Kendall's tau-b: –.167
Kendall's tau-c: –.152
Gamma: –.273
Somer's d (symmetric): –.167
Attention to campaigns dependent: –.174
Level of education dependent: –.161

Source: 1996 National Election Study.

Notes: Numbers of cases are in parentheses. Education categories are coded: 1 = Less than high school, 2 = High school, 3 = More than high school. Campaign interest is coded: 1 = Very interested, 2 = Somewhat interested, 3 = Not very interested. Question: "Some people don't pay much attention to political campaigns. How about you? Would you say that you have been very much interested, somewhat interested, or not much interested in the political campaigns so far this year?"

This example illustrates the calculation of **lambda**, a PRE measure frequently used to gauge the strength of a relationship between two variables, at least one of which is nominal. (Sometimes there is a problem with lambda, which we discuss below.) If both variables are measured at the ordinal level, several PRE statistics are available: gamma, Kendall's tau-b, Kendall's tau-c, and Somer's d. Since you may encounter this confusing array of choices in your own or in others' research, let's work through an example. In doing so, we will anticipate some problems you might have and provide some guidance on which choices to make.

Table 6-8 tests this hypothesis about the relationship between two ordinal-level variables: In comparing individuals, people with higher levels of education are more likely to be interested in political campaigns than are people with lower levels of education. The data have been arranged according to protocol, with the categories of the independent variable on the columns and the dependent variable on the rows. The data appear consistent with the hypothesis. Reading across the columns at the "very interested" value of the dependent variable, we see a systematic—and positive—pattern: As education increases, so does the percentage of respondents who say they are "very interested" in the campaign. Chi-square for Table 6-8 is 61.77 with 4 degrees of freedom, which has a P-value of .00. So we can reject H_0.

Now consider the full complement of measures of association that appear at the bottom of Table 6-8. The first thing you may notice is that all of them, despite their other differences, have a negative sign. Since the data clearly show a positive association, why the negative signs? Because all ordinal measures are computed based on a specific model of positive association. If the cases fall along a diagonal from upper left to lower right, the statistic takes on a positive value. If the cases fall, as they do in Table 6-8, from lower left to upper right, the statistic takes on a negative value. Students often find this upper-left-to-lower-right idea of a positive relationship counterintuitive, and they sometimes want to recode the data or rearrange the columns to make things come out right. But remember: The "problem" is with the statistic, not the cross-tabulation. The cross-tabulation is fine. In reporting the strength of the positive relationship between education and campaign interest, you would use your substantive knowledge of the relationship to put the "correct" sign on the measure of strength. So if you were using Kendall's tau-b, you would report a value of +.167.[8]

That raises the next question: Of all these measures, which one should be used? Again notice that all of them, with the exception of gamma, have similar magnitudes, in the .15 to .17 range. Gamma, because of the way it is computed, tends to over-estimate strength, and so is not recommended. The Somer's d and Kendall statistics produce very similar estimates.[9] Though it is largely a matter of personal preference, the measure of choice among many researchers is **Kendall's tau-b** or **Kendall's tau-c**. Well, which Kendall is correct, tau-b or tau-c? Here is a rule: If the table is square—the dependent and independent variables have the same number of categories—use tau-b. If the table is not square—the dependent and independent variables do not have the same number of categories—use tau-c. Because Table 6-8 is square, we would rely on Kendall's tau-b to tell the strength of the relationship between level of education and campaign interest.

The most useful quality of PRE measures is their common metric, ranging from a magnitude of 0, no predictive leverage is gained from the independent variable, to a magnitude of 1, perfect prediction of the dependent variable is gained from the independent variable. You will always get a PRE measure that falls between these poles. Thus, compared with how well we could predict campaign interest without knowing respondents' levels of education, we realized a 16.7-percent improvement by taking into account their education. Is this relationship weak? Or is it moderate, or strong? In the analysis of social science data, especially individual-level survey data, large PRE magnitudes (of, say, .5 or above) are uncommon. Lesser values (of about .3 or lower) are more frequent, even for relationships, like in Table 6-8, that show a clear pattern easily trumping the null hypothesis. Although one independent variable may do part of the work in predicting a dependent variable, the prediction can almost always be improved by taking into account additional independent variables. Keeping these qualifications in mind, the following is a useful guideline for labeling the strength of a PRE statistic: If the magnitude of the PRE statistic is less than .1, then the relationship is weak; if it is greater than .1 but less than .2, then the relationship is moderate; if it is greater than .2 but less than .3, then the relationship is moderately strong; and if the magnitude of the PRE statistic is greater than .3, then the relationship is strong. According to this guideline, for example, the Kendall's tau-b that we obtained from Table 6-8 (tau-b = .167), falls toward the higher end of the moderate range.

Lambda Revisited: The Problem and a Remedy

In addition to their common metric, all PRE measures (with the exception of gamma) are conservative—they tend to give a minimum reading of strength. This is essentially a good thing, because it is consistent with a skeptical scientific attitude toward research results. However, the nominal-level PRE measure of choice, lambda, can be rather too conservative.

Table 6-9   Campaign Interest, by Gender, Controlling for Race

Interested in campaign?	Race					
	White			Black		
	Gender			Gender		
	Male	Female	Total	Male	Female	Total
Very	30.0%	24.1%	26.8%	44.3%	25.8%	32.9%
	(198)	(191)	(389)	(35)	(33)	(68)
Some/not very[a]	70.0%	75.9%	73.2%	55.7%	74.2%	67.1%
	(462)	(603)	(1,065)	(44)	(95)	(139)
Total	100.0%	100.0%	100.0%	100.0%	100.0%	100.0%
	(660)	(794)	(1,454)	(79)	(128)	(207)
Lambda			.000			.000
Cramer's V			.067			.192

Source: 1996 National Election Study.

Notes: Numbers of cases are in parentheses. Question: "Some people don't pay much attention to political campaigns. How about you? Would you say that you have been very much interested, somewhat interested, or not much interested in the political campaigns so far this year?"

[a] Respondents who are "somewhat" or "not very" interested have been collapsed into a single category.

It may return a value of 0, even for tables that clearly show a relationship between the independent and dependent variables.[10] You will often use or interpret nominal-level data in political research, so let's review the problem and settle on a workable solution.

Table 6-9 tests the relationship between a nominal independent variable, gender, and campaign interest, which has been collapsed into two categories. To make things interesting, and to illustrate a separate point about using measures of association, Table 6-9 displays the relationship between gender and campaign interest, controlling for race. By applying your table-reading skills, you could well describe the relationship between the independent and dependent variables for each category of the control. Among whites, gender has some effect, since men are somewhat more likely than women to say that they are "very interested" in the campaign. This difference, about 6 percentage points, is interesting if not particularly earth-shattering. Among blacks, however, the gender difference is huge. A nearly 20-percentage-point difference exists between the percentages of black males (44.3%) and black females (25.8%) who expressed a high level of campaign interest. Clearly, too, interaction is at work, since the effect of the independent variable, gender, depends on the value of the control, race. The calculated values of chi-square are statistically significant for both whites and blacks.[11]

But notice that lambda remains mute on these relationships. For both whites and blacks, this PRE measure says that gender does not help at all in predicting campaign interest. Why is this? Because, guessing the modal value of the dependent variable, "some/not very," produces the same number of errors with knowledge of the independent variable as without knowledge of the independent variable. Among all whites, for example, the modal response is "some/not very," and the modal response among white males and white females also is "some/not very." This is the problem with lambda. When the dependent variable has a low amount of variation—one category is populated much more heavily with cases than are the other categories—lambda becomes an insensitive measure of strength.

In such situations, another measure of association, **Cramer's V**, is recommended. Cramer's V, which is based on chi-square, takes a value of between 0, no relationship, and 1, a perfect relationship.[12] Because Cramer's V is not a PRE measure, the researcher may not interpret its value as a gauge of predictive accuracy. However, when it comes to interpreting controlled comparisons, such as that presented in Table 6-9, Cramer's V is entirely appropriate and quite useful. Just as we learned from our substantive interpretation, Cramer's V reflects a modest relationship between gender and campaign interest for whites ($V = .067$) but a much stronger relationship among blacks ($V = .192$).

SUMMARY

As we have seen in previous chapters of this book, political researchers are interested in describing political variables and constructing explanations for political phenomena. They propose hypotheses and analyze relationships to find out whether their explanations are consistent with what is happening in the political world. Yet we have also seen that political researchers often do not have complete information about each and every unit of analysis they seek to understand. Because they often rely on sample data, researchers learn to be cautious: "I have performed the analysis and found this relationship. If I assert that my findings describe what is really going on 'out there' in the population, will I be making a mistake?"

With random samples, of course, we can never know the answer to this question with absolute certainty. But, thanks to tests of statistical significance, we can determine the probability of making a mistake. As discussed in this chapter, a test of significance tells the researcher the probability of committing an inferential error—asserting the existence of a relationship in the population if, in reality, no relationship exists. The approaches we have discussed—the informal eyeball test, the 1.645 test, the chi-square test—are based on the same idea. If the sample results can be accounted for by random sampling error, then we must say that there is no relationship in the population. We accept the null hypothesis. If, by contrast, the sample results cannot plausibly be attributed to random sampling error, then we can say that a relationship probably does exist in the population. We would take an acceptable chance and reject the null hypothesis. A computer-reported P-value, the exact probability of obtaining the observed relationship if the null hypothesis is correct, affords the researcher a high degree of precision in making this inferential decision.

We have also discussed measures of association, statistics that help the researcher gauge the strength of the relationship between an independent variable and a dependent variable. Over the years, social scientists and statisticians have devised a wide array of these measures. The main decision with which you will be faced, however, is not *how many* measures to use but rather *which one* is most appropriate to use in a particular analysis. Table 6-10 provides a guide you can follow in making this decision. All of the measures in Table 6-10, with one exception, are proportional reduction in error (PRE) measures. As discussed in this chapter, a PRE measure tells you how much better you can predict the values of the dependent variable by knowing the independent variable than by not knowing the independent variable. Thus PRE techniques provide a commonsensical measure of predictive accuracy. If we would do just as well in both situations—predicting the dependent variable with or without knowledge of the independent variable—then a PRE statistic will tell us so by returning a value of 0. If the independent variable provides perfect predictive leverage, allowing us an error-free prediction of the dependent variable, then a PRE statistic will communicate this by returning a value of 1. In this chapter we considered the PRE logic as it applies to nominal and ordinal

Table 6-10 Summary Guide to Measures of Association

Measure of association	What it is	When to use it
Lambda	PRE measure of strength	One variable is nominal level. If the dependent variable has low variation, lambda may underestimate strength.
Kendall's tau-b	PRE measure of strength and direction	Both variables are ordinal level and both variables have the same number of categories—the table is "square."
Kendall's tau-c	PRE measure of strength and direction	Both variables are ordinal level and the variables have different numbers of categories—the table is "nonsquare."
Cramer's V	Non-PRE measure of strength; based on chi-square	Used when lambda underestimates strength. It is also useful in analyzing controlled comparisons.

relationships. Yet the same logic applies to relationships between interval-level variables. The analysis of interval-level relationships is our next topic of discussion.

KEY TERMS

chi-square test of significance (p. 139)
Cramer's V (p. 150)
critical value (p. 143)
Kendall's tau-b (p. 148)
Kendall's tau-c (p. 148)
lambda (p. 147)
measure of association (p. 131)
null hypothesis (p. 132)
one-tailed test of significance (p. 135)
.05 level of significance (p. 133)

proportional reduction in error (PRE) (p. 145)
P-value (p. 136)
standard error of the difference (p. 134)
test of statistical significance (p. 131)
test statistic (p. 135)
t-ratio (p. 136)
two-tailed test of significance (p. 134)
Type I error (p. 132)
Type II error (p. 132)

EXERCISES

1. How could current election laws be changed so that more citizens go to the polls on Election Day? One suggestion is to hold elections on nonworkdays, such as holidays or weekends, instead of workdays, as is the current practice in the United States. Interestingly, however, the mean turnout in democracies holding elections on workdays is actually *higher* than the mean turnout in democracies holding elections on nonworkdays. The following table reports the mean turnouts and standard errors for 18 workday democracies and 40 nonworkday democracies:[13]

Workday or nonworkday?	Mean turnout	Standard error
Workday	71.8	2.75
Nonworkday	68.5	2.24

A. What is the difference between the mean turnout in workday countries and the mean turnout in nonworkday countries? State the null hypothesis for the workday/nonworkday comparison.

B. What is the standard error of the difference between the workday mean and the nonworkday mean? Calculate the t-statistic. $(H_A - H_0) / $ *standard error of difference*

C. Does the mean difference pass the eyeball test of significance? What is your inferential decision: Reject the null hypothesis or do not reject the null hypothesis? Explain.

D. Upon seeing that workday democracies have a higher mean turnout than do nonworkday democracies, an election reformer suggests that, to boost turnout, countries currently holding elections on weekends or holidays should switch to workdays. Is this reformer's suggestion supported by the data? Explain.

2. Scholars of political development have investigated the so-called oil curse, the idea that oil-rich countries tend not to develop democratic systems of governance, that "oil and democracy do not mix."[14] Framing this idea in the form of a hypothesis: In comparing countries, those having economies less dependent on oil wealth will be more democratic than will countries having economies more dependent on oil wealth. Does this hypothesis have merit? Consider the following data, which present information for 20 countries with non-oil-dependent economies and 15 countries with oil dependent economies. The dependent variable is a 7-point level-of-democracy scale, with higher scores denoting more democracy. Here are the mean values and standard errors of the democracy scale for non-oil-dependent and oil-dependent countries:

Oil-dependent economy?	Mean democracy scale	Standard error
No	4.6	.48
Yes	2.6	.28

A. State the null hypothesis for the non-oil-dependent/oil-dependent comparison.

B. Calculate the difference between the means of the democracy scale for non-oil-dependent and oil-dependent countries. Calculate the standard error of the difference. Calculate the t-statistic.

C. Does the mean difference pass the 1.645 test of significance? Explain how you know.

D. Based on these results, suppose a researcher decides to reject the null hypothesis. Is the probability of Type I error acceptably low? Explain.

3. Below are two conventional wisdoms, statements generally believed to be accurate descriptions of the world. Accompanying each statement are data (from the General Social Surveys) that allow you to test each conventional wisdom. For each statement:

A. State the null hypothesis.

B. Calculate the difference between the proportions or means.

C. Calculate the standard error of the difference in proportions or means.

D. Using the eyeball test, state whether you would accept the null hypothesis or reject the null hypothesis.

     Conventional Wisdom One: Catholics have larger families than Protestants. The 1998 General Social Survey asked respondents how many brothers and sisters they have. The 703 Catholic respondents reported an average of 4.13 siblings (standard error = .13), whereas the 1,516 Protestants averaged 4.07 siblings (standard error = .09).

     Conventional Wisdom Two: The divorce rate has increased dramatically over the past 25 years or so. Among respondents in the 1973 General Social Survey, .13 said they had been divorced (standard error = .01). In the 1998 General Social Survey, .23 had been divorced (standard error = .01).

4. In 2001 the U.S. Senate voted on the question of whether to allow oil and gas drilling in the Gulf of Mexico. The relationship between party affiliation and vote is shown in the following table:

Allow drilling?	Party		Total
	Democrat	*Republican*	
No	33	0	33
Yes	18	49	67
Total	51	49	100

A. Calculate lambda for this table. Write a sentence explaining exactly what this value of lambda means.
B. Would you say that this relationship is weak, moderate, or strong?
C. Assume that the data in this table were drawn from a random sample. Use chi-square to test the null hypothesis that, in the population from which the sample was drawn, there is no relationship between party and vote. Using Table 6-6, find the appropriate critical value (use the .05 level of significance). What do you think? Can you safely infer that party and vote are related? Explain how you know.

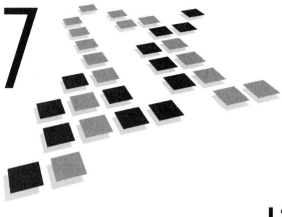

7

Correlation and Linear Regression

LEARNING OBJECTIVES

In this chapter you will learn:
- How to use correlation analysis to describe the relationship between two interval-level variables
- How to use regression analysis to estimate the effect of an independent variable on a dependent variable
- How to perform and interpret dummy variable regression
- How to use multiple regression to make controlled comparisons

By this point you have covered a fair amount of methodological ground. In Chapter 3 you learned two essential methods for analyzing the relationship between an independent variable and a dependent variable: cross-tabulation analysis and mean comparison analysis. Chapter 4 covered the logic and practice of controlled comparison—how to set up and interpret the relationship between an independent variable and a dependent variable, controlling for a third variable. In Chapters 5 and 6 you learned about the role of inferential statistics in evaluating the statistical significance of a relationship, and you became familiar with measures of association. You can now frame a testable hypothesis, set up the appropriate analysis, interpret your findings, and figure out the probability that your observed results occurred by chance.

In many ways, correlation and regression are similar to the methods you have learned. **Correlation analysis** produces a measure of association, Pearson's correlation coefficient, that gauges the direction and strength of a relationship between two interval-level variables. **Regression analysis** produces a statistic, a regression coefficient, that estimates the size of the effect of the independent variable on the dependent variable.

Suppose, for example, we were working with survey data and we wanted to investigate the relationship between individuals' ages and the number of hours they spend watching television each day. Is the relationship positive, with older individuals watching more hours of TV than younger people? Or is the relationship negative, with older people watching less

TV than younger people? How strong is the relationship between age and the number of hours devoted to TV? Correlation analysis would help us address these questions.

Regression analysis is similar to mean comparison analysis. In performing mean comparison analysis, you learned to divide subjects on the independent variable—females and males, for example—and compare values on the dependent variable—such as mean Hillary Clinton thermometer ratings. Furthermore, you learned how to test the null hypothesis, the assumption that the observed sample difference between females and males was produced by random sampling error. Similarly, regression analysis communicates the mean difference on the dependent variable, such as thermometer ratings, for subjects who differ on the independent variable, females compared with males. And, just as in the comparison of two sample means, regression analysis provides information that permits the researcher to determine the probability that the observed difference was produced by chance.

However, regression is different from the previously discussed methods in two ways. First, regression analysis is very precise. It produces the statistic, the regression coefficient that reveals the exact nature of the relationship between an independent variable and a dependent variable. A regression coefficient reports the amount of change in the dependent variable that is associated with a one-unit change in the independent variable. Strictly speaking, regression may be used only when the dependent variable is measured at the interval level.[1] The independent variable, however, can come in any form: nominal, ordinal, or interval. In this chapter we show how to interpret regression analysis in which the independent variable is interval level. We also discuss a technique called dummy variable regression, which uses nominal or ordinal variables as independent variables.

A second distinguishing feature of regression is the ease with which it can be extended to the analysis of controlled comparisons. In setting up a cross-tabulation analysis, controlling for a third variable, we performed mechanical control—separating units of analysis on the control variable, then reexamining the relationships between the independent and dependent variables. Regression also analyzes the relationship between a dependent variable and a single independent variable. This is simple or bivariate regression. However, regression easily accommodates additional control variables that the researcher may want to include. In multivariate or multiple regression mode, regression uses statistical control to adjust for the possible effects of the additional variables. Regression is remarkably flexible in this regard. Properly applied, regression can be used to detect and evaluate spuriousness, and it allows the researcher to model additive relationships and interaction effects.

CORRELATION

Figure 7-1 shows the relationship between two variables: the percentage of a state's population that graduated from high school (the independent variable) and the percentage of the eligible population that voted in the 1994 elections (the dependent variable). This display is called a **scatterplot.** In a scatterplot, the independent variable is measured along the horizontal axis and the dependent variable is measured along the vertical axis. Figure 7-1, then, locates each of the 50 states in two-dimensional space. Consider the overall pattern of this relationship. Would you say that the relationship is strong, moderate, or weak? And what, if any, is the direction of the relationship—positive or negative? Even without the help of a numeric measure of strength and direction, you can probably arrive at reasonable answers to these questions. Direction is easily ascertained. Clearly, as you move from lower to higher values of the independent variable—comparing states with lower levels of education to states

Figure 7-1 Scatterplot: High School Graduates and Turnout, 1994 (percent)

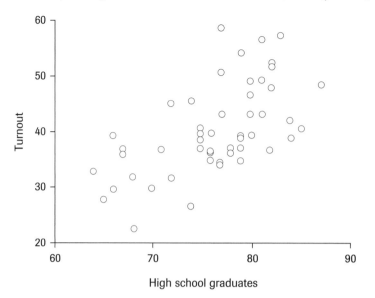

Source: State Politics and Policy Data Archive, Illinois Legislative Studies Center, University of Illinois at Springfield.

with higher education levels—the values of the dependent variable tend to adjust themselves accordingly, clustering a bit higher on the turnout axis. So the direction is positive. But how strong is the relationship? In assessing strength, you need to consider the consistency of the pattern. If the relationship is strong, then just about every time you compare a state that has lower education with a state that has higher education, the second state would also have higher turnout. So an increase in X would be associated with an increase in Y most of the time. If the relationship is weak, you would encounter many cases that do not fit the positive pattern, many higher-education states with turnouts that are about the same as, or perhaps less than, lower-education states. So an increase in X would not consistently occasion an increase in Y. Now suppose you had to rate the relationship in Figure 7-1 on a scale from 0 to 1, where a rating close to 0 denotes a weak relationship, a rating of around .5 denotes a moderate relationship, and a rating close to 1 denotes a strong relationship. What rating would you give? A rating close to 0 would not seem correct, because the pattern has some predictability. Yet the other pole, a rating of 1, does not seem right either, because you can find quite a few states that are in the "wrong" place on the turnout variable, given their levels of education. A rating of around .5, somewhere in the moderate range, would seem a reasonable gauge of the strength of the relationship.

The **Pearson's correlation coefficient**, which is symbolized by a lowercase *r*, uses just this approach in determining the direction and strength of an interval-level relationship. Pearson's r always has a value that falls between −1, signifying a perfectly negative association between the variables, and +1, a perfectly positive association between them. If no relationship exists between the variables, Pearson's r takes on the value of 0. Though the exact computation of r need not be discussed, it is important to understand the statistical basis of the correlation coefficient.[2] Conceptually, the correlation coefficient is defined by

Covariation of X and Y / Separate variation of X and Y.

The numerator, "Covariation of X and Y," measures the degree to which variation in X is associated with variation in Y. This value quantifies the thinking we applied to the scatterplot of states. Suppose we were comparing two states, one having a low value on X, a low percentage of high school graduates, and one having a higher value on X. If the second state also has higher turnout than the first state, then the numerator will be positive. If, by contrast, the state with a higher value on X has a lower value on Y, a higher percentage of high school graduates but a lower turnout rate, the numerator will be negative. If the pattern is inconsistent—the states have different values on X but similar values on Y—the numerator records this inconsistent pattern and assumes a value close to 0. The denominator, by contrast, does not measure the relationship between the variables. Rather, it summarizes all the variation in both variables considered separately.[3] If the covariation of X and Y is equal to the measure of the total variation in both variables, then r takes on a value of +1 (perfectly positive covariation) or −1 (perfectly negative covariation). If X and Y do not move together in a systematic way, then r assumes a value close to 0. What is the correlation coefficient for the relationship depicted in Figure 7-1? According to a computer analysis of this relationship, Pearson's r = +.6.

It should be pointed out that Pearson's r is a symmetrical measure of association between two variables. This means that the correlation between X and Y is the same as the correlation between Y and X. So if the axes in Figure 7-1 were reversed—with percent high school graduates appearing on the vertical axis and percent turnout appearing on the horizontal axis—Pearson's r would still be +.6. This makes correlation analysis quite useful during the early stages of research, when the researcher is getting an idea of the overall relationship between two variables. However, Pearson's r is neutral on the question of whether X causes Y or Y causes X. Therefore, one cannot attribute causation based on a correlation coefficient. As always, the researcher's explanation, the process the researcher has described to explain the connection between X and Y, is the source of causal reasoning. Furthermore, Pearson's r is not a PRE (proportional reduction in error) measure of association. It is neatly bounded by −1 and +1, and so communicates strength and direction by a common metric. But the specific magnitude of r does not tell us how much better we can predict the dependent variable by knowing the independent variable than by not knowing the independent variable. Happily, another measure can do that job for us, but first we need to understand regression analysis, to which we now turn.

BIVARIATE REGRESSION

By way of introducing bivariate regression, consider a hypothetical example. Let's say that an instructor wishes to analyze the relationship between the scores that her students received on an exam (the dependent variable, Y) and the number of hours they spent studying for the test (the independent variable, X). The raw data for each of her eight students are presented in Table 7-1. Examine these numbers closely. Can you identify a pattern to the relationship (other than that it must have been a hard exam!)? You can see that the relationship is positive: Students who studied more received better scores than did students who studied less. And you can be sure that the correlation between the variables is indeed strong. But regression analysis permits us to put a finer point on the relationship. In this case, each additional hour spent studying results in exactly a 6-point increase in exam score. The student who studied 1 hour did 6 points better than the student who didn't study at all. And the student who studied 2 hours received a score that was 6 points better than the student who studied 1 hour, and so on. More than this, the XY pattern can be summarized by a line. Visualize this for a

Table 7-1   Hours Spent Studying (X) and
Test Score (Y)

Hours (X)	Score (Y)
0	55
1	61
2	67
3	73
4	79
5	85
6	91
7	97

Note: Hypothetical data.

moment. What linear equation would summarize the relationship between hours spent studying and exam score?

To visualize or draw a line, you must know two things: the Y-intercept and the slope of the line. The Y-intercept is the point at which the line crosses the Y-axis—the value of Y when X is 0. The slope of a line, called the **regression coefficient**, is "rise over run," the amount of change in Y for each unit change in X. With these two elements, we arrive at the general formula for a **regression line**, a linear equation that summarizes the relationship between X and Y:

$$Y = a + b(X)$$

The term *a* represents the Y-intercept. Based on the information in Table 7-1, the Y-intercept is 55, the score received by the student who did not study at all (X = 0). The term *b* represents the slope of the line. The slope, or regression coefficient, is the workhorse of regression. When you first considered Table 7-1, you probably figured out the regression coefficient right away. With each one-unit change in the independent variable, there is a six-unit change in the dependent variable. So in the example, the regression coefficient (b) is equal to 6. Thus the regression line for Table 7-1 is

$$\text{Test score} = 55 + 6(\text{Number of hours}).$$

Notice a few aspects of this approach. First, the regression equation provides a general summary of the relationship between X and Y. For any given student in Table 7-1, we can plug in the number of hours spent studying, do the arithmetic, and arrive at his or her exam score. Second, the formula would seem to hold some predictive power, the ability to estimate scores for students who do not appear in the data. For example, if information about the studying efforts of a new student were introduced—she or he spent, say, 3.5 hours studying—we would have a predictive tool for estimating that student's score. Our estimate: 55 + 6(3.5) = 76. Using an established regression formula to predict values of a dependent variable for new values of an independent variable is a common application of regression analysis.

In any event, empirical relationships are never as well behaved as the data in Table 7-1. Let's modify the example to make it somewhat more realistic. Assume that the instructor is

Table 7-2 Hours Spent Studying (X), Test Score (Y), and Estimated Score ($\hat{Y}$)

Hours (X)	Score (Y)	Estimated score ($\hat{Y}$) for a given value of X
0	53	55
0	57	
1	59	61
1	63	
2	65	67
2	69	
3	71	73
3	75	
4	77	79
4	81	
5	83	85
5	87	
6	89	91
6	93	
7	95	97
7	99	

Note: Hypothetical data.

working with a sample of 16 students drawn at random from the student population. Table 7-2 groups these cases on the independent variable. Let's look at the data. According to Table 7-2, neither of the first two students spent any time studying (for each, X = 0). One received a 53, and the other did somewhat better, a 57. The next two students share the same value on the independent variable, 1 hour, but their scores, too, were different, a 59 and a 63, and so on for the other pairs of cases. Now suppose you had to calculate, for each pair of cases, a one-number summary of their value on the dependent variable. How would you proceed? You would probably do what regression does—calculate the mean value of the dependent variable for each value of the independent variable. So for the two nonstudiers you would average their scores: (53 + 57)/2 = 55; for the two 1-hour cases, (59 + 63)/2 = 61, and so on. Notice that this averaging process does not reproduce the actual data. Instead, it produces estimates of the actual test scores for each number of hours spent studying. Because these estimates of Y do not represent real values of Y, they are given a separate label, $\hat{Y}$ ("Y-hat"), the letter Y with a "hat" on top. Now if, based on Table 7-2, the instructor had to describe the relationship between X and Y, she might say, "Based on my sample, each additional hour spent studying produced, *on average*, a 6-point increase in exam score." So the regression coefficient, b, communicates the average change in Y for each unit change in X. A linear regression equation takes this general form:

$$\hat{Y} = \hat{a} + \hat{b}(X)$$

$\hat{Y}$ ("Y-hat") is the estimated mean value of the dependent variable, $\hat{a}$ ("a-hat") is the average value of Y when X is 0, and $\hat{b}$ ("b-hat") is the average change in Y for each unit change in X. For Table 7-2 we would have:

$$\text{Estimated score} = 55 + 6(\text{Number of hours})$$

Regression analysis is built on the estimation of averages. Suppose that there were no students in the sample who had not studied at all. No matter. Regression will use the available information to calculate a Y-intercept, an estimate of the average score that students would have received, had they not studied. By the same token, if no empirical examples existed for X = 5 hours, regression nonetheless will yield an estimate, 55 + 6(5) = 85, an estimated average score. A regression line travels through the two-dimensional space defined by X and Y, estimating mean values along the way.[4]

Regression relentlessly summarizes linear relationships. Feed it some sample values for X and Y, and it will return estimates for a and b. But because these coefficients are means— means calculated from sample data—they will contain random sampling error, as do any sample means. Focus on the workhorse, the regression coefficient, $\hat{b}$. Based on Table 7-2, the instructor can infer that, in the population from which the sample was drawn, the average change in score for each additional hour spent studying is +6 points. But obviously this estimate contains some error, because the actual student scores fall a bit above or below the average, for any given value of X. Just like any sample mean, the size of the error in a regression coefficient is measured by a familiar statistic, its standard error. So we know that the real value of b in the population (labeled with the Greek letter β ["beta"]) is equal to the sample estimate, $\hat{b}$, within the bounds of standard error:

$$\beta = \hat{b} \pm (\text{standard error of } \hat{b})$$

There is nothing mysterious or special about regression analysis in this regard. All of the statistical rules you have learned—the informal ± 2 rule of thumb, the more formal 1.645 test, the calculation of P-values, the inferential set-up for testing the null hypothesis—apply to regression analysis. In evaluating the difference between two sample means, we tested the null hypothesis that the difference in the population is equal to 0. In its regression guise, the null hypothesis says much the same thing—that the true value of β in the population is equal to zero, that $\beta = 0$. Put another way, H_0 claims that a one-unit change in the independent variable produces zero units of change in the dependent variable, that the true regression line is flat and horizontal. Just as in the comparison of two sample means, we test the null hypothesis by calculating a t-statistic, or t-ratio:

$$t = (\hat{b} - \beta) / (\text{Standard error of } \hat{b}), \text{ with degrees of freedom (d.f.)} = n - 2.$$

Informally, if the t-ratio is equal to or greater than 2, then we can reject the null hypothesis. And of course a precise P-value for t can be obtained in the familiar way.[5] For each 1-hour increase in studying time, we estimated a 6-point increase in exam score ($\hat{b} = +6$). Calculated by computer, the standard error of $\hat{b}$ is .233. So the t-statistic is 6/.233 = 25.75, which has a P-value that rounds to .000. If the true value of β in the population really is 0, then the probability of obtaining a sample estimate of $\hat{b} = 6$ is highly remote.

Figure 7-2 Regression: High School Graduates and Turnout, 1994 (percent)

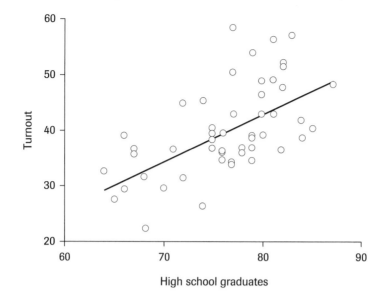

Source: State Politics and Policy Data Archive.
Note: Regression line: percent turnout = –26.27 + .87 (percent high school graduates).

This hypothetical example has demonstrated some basic points. But let's return to a real-world relationship, the education-turnout example introduced in Figure 7-1, and discuss some further properties of regression analysis. Figure 7-2 again displays the scatterplot of states, only this time the estimated regression line has been superimposed within plot. Where did this line originate?

In the hypothetical example of exam scores, we could easily discern the regression line by averaging the scores for each value of X. Though the estimation of a regression line for actual data is a bit more complicated, the principle is the same. Linear regression finds a line that provides the best fit to the data points. Using each case's value on X, it finds $\hat{Y}$, an estimated value of Y. It then calculates the difference between this estimate and the case's actual value of Y. This difference is called **prediction error**. Prediction error is represented by the expression $Y - \hat{Y}$, the actual value of Y minus the estimated value of Y. So regression would use the values of the independent variable, percent high school graduates, to determine an estimated value on the dependent variable, percent turnout. Prediction error, for each state, would be the difference between the state's actual level of turnout, Y, and the estimated turnout, $\hat{Y}$.

Now, the prediction error for any given state may be positive—its actual turnout is higher than its estimated turnout—or it may be negative—its actual turnout is lower than its estimated turnout. In fact, if one were to add up all of the positive and negative prediction errors across all states, they would sum to zero. When it finds the best-fitting line, therefore, regression does not work with the simple difference between Y and $\hat{Y}$. Rather, it works with the square of the difference, $(Y - \hat{Y})^2$. So for each state, regression would square the difference between the state's actual level of turnout and its estimated level of turnout. In the regression logic, the best-fitting line is the one that minimizes the sum of these squared prediction errors across all cases. That is, regression finds the line that minimizes the quantity $\Sigma (Y - \hat{Y})^2$. This criterion of best fit—the line that minimizes the sum of the squared differences between real values of Y and estimated values of Y—is frequently used to distinguish garden-variety ordinary least squares (OLS) regression from other regression-based techniques. The line represented in Figure 7-2, then, is an OLS regression line. True to form, regression reported the equation that provides the best fit for the relationship between X and Y:

Estimated turnout = −26.27 + .87(Percent high school graduates)

How would you interpret each of the estimates for a and b? First consider the estimate for a, the level of turnout when X is 0. What can a turnout level of −26.27 possibly mean? In this case, not much. In the actual data, of course, no state has a value of 0 on the independent variable, 0 percent who graduated from high school. Nonetheless, regression produced an estimate for â, anchoring the line at a −26.27 turnout rate.[6] (That must be a situation in which 26.27 percent of the electorate goes to the polls and declares that they are not going to vote!) For some applications of regression, the value of the Y-intercept, the estimate â, has no meaningful interpretation. (Sometimes â is essential, however. This is discussed below.) What about $\hat{b}$, the estimated effect of education on turnout?

There are two rules for interpreting a regression coefficient. The first rule is to be clear about the units in which the independent and dependent variables are measured. In this example, the dependent variable, Y, is measured by percentages—the percentage of each state's eligible population that voted in the 1994 election. The independent variable, X, also is expressed in percentages—the percentage of each state's population that has a high school degree. The second rule is that the regression coefficient, $\hat{b}$, is expressed in units of the dependent variable, not the independent variable. Therefore, the coefficient, .87, tells us that turnout (Y) increases, on average, by .87 of a percentage point for each 1-percentage-point increase in education (X).

Indeed, a common mistake made by beginners is to interpret $\hat{b}$ in terms of the independent variable. It might seem reasonable to say something like, "If the percentage of high school graduates increases by .87 percent, then turnout increases by 1 percent." This would be incorrect. Remember that all the coefficients in a regression equation are measured in units of the dependent variable. The intercept is the value of the dependent variable when X is zero. The slope is the estimated change in the dependent variable for a one-unit change in the independent variable.

The data in Figure 7-2 were calculated on a population, all 50 states, not a random sample of states. Strictly speaking, of course, when one is dealing with a population, questions of statistical inference do not enter the picture. But let's assume, for the sake of illustration, that we have a sample here, and that we obtained a sample estimate of .87 for the true population value of β.[7] The null hypothesis would claim that β is really 0, and that the sample estimate we obtained, .87, is within the bounds of sampling error. As before, we enlist the regression coefficient's standard error, which the computer calculated to be .17, and arrive at a t-ratio:

$$t = (\hat{b} - \beta) / (\text{Standard error of } \hat{b}), \text{ with d.f.} = n - 2$$
$$= .87 / .17$$
$$= 5.12, \text{ with d.f.} = 50 - 2 = 48.$$

The informal ± 2 rule of thumb advises us to reject the null hypothesis. The P-value, a probability of 2.68-E06, verifies that advice.

R-SQUARE

Regression analysis gives a precise estimate of the effect of an independent variable on a dependent variable. It looks at a relationship and reports the relationship's exact nature. So if someone were to inquire, "What, exactly, is the effect of education on turnout in the states?," the regression coefficient provides an answer: "Turnout increases by .87 percent for each 1-percent increase in the percentage of the states' population with a high school diploma. Plus, the regression coefficient has a P-value of .000." By itself, however, the regression coefficient does not measure the completeness of the relationship, the degree to which Y is explained by X. A skeptic, on viewing Figure 7-2, might point this out. Certainly but a handful of states fall exactly on the regression line. Most have lower levels of turnout—or higher levels of turnout—than the regression line would predict. Overall, just how good a job does the independent variable do in explaining the dependent variable? How much better can we predict a state's turnout by knowing its education level than by not knowing its education level?

These are not questions about the precise nature of the relationship. They are questions about the size of the contribution X makes to the explanation of Y. You can probably think of several variables that may explain why states are below or above the line. Perhaps below-the-line cases tend to be Southern states, which historically have lower turnouts, and above-the-line cases are non-Southern states. Or maybe states with lower-than-predicted turnout rates have more stringent voter registration requirements than do states with higher-than-predicted turnouts. Hard to tell. In any event, states' education levels, though clearly related to turnout, provide an incomplete explanation of it.

In regression analysis, the completeness of a relationship is measured by the statistic R^2 ("R-square"). **R-square** is a PRE measure, and so it poses the question of strength the same way as lambda or Kendall's tau: "How much better can we predict the dependent variable by knowing the independent variable than by not knowing the independent variable?" Consider the state turnout data. If you had to guess a state's turnout without knowing its education level, what is your best guess? As we saw in the Chapter 6 illustration of lambda, the best guess for a nominal-level variable is the variable's measure of central tendency, its mode. In the case of an interval-level dependent variable, such as percent turnout, the best guess also is provided by the variable's measure of central tendency, its mean. This guess, the mean value of Y, is represented by the symbol $\overline{Y}$ ("Y-bar"), Y with a bar across the top.

Let's return to the state turnout data. Figure 7-3 again shows the scatterplot of states and the regression line. This time, however, a flat line is drawn at 40-percent turnout. This value is the mean turnout for all 50 states, and it was calculated like any mean—by summing the turnouts for all states and dividing by the number of states. So $\overline{Y} = 40$ percent. If we had no knowledge of the independent variable, we would guess a turnout rate of 40 for each state taken one at a time. This guess would serve us fairly well for many states, but it would produce quite a few errors. Consider the case of one state, Wyoming, which appears as a solid dot in the scatterplot. Wyoming had a turnout rate of about 57 percent in 1994. So our guess of 40 for Wyoming would have a large dose of error. How big of a dose? Since Wyoming's actual turnout was 57 and our guess, based on the mean for all states, is 40, the size of this error would be $57 - 40 = 17$. Wyoming's turnout rate is 17 units higher than predicted, based only on the mean turnout for all states. Formally, this error can be labeled as $Y - \overline{Y}$, the actual value of Y minus the overall mean of Y. This value, calculated for every case, is the starting point for R-square. Specifically, R-square finds $(Y - \overline{Y})$ for each case, squares it, and then sums these squared values across all observations. The result is the total sum of squares of all deviations from the mean value of Y: $\Sigma (Y - \overline{Y})^2$. Let's label the total sum of squares TSS. The

Figure 7-3 Scatterplot with Mean of Y and Regression Estimate Ŷ: High School Graduates and Turnout, 1994 (percent)

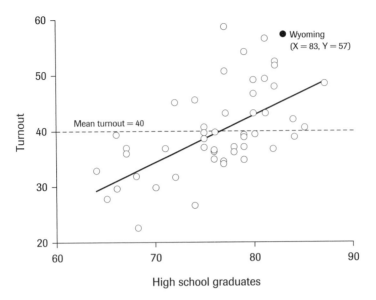

Source: State Politics and Policy Data Archive.
Note: Wyoming's estimated turnout = −26.27 + .87 (83) ≈ 46.

total sum of squares or TSS is an overall summary of all our missed guesses of turnout, based *only* on knowledge of the dependent variable.[8]

Now let's reconsider the regression line in Figure 7-3 and see how much it improves the prediction of Y. The regression line is the estimated level of turnout calculated *with* knowledge of the independent variable, education level. Now for each state, taken one at a time, we would not guess $\overline{Y}$, the overall mean of Y. Rather, we would guess $\hat{Y}$, the mean value of Y for a given value of X. Wyoming, for example, has a value of 83 on the independent variable, since 83 percent of its population has a high school diploma. What would be our estimate of its turnout level? Plugging 83 into the regression equation, for Wyoming we obtain −26.27 + .87(83) ≈ 46 on the turnout scale. Is our new guess, 46, better than our old guess, 40? Well, somewhat better. By guessing the mean, we "missed" Wyoming's actual turnout by 17 units. Our new estimate, 46, improves on our old guess by 6 units, since $\hat{Y} - \overline{Y}$ is equal to 46 − 40 = 6. So $\hat{Y}$ puts us a bit closer to the real value of Y. But the distance between Wyoming's actual turnout (Y) and our new estimate ($\hat{Y}$) remains unexplained. This is prediction error. For Wyoming, the size of the prediction error would be Y − $\hat{Y}$, or 57 − 46 = 11. Thus for Wyoming we could divide its total distance from the mean, 17 units, into two parts: the amount accounted for by the regression estimate, an amount equal to 6, and the amount left unaccounted for by the regression estimate, an amount equal to 11. More generally, in regression analysis the TSS has two components:

$$\text{Total Sum of Squares} = \text{Regression Sum of Squares} + \text{Error Sum of Squares}$$

$$\text{TSS} = \text{RSS} + \text{ESS}$$

$$\Sigma\,(Y - \overline{Y})^2 = \Sigma\,(\hat{Y} - \overline{Y})^2 + \Sigma\,(Y - \hat{Y})^2$$

TSS, as we saw, is a summary of all the variation in the dependent variable. RSS is the **regression sum of squares**, which is the component of TSS that we pick up by knowing the independent variable. ESS, the **error sum of squares** is the component of TSS that is left over, or not explained by the regression equation.[9] Obviously, if RSS is a large chunk of TSS, then the independent variable is doing a lot of work in explaining the dependent variable. As the contribution of RSS declines, and the contribution of ESS increases, knowledge of the independent variable provides less help in explaining the dependent variable. R-square is simply the ratio of RSS to TSS:

$$R^2 = RSS / TSS.$$

R-square measures the goodness of fit between the regression line and the actual data. If X completely explains Y, if RSS equals TSS, then R-square is 1. If RSS makes no contribution—if we would do just as well in accounting for Y without knowledge of X as with knowledge of X—then R-square is 0. R-square is a PRE measure and is always bracketed by 0 and 1. Its value may be interpreted as the proportion of the variation in Y that is explained by X. The computer reports that the R-square for the state data is equal to .36. Therefore, 36 percent of the variation among states in their turnout rates is accounted for by their levels of education. The leftover variation among states, 64 percent, may be explained by other variables, but it is not accounted for by differences in education.[10]

R-square, which sometimes goes by the serious-sounding label *coefficient of determination,* bears a family resemblance to r, Pearson's correlation coefficient. In fact, $R^2 = r^2$. So the value of R^2, just computed to be .36 for the state data, is the square of r, reported earlier to be +.6 for the same data. Pearson's r is widely used and well understood in political analysis, and it is a good measure to be familiar with. The problem with r is that it may mislead the consumer of political research into overestimating the relationship between two variables. Though researchers and instructors may hold different opinions on this point, R-square, because it is tied to the PRE standard, is the generally preferred measure of strength.[11]

DUMMY VARIABLE REGRESSION

As noted earlier, one attraction of regression analysis is its adaptability to a variety of research problems. In one very common situation, the researcher has a nominal or ordinal independent variable, not an interval-level independent variable. No problem. Regression will adapt. Consider the following regression equation, which sets up an analysis of the relationship between state turnout (again appearing as the dependent variable) and an independent variable labeled "South." The independent variable, which is categorical, identifies states as Southern or non-Southern.

$\hat{Y}$	=	$\hat{a}$	+	$\hat{b}$ (South)
Estimated turnout	=	Estimated turnout when South is 0	+	Mean change in turnout (South)

All of the elements of the equation are by now familiar. $\hat{Y}$ is the estimate of Y, turnout. The intercept, $\hat{a}$, "Estimated turnout when South is 0," is the value of $\hat{Y}$ when the independent variable, X, is 0. And $\hat{b}$, "Mean change in turnout," as before, is the average change in the dependent variable for each unit change in X. Now suppose that the independent variable,

Table 7-3 Voter Turnout in Southern and Non-Southern States

$\hat{Y}$	=	$\hat{a}$	+	$\hat{b}$	(X)
Estimated turnout	=	Estimated turnout when South is 0	+	Mean change in turnout	(South)
Estimated turnout	=	43.5	+	−10.4	(South)
Standard error of $\hat{b}$				2.01	
t-statistic				−5.19	
P-value				.000	
R-square = .36					

Source: State Politics and Policy Data Archive.

South, is coded so that non-Southern states have a value of 0. So South = 0 for all non-Southern states in the dataset. Suppose further that South is coded 1 for all Southern states, so that South = 1 for each Southern state in the dataset. South is a dummy variable. A **dummy variable** is a variable for which all cases falling into a specific category assume the value of 1, and all cases not falling into that category assume a value of 0. Now apply the regression logic. Since $\hat{a}$ is the value of $\hat{Y}$ when X is 0, $\hat{a}$ in the above equation will estimate the average level of turnout for non-Southern states. Why? Non-Southern states are coded 0 on South, so their estimated turnout is equal to

$$\hat{a} + \hat{b}\,(0) = \hat{a}.$$

Furthermore, the estimated turnout for Southern states will be equal to $\hat{a} + \hat{b}$. Why so? Because Southern states are coded 1 on South, making our estimate for their turnout

$$\hat{a} + \hat{b}\,(1) = \hat{a} + \hat{b}.$$

Nifty. Since regression is in the business of estimating means, it can be applied, by using dummy variables, to problems that compare the means on a dependent variable for subjects that differ on a nominal or ordinal variable. Table 7-3 reports the estimates obtained for the comparison of turnouts in Southern and non-Southern states.

Let's interpret these numbers. The estimate for the Y-intercept, in this case, is clearly meaningful. It communicates the average turnout for non-Southern states, a turnout rate of 43.5. The coefficient for $\hat{b}$, −10.4, tells us to adjust our estimate for Southern states relative to non-Southern states by minus 10.4 percent. So Southern states, on average, fall about 10 units below non-Southern states on the turnout scale. Remember that the regression coefficient, by itself, does not estimate turnout for Southern states. Rather, it reflects the average difference between states that have a value of 0 on South and states that have a value of 1 on South. When South switches from 0 to 1, average turnout drops by 10.4 units. We can, of course, use this information to arrive at an estimate of the average turnout for Southern states: 43.5 − 10.4 = 33.1.

What would the null hypothesis have to say about these results? The null hypothesis would assert that, in the population, no difference exists in the turnout rates of Southern and non-Southern states, that $\beta = 0$. Is the estimated average difference of -10.4 large enough to reject the null hypothesis? The t-ratio says so. Dividing the regression coefficient by its standard error, $-10.40/2.01$, yields a t-statistic of -5.19, well beyond the acceptable realm of random error. Finally, R-square, which is equal to .36, gives us an overall reading of how well we can explain differences in turnout by knowing whether states are Southern or non-Southern. The independent variable accounts for 36 percent of the variation among states in turnout rates.[12]

The dummy logic can be easily extended to nominal or ordinal variables that have more than two values. In the state data, for example, region is measured by four categories: Northeast, Midwest, West, and South. In the dummy regression just discussed, states in the Northeast, Midwest, and West were lumped together and coded 0 on the dummy variable, South. Southern states were given a value of 1 on the dummy. But suppose that you wanted to compare the turnout rates of all four regions. Again, regression adapts. Consider the following regression equation:

$$\text{Estimated turnout} = \hat{a} + \hat{b}_1 (\text{Northeast}) + \hat{b}_2 (\text{West}) + \hat{b}_3 (\text{South}).$$

Northeast is a dummy variable that takes on the value of 1 for Northeastern states, and a value of 0 for all other states. West too is a dummy, coded 1 for Western states and 0 otherwise. Similarly, South is 1 for Southern states, and 0 for all states not in the South. What about states located in the Midwest? Have we mistakenly excluded them from the equation? Not at all. Keep the "0 or 1" dummy idea in mind. A Midwestern state would have a value of 0 on Northeast, a value of 0 on West, and a value of 0 on South. The estimated turnout for Midwestern states, then, is captured by the Y-intercept, $\hat{a}$. As always, the intercept gives you the average value of the dependent variable when the independent variable is equal to 0. In this example, there are three dummies, each of which identifies a different category of region. When all these categories are 0, the intercept records the dependent variable for all the cases not included in any of the other categories. In the parlance of dummy variable regression, the intercept estimates the value of Y for the "base" or "excluded" category of X.

There are a few rules to keep in mind when setting up a regression with dummy variables. First, in doing dummy regression with an independent variable that has K categories, the number of dummies should be equal to $K - 1$. Since region has four categories, we include three dummies in the equation. This rule was applied in the earlier example, too. The independent variable had two categories, non-South and South, so the regression had one dummy, South. A second rule is that the categories must be mutually exclusive and jointly exhaustive. Mutually exclusive means that any case that is coded 1 in one category must be coded 0 in all other categories. Jointly exhaustive means that all the categories account for all the cases, so that no cases are left unclassified. Cases in the base or excluded category meet these conditions, since they are uniquely classified by their absence from all the other categories.

Now consider the notation and meaning of the regression coefficients. To keep their identities separate, each coefficient has its own subscript: $\hat{b}_1$, $\hat{b}_2$, and $\hat{b}_3$. What does each coefficient mean? The coefficient for $\hat{b}_1$ will tell us the average difference in turnout between Northeastern states and the average turnout for the base category, Midwestern states. Similarly, $\hat{b}_2$ adjusts the value of the intercept for states in the West, and $\hat{b}_3$ gives us the average difference between Southern states and the base category. Let's look at the results of the analy-

Table 7-4 Estimating Voter Turnout in Four Regions

Estimated turnout =	â	+	$\hat{b}_1$ (Northeast)	+	$\hat{b}_2$ (West)	+	$\hat{b}_3$ (South)
	44.7 +		− 3.4	+	−.7	+	−11.6
Standard error of $\hat{b}$			2.93		2.66		2.54
t-statistic			−1.16		−.26		−4.57
P-value			.25		.79		.00
R-square = .38							

Source: State Politics and Policy Data Archive.

sis, presented in Table 7-4, and clarify these points. According to the regression estimates, the turnout rate for states in the base category, Midwestern states, is 44.7, since â = 44.7. Do the other three regions have higher or lower turnouts than this? Well, the coefficient for Northeast is −3.4, telling us that, on average, the turnout rate for these states is 3.4 units lower than the base, or 44.7 − 3.4 = 41.3. The average for Western states, too, is a bit lower than the base rate of 44.7. However, judging from the estimate for $\hat{b}_2$, −.7, the mean turnout for Western states is only slightly less than turnout in the Midwest. A much larger adjustment is called for in the case of Southern states. Southern states, on average, score 11.6 units below the intercept, since $\hat{b}_3$ = −11.6. That places their mean turnout at 44.7 − 11.6 = 33.1.

The interpretation of the t-statistics and P-values is exactly the same as before. You can see that the coefficients for $\hat{b}_1$ and $\hat{b}_2$ do not pass muster with the null hypothesis. The t-ratio for $\hat{b}_1$, −1.16, and its accompanying P-value, .25, suggest that the average difference between Midwestern and Northeastern can be accounted for by sampling error. Ditto for $\hat{b}_2$, with t = −.26 and P = .79. The coefficient for South, though, is significantly different from zero. Its t-ratio of −4.57 and P-value of .00 suggest that the estimate of $\hat{b}_3$ is too large to have occurred by chance.

MULTIPLE REGRESSION

By now you are getting a feel for regression analysis, and you may be gaining an appreciation for its malleability. Ordinary least squares regression, along with its more sophisticated relatives, is one of the most powerful techniques available to the political researcher. Indeed, once you become comfortable with this method, you can begin using it to model and estimate complex relationships. In **multiple regression**, for example, we are able to isolate the effect of one independent variable on the dependent variable, while controlling for the effects of other independent variables.

Consider some of the variables we have used in this chapter to explain differences in turnout. In discussing simple bivariate regression, we analyzed the relationship between turnout and state education level. In looking at dummy regression, we analyzed the relationship between turnout and the two-category dummy, South. In each case we found the independent variable to be related to turnout. But there is a problem. What if these two independent variables, education and South, are themselves related? That is, what if Southern states tend to have lower high school graduation rates than non-Southern states? If they are related, then at least some of the education-turnout relationship includes the effect of South. By the same token, some of the bivariate relationship between South and turnout is being confounded by educational differences between Southern and non-Southern states.

Table 7-5 Regression Estimates for Education Level and South, for Dependent Variable, Voter Turnout

Estimated turnout	=	â	+	$\hat{b}_1$ (Education)	+	$\hat{b}_2$(South)
		3.4	+	.5	+	−5.9
Standard error of $\hat{b}$				.24		2.92
t-statistic				2.08		−2.02
P-value				.04		.05
R-square = .41						

Source: State Politics and Policy Data Archive.

The logic of controlled comparison tells us how to sort this out. If we had categorical variables and were doing cross-tabulation analysis, we would separate the states into two categories, non-Southern states and Southern states. (This would make South the control variable, Z.) We would then reexamine the relationship between education level (X) and turnout (Y) separately for each category of the control. Thus we would isolate the effect of education on turnout—the partial effect of X on Y, controlling for Z. As you know, by jumping between control tables, we also could isolate the effect of South on turnout—the partial effect of Z on Y, controlling for X.

Multiple regression does the same thing. Multiple regression estimates a partial slope—the pure effect of X on Y, controlling for Z. And just as in the analysis of control tables, regression will estimate the partial effect of Z on Y, controlling for X. In this case, the multiple regression model would take the form

$$Y = â + \hat{b}_1 (X) + \hat{b}_2 (Z).$$

There is but one difference between this equation and the model for bivariate regression. But it is an important difference. The coefficient, $\hat{b}_1$, estimates the average change in Y for each unit change in X, controlling for Z. The coefficient, $\hat{b}_2$, estimates the average change in Y for each unit change in Z, controlling for X. Thus $\hat{b}_1$ and $\hat{b}_2$ tell us the partial effects of each independent variable on the dependent variable. The intercept, â, estimates the mean of Y when both X and Z are zero. To illustrate the basic properties of multiple regression—and to point out some of its limitations and pitfalls—we return to the state turnout data.

Here is the regression model we want to estimate:

$$\text{Estimated turnout} = â + \hat{b}_1 \text{ (Education level)} + \hat{b}_2 \text{ (South)}.$$

The coefficient $\hat{b}_1$ will estimate the partial effect of education level, controlling for South. The coefficient $\hat{b}_2$ will estimate the partial effect of South, controlling for education level. Table 7-5 reports the results.

Let's consider Table 7-5 and interpret the coefficients. According to Table 7-5, the regression coefficient for the effect of education on turnout is .5. In the context of multiple regression, what does this mean? Regression statistically divided the cases into categories of Z (South) and then found the best estimate of the partial effect of education on turnout. So the estimate for $\hat{b}_1$, .5, means that, if South is held constant, a one-unit increase in education is associated with about a half-unit increase in turnout. Similarly, the coefficient for South, −5.9, says that, after we control for educational differences (X) between Southern and non-Southern states, Southern states still averaged 5.9 units lower on the turnout scale. Is the effect of education contaminated by the possible relationship between X and Z? No, the regression has controlled for Z. Might Southern states have lower turnouts because they have proportionately fewer high school graduates than non-Southern states? No, again. Multiple regression has taken this into account.

The interpretation of most of the remaining numbers in Table 7-5—the standard errors, the t-ratios, and the P-values—follows much the same protocol as for bivariate regression. The t-statistics and P-values suggest that each variable has an independent effect on turnout. In fact, with t-ratios at around 2, both pass the eyeball test of significance. In multiple regression, R-square takes on a more expansive PRE meaning. Its value communicates how completely *all* the independent variables explain the dependent variable. An R-square of .41 says that by knowing two things about states, the percentage of the population with a high school education and whether or not they are located in the South, we can account for 41 percent of their differences in turnout. Again, the other 59 percent remains unexplained by the two variables in the model.

Interaction Effects in Multiple Regression

The multiple regression technique is linear and additive. It controls for one independent variable (Z) and then estimates a single partial effect of the other independent variable (X). In doing this, regression assumes the effect of X on Y is the same for all values of Z. In the example just discussed, for instance, regression estimated the partial effect of education level on turnout, controlling for South. The estimates produced by the technique were based on the assumption that the effect of education on turnout is the same for non-Southern states and Southern states. So, according to the results, in non-Southern and Southern states alike, a one-unit increase in education is associated with a half-unit increase in turnout.

In its natural form, multiple regression is ready-made for detecting spurious relationships and for modeling additive relationships. If the researcher thinks that the relationship between South and turnout might be spurious—that the apparent regional difference in turnout is the spurious result of educational differences between non-Southern and Southern states—then multiple regression will ferret out this spurious effect. If additive relationships are at work, with both variables contributing to our understanding of turnout, regression will estimate the partial effects of each one.

In Chapter 4 we discussed interaction relationships. In an interaction relationship, you will recall, the effect of the independent variable (X) on the dependent variable (Y) is not the same for all values of the control variable (Z). In multiple regression analysis, an interaction relationship is often called an **interaction effect**. An interaction effect occurs when the combined effect of two independent variables is greater than their separate, partial effects. In the regression we just estimated, for example, multiple regression's linear-additive coefficients would tell us to estimate turnout by adding the partial effect of education level (X) to the partial effect of South (Z). But what if states having a combination of these characteristics—Southern states with high percentages of high school graduates—had significantly higher turnouts than one would predict on the basis of X and Z alone? That is, what if the effect of education on turnout was much greater in the South than in the non-South? If this were the case, then the model we have described and estimated would be an incorrect depiction of the relationship. Most of the time, multiple regression's linear-additive assumptions work pretty

Table 7-6 Mean Pro-Choice Scale, by Gender and Level of Education (tabular)[a]

| Gender | Education | | Total |
	High school or less	*More than high school*	
Male	4.04	5.14	4.43
	(460)	(255)	(715)
Female	3.50	5.76	4.20
	(690)	(311)	(1001)
Total	3.72	5.48	4.30
	(1,150)	(566)	(1,716)

Source: James A. Davis, Tom W. Smith, and Peter V. Marsden, *General Social Surveys, 1972–2002* (Chicago, Ill.: National Opinion Research Center [producer], 2003; Storrs, Conn.: Roper Center for Public Opinion Research, University of Connecticut/Ann Arbor, Mich.: Inter-university Consortium for Political and Social Research [distributors], 2003).

Note: Displayed data are from the 1998 General Social Survey.

[a] Interviewer prompt: "Please tell me whether or not you think it should be possible for a pregnant women to obtain a legal abortion if. . . ." The pro-choice scale was constructed by summing the number of "yes" responses to the prompts "If she is married and does not want any more children?," "If the family has very low income and cannot afford any more children?," and "If she is not married and does not want to marry the man?" The scale was rescaled to vary between 0 (low pro-choice opinion) and 10 (high pro-choice opinion).

well. However, if interaction is going on in the data, or the researcher has described an explanation or process that implies interaction, then a different model needs to be identified.

The analysis of interaction effects using regression is a somewhat advanced application of the method. So let's begin by looking at a highly simplified example of interaction using mean comparison analysis. We then show how to model the same relationship using multiple regression.

An interesting perspective on public opinion in American politics says that political disagreements often become more intense as one ascends the socioeconomic ladder. People with more education and income, according to this view, are more polarized on important issues than are people with less education and income. Consider a phenomenon used throughout this book, the gender gap. If the polarization perspective has merit, then the gender gap should be more pronounced among individuals with higher education and income than among individuals with lower education and income. From a methodological standpoint, this perspective implies interaction: In comparing males and females on an important issue, the size of the gender gap will be greater for men and women with higher education or income than for men and women with lower education or income. So the effect of gender (X) on a political issue (Y) will be greater for one value of Z (higher education or income) than for another value of Z (lower education or income).

We use data from the 1998 General Social Survey (GSS) to test this idea, first using mean comparison analysis. The independent variable, X, is gender, male and female. For the dependent variable, Y, we use a measure of pro-choice abortion opinions. Higher scores on this variable denote stronger pro-choice views. The control variable, Z, categorizes respondents by level of education: high school or less and more than high school. Table 7-6 compares mean values on the pro-choice scale for males and females at two levels of education. Figure 7-4 is the line graph based on Table 7-6.

Figure 7-4 Mean Pro-Choice Scale, by Gender and Level of Education (1998) (graphic)

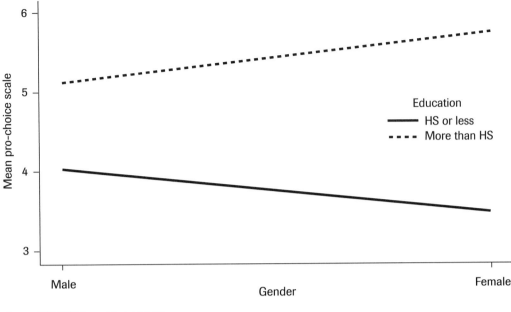

Source: 1972–2002 General Social Surveys.
Note: Displayed data are from 1998.

Examine these (somewhat surprising) relationships for a few moments. In both tabular and graphic forms, you will recognize the signature of interaction. Notice that, as expected, men and women with more education are divided on this issue. Tracing from left to right along the "More than high school" line in Figure 7-4, you see that mean scores rise about .6 of a unit on the 10-point scale, communicating that women, on average, are more pro-choice than men. Unexpectedly, however, a gender gap of similar magnitude also appears among less-educated respondents—a *reverse* gender gap. Whereas males with lower levels of education averaged 4.04, less-educated females were even less favorably disposed toward the pro-choice position, averaging 3.50, or about .5 of a unit lower than their male counterparts. Notice, too, that the partial effect of education is much larger for women than for men—more than a 2-unit effect for women (from 3.50 to 5.76) but only a bit more than a 1-unit effect for men (from 4.04 to 5.14).

Clearly we are not dealing with linear-additive effects here. What regression equation would accurately depict these relationships? Consider the following model:

$$\hat{Y} = \hat{a} + \hat{b}_1(\text{female}) + \hat{b}_2(\text{high education}) + \hat{b}_3(\text{female} * \text{high education}), \text{ where}$$

$\hat{Y}$ is estimated pro-choice scale score;

female is a dummy variable, coded 1 for women and 0 for men; and

high education is a dummy variable, coded 1 for respondents with more than a high school education and 0 for respondents with a high school education or less.

This equation is, in most respects, a no-frills multiple regression with dummy variables. Female is a dummy, coded 1 for women and 0 for men. The variable high education is a

Table 7-7 Modeling Interaction in Regression: Gender, Education, and Pro-Choice Opinions

Estimated pro-choice scale	= â	+ $\hat{b}_1$ (female) +	$\hat{b}_2$ (high education)	+ $\hat{b}_3$ (female * high education)
	4.04	+ −.55 (female) +	1.09 (high education)	+ 1.16 (female * high education)
Standard error of $\hat{b}$		.276	.358	.476
t-statistic		−1.98	3.06	2.45
P-value		.05	.00	.01

Source: 1998 General Social Survey.

dummy, coded 1 for respondents having more than a high school education and 0 for people with a high school education or less. The estimated value of Y for the base categories of both variables is captured by the intercept. In this model, â will report the average pro-choice score for males (since female = 0) who have low education (since high education = 0). The coefficient $\hat{b}_1$ adjusts the Y-intercept for women, telling us how much to add or subtract from the base category for females. Thus the estimate of Y for less-educated women would be $\hat{a} + \hat{b}_1$, since female = 1 and high education = 0. The coefficient $\hat{b}_2$ does the adjustment for education, telling us how much to add or subtract to the base for males with higher levels of education. So to estimate the value of Y for more-educated males we calculate the sum, $\hat{a} + \hat{b}_2$.

What about women with more education? Don't the coefficients for female and high education allow us to estimate the value of Y for more highly educated women? In part they do. When both dummies switch to 1, our estimate of Y would begin with $\hat{a} + \hat{b}_1 + \hat{b}_2$, adding the effect of being female to the effect of being more highly educated. But the data in Table 7-6 clearly show interaction between gender and education, with more-educated women having much stronger pro-choice views than one would predict on the basis of their education alone. This effect is represented by the term female * high education and its accompanying coefficient, $\hat{b}_3$. The term female * high education captures the interaction effect. It takes on the value of 1 for only one combination of gender and education: females with higher levels of education, respondents for whom female = 1 *and* high education = 1. For this subgroup of respondents, $\hat{b}_3$ will tell us how much more to adjust Y, over and above the partial effects of gender and education considered by themselves.

The estimates are reported in Table 7-7. Notice that the effect of female ($\hat{b}_1$) alone is negative and statistically significant. This communicates that, among the less educated, women scored significantly lower than men on the pro-choice scale. Less-educated men averaged 4.04, and less-educated women about .55 less—thus the reverse gender gap we noted earlier. Notice too the positive and significant coefficient on high education. This tells us that men with more education, on average, score about 1 unit higher on the scale than do men with less education, or 4.04 + 1.09 = 5.13. Now let's estimate the dependent variable for women with more education. All the coefficients are switched on for this estimation. We start with the intercept, 4.04; adjust for the effect of being female (−.55); and then add the effect of having more education (1.09). Summing these three coefficients, we get 4.04 + (−.55) + 1.09 = 4.58. Obviously this estimate leaves us short of the mark, since more-educated females have stronger pro-choice opinions than one would predict on the basis of the independent effects of gender and high education. It is here that the interaction effect, the coefficient on female * high education, enters the picture. This effect, equal to 1.16, is positive and significant. It tells us to add another 1.16 units for more-educated women, to further adjust for the combined effect of being female *and* having more education. Doing so yields an estimate that reproduces (with some rounding error) the mean pro-choice scale score in Table 7-6 for women with higher levels of education: $4.04 + (-.55) + 1.09 + 1.16 = 5.74$.[13]

A Problem to Look Out For: Multicollinearity

In several examples in this chapter, multiple regression was used to estimate the partial effects of two independent variables on a dependent variable. However, the technique is not limited to two independent variables. In fact, the researcher may include any number of independent variables in the equation. In explaining state turnout, for example, we could hypothesize that yet another state-level variable—say, the degree of interparty competition in the state—has an effect on turnout. We could easily enter this variable into the equation and estimate its partial effects. By the same token, in accounting for differences in pro-choice opinions, we could come up with other plausible variables, such as partisanship or religiosity, and further expand the model. Multiple regression would oblige by returning regression coefficients, t-statistics, R-square, and all the rest. If the researcher becomes too enamored of the power and flexibility of multiple regression, however, a serious statistical problem may be overlooked.

This problem can best be appreciated by thinking of controlled comparisons in cross-tabulations. Consider a realistic example. Suppose that you were using survey data, and you wanted to figure out the relationship between an independent variable, race (white/black), and a dependent variable, turnout (voted/did not vote). The bivariate analysis would be easy enough: Compare the percentage of whites who voted with the percentage of blacks who voted. But suppose further that you wanted to control for partisanship (Democrat/Republican). Logically, this too is easily accomplished. You would divide the subjects on the basis of partisanship—Democrats in one group, Republicans in the other—and then reexamine the race-turnout relationship separately for Democrats and Republicans. At that point you would encounter a classic problem. When you looked at the group of Republicans and sought to compare whites with blacks, you would find very few blacks—too few, in fact, to make a reasonable comparison. The problem, of course, is that the two independent variables, race and partisanship, are very strongly related. Blacks are overwhelmingly Democratic. So when you divide the sample into Democrats and Republicans, most of the blacks remain in one category of the control, Democrat. You might have a few black Republicans, but the percentages you calculated would be highly suspect, because they would be computed on so few cases.

The same problem occurs in multiple regression, and it has an intimidating name—**multicollinearity**. Multicollinearity occurs when the independent variables are so strongly related to each other that it becomes difficult to estimate the partial effect of each independent variable on the dependent variable. In its attempt to statistically control for one independent variable so that it can estimate the partial effect of the other independent variable, regression runs into the same problem encountered in the cross-tabulation example: too few cases. Now, it is okay for the independent variables to be related. After all, the beauty of multiple regression is its ability to partial out the shared variance of the independent variables and arrive at estimates of the regression coefficients. The problem lies in the degree of relationship between the independent variables.

How can you tell if multicollinearity is a problem? If the magnitude of the correlation coefficient between the independent variables is less than .8, then multiple regression will work fine. If the correlation is .8 or higher, then multiple regression will not return good estimates. The regression model estimating state turnout from education and South, for example, suffers from only a mild case of the multicollinearity disease, since the correlation between the two independent variables is about .6. Another important clue is provided by comparing the value of R-square when one independent variable is included in the regression to the value of R-square when both variables are included. This comparison tells you how much better you can account for the dependent variable by knowing both independent variables. If the two independent variables are strongly related, then there will not be much improvement in R-square. In the state turnout example, we improved our explanation of turnout to some degree. R-square using education level was .36. Using education and South produced an R-square of .41.

SUMMARY

In this chapter we introduced two powerful techniques of political analysis, correlation and regression. Correlation and regression together provide the answers to four questions about a relationship: (1) How strong is the relationship? (2) What is the direction of the relationship? (3) What is the exact nature of the relationship? (4) Could the observed relationship have occurred by chance? As we have seen, correlation speaks to questions of strength and direction. If the researcher has interval-level measurements for two variables, Pearson's r will summarize direction with a positive or negative sign on r, and it will give a reading of strength, from −1 to +1. Researchers typically use correlation analysis during the early stages of the research process, to explore the overall relationships between variables of interest.

Regression analysis is somewhat more specialized than correlation. Regression, too, reveals the direction of the relationship between an independent variable and a dependent variable. A positive or negative sign on a regression coefficient indicates which way the relationship runs, with a positive slope indicating a positive relationship and a negative slope indicating an inverse relationship. Regression is often used to examine the causal connection between the variables. The regression coefficient, as we have seen, reveals the exact nature of this connection: the mean change in the dependent variable for each unit change in the independent variable. Thanks to the statistics provided by regression, the researcher also can test the null hypothesis that the true regression coefficient is equal to zero. Regression analysis provides a measure of strength as well. R-square is a PRE measure that tells the researcher how completely the independent variable explains the dependent variable.

KEY TERMS

correlation analysis (p. 154)
dummy variable (p. 166)
error sum of squares (ESS) (p. 165)
interaction effect (p. 170)
multicollinearity (p. 174)
multiple regression (p. 168)
Pearson's correlation coefficient (p. 156)
prediction error (p. 161)

regression analysis (p. 154)
regression coefficient (p. 158)
regression line (p. 158)
regression sum of squares (RSS) (p. 165)
R-square (p. 163)
scatterplot (p. 155)
total sum of squares (TSS) (p. 164)

EXERCISES

1. A researcher is investigating the relationship between economic development (X) and level of religiosity (Y) in 10 countries. (The researcher has interval-level measurements for both variables.) The researcher theorizes that citizens of countries at the lower end of the development scale will profess higher levels of religiosity than will citizens of countries at the higher end of the development scale. As development increases, religiosity decreases. Draw and label four sets of axes, like the one below:

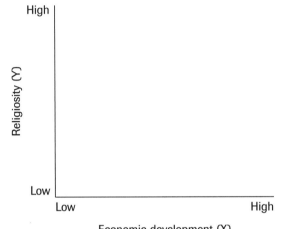

A. Is the researcher hypothesizing a positive correlation between X and Y, a negative correlation between X and Y, or no correlation between X and Y? Explain.

B. In the first set of axes you have drawn, and using a dot to represent each of the 10 countries, depict a correlation of −1 between economic development and level of religiosity.

C. In the second set of axes, depict a correlation of +1 between economic development and level of religiosity.

D. In the third set of axes, depict a correlation of 0 between economic development and level of religiosity.

E. Suppose the researcher finds a correlation of −.7 between the independent and dependent variables. In the fourth set of axes, show what a correlation of −.7 would look like. (Just make it look plausible. It doesn't have to be precise.)

F. Based on a correlation of −.7, the researcher concludes, "Level of economic development explains 70 percent of the variation in level of religiosity." Is this correct? Explain. (Hint: Review the difference between Pearson's r and R-square.)

2. *Environmental equity* is an interesting, and somewhat controversial, area of research. Some observers have argued that when state and local governments decide where to locate undesirable facilities, such as hazardous waste treatment plants, they choose areas more heavily populated with minorities. So, in this view, the racial composition of an area (X) should predict the area's proximity (Y) to environmental and health hazards. Below are fabricated data for 10 census blocks. The independent variable is percent black, and the dependent variable is the distance (in miles) between each block and the nearest hazardous waste treatment facility. The hypothesis: In comparing census blocks, those with higher percentages of blacks will be closer to hazards than will blocks having lower percentages of blacks.

Census block:	Percent black (X)	Distance in miles (Y)
Block 1	0	27
Block 2	0	23
Block 3	10	22
Block 4	10	18
Block 5	20	17
Block 6	20	13
Block 7	30	12
Block 8	30	8
Block 9	40	6
Block 10	40	4

A. What is the regression equation for this relationship? Interpret the regression coefficient. What is the effect of X on Y?

B. Interpret the Y-intercept. What does the intercept tell you, exactly?

C. Based on this equation, what is the predicted value of Y for census blocks that are 15 percent black? Census blocks that are 25 percent black?

D. The R-square for these data is .94. Interpret this value.

3. Are Catholics more likely to oppose abortion rights than are non-Catholics? To find out, a researcher first constructs an abortion scale from responses to the 1998 GSS. Scores range from 0 (abortion should be permitted under all circumstances) to 7 (abortion should not be permitted under any circumstances). So respondents with lower scores are more pro-choice, and respondents with higher scores are more pro-life. This is the dependent variable, Y. The researcher then creates a dummy variable. Catholics are coded 1 on this dummy, and non-Catholics are coded 0. This is the independent variable, X. Here are the regression results:

$$Y = 2.6 + .56(X)$$
$$\text{Standard error of } b = .15$$
$$R^2 = .01$$

A. Based on these findings, the researcher concludes: "While non-Catholics averaged 2.6 on the abortion scale, Catholics averaged only .56 on the scale. Therefore, Catholics are more pro-choice than are non-Catholics." Is this inference correct? Why or why not?

B. Another conclusion reached by the researcher: "The independent variable does not have a statistically significant effect on the dependent variable." Is this inference correct? Why or why not?

C. Yet another of the researcher's conclusions: "The independent variable explains very little of the variation in the dependent variable." Is this inference correct? Why or why not?

4. Another researcher, after viewing the puny value of R^2 in Exercise 3, suggests that another variable, the frequency with which individuals attend religious services, may contribute to the explanation of abortion beliefs. This researcher defines a dummy variable, which is coded 1 for individuals who report high levels of religious attendance and coded 0 for people who have low levels of attendance. The regression to be estimated: $Y = a + b_1(X_1) + b_2(X_2)$, where X_1 is the Catholic/non-Catholic dummy (Catholics are coded 1, non-Catholics coded 0) and X_2 is the high attendance/low attendance dummy. Here are the results (the standard errors for the regression coefficients are in parentheses):

$$Y = 2.14 + .50(X_1) + 1.95(X_2)$$
$$(.14) (.14)$$

$R^2 = .12$

A. What is the *partial* effect of Catholicism on the abortion scale, controlling for attendance at religious services? Is it reasonable to infer that, in the population, Catholics are more opposed to abortion than are non-Catholics? Explain.

B. What is the partial effect of attendance on the abortion scale, controlling for differences between Catholics and non-Catholics? Is it reasonable to infer that, in the population, people who attend services more frequently are more opposed to abortion than are people who attend less frequently? Explain.

C. Based on this regression, what is the mean abortion score for non-Catholic low-attenders? For Catholic high-attenders?

D. The R^2 value is .12. This means that ____ percent of the variation in abortion scores is explained by both variables in the model. It also means that ____ percent is explained by variables *not* in the model. Name one other variable that may account for differences in the dependent variable. Briefly describe why you think this variable may contribute to the explanation of abortion attitudes.[14]

8

Logistic Regression

LEARNING OBJECTIVES

In this chapter you will learn:
- How to use logistic regression to describe the relationship between an interval-level independent variable and a dichotomous dependent variable
- How logistic regression is similar to—and different from—ordinary least squares regression
- How maximum likelihood estimation works
- How to use logistic regression with multiple independent variables

Political analysis is not unlike using a toolbox. The researcher looks at the substantive problem at hand, selects the methodological tool most appropriate for analyzing the relationship, and then proceeds with the analysis. Selection of the correct tool is determined largely by the levels of measurement of the variables of interest. If both the independent and dependent variables are measured by nominal or ordinal categories—a common situation, particularly in survey research—the researcher would most likely select cross-tabulation analysis. If both the independent and dependent variables are interval level, then ordinary least squares (OLS) regression would be applied. Finally, if you wanted to analyze the relationship between an interval-level dependent variable and a categorical independent variable, then you might use mean comparison analysis or, alternatively, you could specify and test a linear regression model using dummy variables. These techniques, all of which have been discussed in earlier chapters, add up to a well-stocked toolbox. Even so, one set of tools is missing.

Logistic regression is part of a family of techniques designed to analyze the relationship between an interval-level independent variable and a categorical dependent variable, a dependent variable measured by nominal or ordinal values. The dependent variable might have any number of categories—from several, to a few, to two. In this chapter we discuss how to use and interpret logistic regression in the simplest of these situations, when the dependent variable takes on only two values. For example, suppose we are using survey data to investigate the relationship between education and voter turnout. We think that a positive relationship exists here: As education increases, so does the likelihood of voting. The independent variable, education, is measured in precise 1-year increments, from 0 (no formal education) to 20 (20 years of schooling). The dependent variable, however, takes on only two values—respondents either voted or they did not vote. In this situation, we have a binary dependent variable. A **binary variable** is a dichotomous variable, one that can assume only two values. Binary variables are identical to dummy variables, discussed in Chapter 7. Thus voted/did not vote, smoker/nonsmoker, approve/do not approve, and married/unmarried are all examples of dummy variables or binary variables.[1]

In some ways, logistic regression is similar to OLS regression. Like OLS, logistic regression gauges the effect of the independent variable by estimating an intercept and a slope, both familiar fixtures of linear regression. Plus logistic regression provides a standard error for the slope, which allows the researcher to test hypotheses about the effect of the independent variable on the dependent variable. And like OLS, logistic regression is remarkably flexible, permitting the use of multiple independent variables, including dummy independent variables.

In one fundamental way, however, logistic regression is a different breed of cat. When we perform OLS regression, we can reasonably assume a linear relationship between an independent variable (X) and a dependent variable (Y). For example, for the relationship between years of schooling (X) and income in dollars (Y), we can use a linear model to estimate the average dollar-change in income for each 1-year increase in education. OLS would give us an idea of how closely the relationship between X and Y fits this linear pattern. However, when we have a binary dependent variable, we must assume that it bears a nonlinear relationship to X. So as education (X) increases from 8 years to 9 years to 10 years, we most plausibly assume that the likelihood of voting (Y) is low and increases slightly for each of these 1-year increments. But as education increases from 11 years to 12 years to 13 years, we would expect voter turnout to show large increases for each 1-year increment in this range of X. In the higher values of education—say, beyond 13 years—we would assume that turnout is already high and that each additional year of schooling would have a weaker effect on voting. A logistic regression analysis would give us an idea of how closely the relationship between X and Y fits this nonlinear pattern.

This chapter is divided into four sections. In the first section we use both hypothetical and real-world data to illustrate the logic behind logistic regression. Here you will be introduced to some unfamiliar terms—such as odds and logged odds—that define the workings of the technique, and you will learn what to look for in your own analyses and how to describe and interpret your findings. In the second section we take a closer look at maximum likelihood estimation, the method logistic regression uses to estimate the effect of the independent variable (or variables) on the dependent variable. Here you will see how logistic regression is similar to other techniques and statistics we discussed previously, particularly chi-square. In the third section we demonstrate how the logistic regression model, much like multiple linear regression, can be extended to accommodate several independent variables. Finally, we will consider some additional ways to present and interpret logistic regression results. By the end of this chapter you will have added another powerful technique to your toolbox of political research methods.

THE LOGISTIC REGRESSION APPROACH

Let's begin with a hypothetical example. Suppose we are investigating whether education (X) affects voter turnout (Y) among a random sample of respondents (n = 500). For purposes of

Table 8-1 Education and the Probability of Voting

Did respondent vote?	Education					
	0. Low	*1. Middle-low*	*2. Middle*	*3. Middle-high*	*4. High*	*Total*
1. Yes, voted	6	20	50	80	94	250
0. No, did not vote	94	80	50	20	6	250
Total (n)	100	100	100	100	100	500
Probability of voting	.06	.20	.50	.80	.94	.50

Note: Hypothetical data.

illustration, let's assume that the independent variable, education, is an interval-level variable that varies from 0 (low) to 4 (high), and that voter turnout is a binary dependent variable, coded 1 if the individual voted and 0 if he or she did not vote. Table 8-1 shows the results from a cross-tabulation analysis of the hypothetical sample data. Although column percentages have not been supplied in Table 8-1, they are easy to figure out because each value of education contains exactly 100 cases. For example, of the 100 people in the low-education category, 6 voted—a percentage equal to 6 or a proportion equal to .06. Twenty percent (.20) of the 100 middle-low education individuals voted, 50 percent (.50) of the middle group voted, and so on. The bottom row of Table 8-1 presents the proportion of voters for each value of education, but it uses the label "Probability of voting." Why use *probability* instead of *proportion*? The two terms are synonymous. Think of it this way: If you were to randomly select one individual from the group of 100 low-education respondents, what is the probability that this randomly selected person voted? Because random selection guarantees that each case has an equal chance of being picked, there are 6 chances in 100—a probability of .06—of selecting a voter from this group. Similarly, you could say that there is a random probability of voting equal to .06 for any individual in the low-education category, a probability of .20 for any respondent in the middle-low group, and so on. It is important to shift your thinking from proportions to probabilities, because logistic regression is aimed at determining how well an independent variable (or set of independent variables) predicts the probability of an occurrence, such as the probability of voting.

Consider the Table 8-1 probabilities and make some substantive observations. Clearly a positive relationship exists between education and the probability of voting: As education (X) goes up, so does the probability of voting (Y). Now examine this pattern more closely and apply the logic of linear regression. Does a one-unit increase in the independent variable produce a consistent increase in the probability of voting? Starting with the interval between low and middle-low, the probability goes from .06 to .20—an increase of .14. So by increasing the independent variable by 1 in this interval, we see a .14 increase in the probability of voting. Between middle-low and middle, however, this effect increases substantially, from .20 to .50— a jump of .30. The next increment, from middle to middle-high, produces another .30 increase in the probability of voting, from .50 to .80. But this effect levels off again between the two highest values of the independent variable. Moving from middle-high to high education occasions a more modest increase of .14 in the probability of voting. Thus the linear logic does not work very well. A unit change in education produces a change in the probability of voting of either .14 or .30, depending on the range of the independent variable examined. Put another way, the probability of voting (Y) has a nonlinear relationship to education (X).

Rest assured that there are very good statistical reasons the researcher should not use OLS regression to estimate the effect of an interval-level independent variable on a binary dependent variable.[2] Perhaps as important, there are compelling substantive reasons you would not expect a linear model to fit a relationship such as the one depicted in Table 8-1. Think about this for a moment. Suppose you made $10,000 a year and were faced with the decision of whether to make a major purchase, such as buying a home. There is a good chance that you would decide not to make the purchase. Now suppose that your income rose to $20,000, a $10,000 increase. To be sure, this rise in income might affect your reasoning, but most likely it would not push your decision over the purchasing threshold, from a decision not to buy to a decision to buy. Similarly, if your initial income were $95,000, you would probably decide to buy the house, and an incremental $10,000 change, to $105,000, would have a weak effect on this decision—you were very likely to make the purchase in the first place. But suppose that you made $45,000. At this income level, you might look at your decision a bit differently: "If I made more money, I could afford a house." Thus that $10,000 pay raise would push you over the threshold. Going from $45,000 to $55,000 greatly enhances the probability that you would make the move from "do not buy" to "buy." So at low and high initial levels of income, an incremental change in the causal variable has a weaker effect on your dichotomous decision (do not buy/buy) than does the same incremental change in the middle range of income.

Although fabricated, the probabilities in Table 8-1 show a plausible pattern. Less-educated individuals are unlikely to vote, and you would not expect a small increment in education to make a huge difference in the probability of voting. The same idea applies to people in the upper education range. Individuals in the middle-high to high category are already quite likely to vote. It would be unreasonable to suggest that, for highly educated people, a one-unit increase in the independent variable would have a big effect on the likelihood of voting. It is in the middle intervals of the independent variable—from middle-low to middle-high—where you might predict that education would have its strongest effect on the dependent variable. As people in this range gain more of the resource (education) theoretically linked to voting, a marginal change in the independent variable is most likely to switch their dichotomous decision from "do not vote" to "vote." Logistic regression allows us to specify a model that takes into account this nonlinear relationship between education and the probability of voting.

As we have seen, the first step in understanding logistic regression is to think in terms of the probability of an outcome. The next step is to get into the habit of thinking in terms of the odds of an outcome. This transition really is not too difficult, because odds are an alternative way of expressing probabilities. Whereas probabilities are based on the number of occurrences of one outcome (such as voting) divided by the total number of outcomes (voting plus nonvoting), **odds** are based on the number of occurrences of one outcome (voting) divided by the number of occurrences of the other outcome (nonvoting). According to Table 8-1, for example, among the 100 people in the middle-high education group, there were 80 voters—a probability of voting equal to 80/100 or .80. What are the odds of voting for this group? Using the raw numbers of voters and nonvoters, the odds would be 80 to 20, or, to use a more conventional way of verbalizing odds, 4 to 1, four voters to every nonvoter. In describing odds, we ordinarily drop the ". . . to 1" part of the verbalization and say that the odds of voting are 4. So for the middle-high education group, the probability of voting is .80 and the odds of voting are 4. In figuring odds, you can use the raw numbers of cases, as we have just done, or you can use probabilities to compute odds. The formula for converting probabilities to odds is as follows:

$$\text{Odds} = \text{Probability} / (1 - \text{Probability}).$$

Table 8-2 The Probability of Voting, Odds of Voting, and Logged Odds of Voting at Five Levels of Education (hypothetical data)

Education (X)	Probability of voting (Y)	Odds of voting (Y)	Logged odds of voting (Y)
0. Low	.06	.06/.94 = .06	−2.8
1. Middle-low	.20	.20/.80 = .25	−1.4
2. Middle	.50	.50/.50 = 1	0
3. Middle-high	.80	.80/.20 = 4	+1.4
4. High	.94	.94/.06 = 16	+2.8

Note: Hypothetical data.

Apply this conversion to the example just discussed. For middle-high education respondents, the odds would be .80 divided by (1 minus .80), which is equal to .80 / .20, or 4. The "Odds of voting" column in Table 8-2 shows this conversion for the five education groups.

Consider the numbers in the "Odds of voting" column and note some further properties of odds. Note that probabilities of less than .50 produce odds of less than 1 and probabilities of greater than .50 convert to odds of greater than 1. The probabilities for low and middle-low education respondents (.06 and .20, respectively) convert to odds of .06 and .25, and the probabilities among the highest education groups translate into odds of 4 and 16. If an event is as likely to occur as not to occur, as among the middle education people, then the probability is .50 and the odds are equal to 1 (.50 / .50 = 1).

Now examine the "Odds of voting" column in Table 8-2 more closely. Can you discern a systematic pattern in these numbers, as you proceed down the column from low education to high education? Indeed, you may have noticed that the odds of voting for the middle-low education group is (very nearly) four times the odds of voting for the low education category, since 4 times .06 is about equal to .25. And the odds of voting for the middle education group is four times the odds for the middle-low group, since 4 times .25 equals 1. Each additional move, from middle to middle-high (from an odds of 1 to an odds of 4) and from middle-high to high (from 4 to 16), occasions another fourfold increase in the odds. So, as we proceed from lower to higher values of the independent variable, the odds of voting for any education group is four times the odds for the next-lower group. In the language of logistic regression, the relationship between the odds at one value of the independent variable compared with the odds at the next-lower value of the independent variable is called the **odds ratio**. Using this terminology to describe the "Odds of voting" column of Table 8-2, we would say that the odds ratio increases by 4 for each one-unit increase in education.

The pattern of odds shown in Table 8-2 may be described in another way. Instead of figuring out the odds ratio for each change in education, we could calculate the **percentage change in the odds** of voting for each unit change in education. This would be accomplished by seeing how much the odds increase and then converting this number to a percentage. Between low and middle-low, for example, the odds of voting go from .06 to .25, an increase of .19. The percentage change in the odds would be .19 divided by .06, which is equal to 3.17—a bit more than a 300-percent increase in the odds of voting. For the move from middle-low to middle we would have (1 − .25) / .25 = 3.00, another 300-percent increase in the odds of voting. In fact, the odds of voting increases by 300 percent for each additional unit increase in education: From middle to middle-high ([4 − 1] / 1 = 3.00) and from middle-high to high ([16 − 4] / 4 = 3.00). Using this method to describe the Table 8-2 data, we could conclude that the odds of voting increase by 300 percent for each one-unit increase in education.

Let's review what we have found so far. When we looked at the relationship between education and the probability of voting, we saw that an increase in the independent variable does not produce a consistent change in the dependent variable. In examining the relationship between education and the odds of voting, however, we saw that a unit change in education does produce a constant change in the odds ratio of voting—equal to 4 for each unit change in X. Alternatively, each change in the independent variable produces a consistent percentage increase in the odds of voting, a change equal to 300 percent for each unit change in X. What sort of model would summarize this consistent pattern?

The answer to this question lies at the heart of logistic regression. Logistic regression does not estimate the change in the probability of Y for each unit change in X. Rather, it estimates the change in the *log of the odds of Y* for each unit change in X. Consider the third column of numbers in Table 8-2. This column reports an additional conversion, labeled "Logged odds of voting." For low education, this number is equal to –2.8, for middle-low education it is equal to –1.4, for middle education 0, for the middle-high group +1.4, and for high education +2.8. Where did these numbers come from?

A logarithm, or log for short, expresses a number as an exponent of some constant or base. If we chose a base of 10, for example, the number 100 would be expressed as 2, since 100 equals the base of 10 raised to the power of 2 ($10^2 = 100$). We would say, "The base-10 log of 100 equals 2." Base-10 logs are called **common logarithms**, and they are used widely in electronics and the experimental sciences. Statisticians generally work with a different base, denoted as *e*.

The base *e* is approximately equal to 2.72. Base-*e* logs are called **natural logarithms** and are abbreviated *ln*. Using the base *e*, we would express the number 100 as 4.61, since 100 equals the base *e* raised to the power of 4.61 ($e^{4.61} \approx 100$, or $\ln(100) \approx 4.61$). We would say, "The natural log of 100 equals 4.61." The five numbers in the Table 8-2 column "Logged odds of voting" are simply the natural logs of .06 ($e^{-2.8} = .06$), .25 ($e^{-1.4} = .25$), 1 ($e^0 = 1$), 4 ($e^{1.4} = 4$), and 16 ($e^{2.8} = 16$). Using conventional notation: $\ln(.06) = -2.8$, $\ln(.25) = -1.4$, $\ln(1) = 0$, $\ln(4) = 1.4$, and $\ln(16) = 2.8$.

These five numbers illustrate some general features of logarithmic transformations. Any number less than 1 has a negatively signed log. So to express .25 as a natural log, we would raise the base *e* to a negative power, –1.4. Any number greater than 1 has a positively signed log. To convert 4 to a natural log, we would raise *e* to the power of 1.4. And 1 has a log of 0, since *e* raised to the power of 0 equals 1. Natural log transformations of odds are often called logit transformations or **logits** for short. So the logit ("lowjit") of 4 is 1.4.[3]

You are probably unaccustomed to thinking in terms of odds instead of probabilities. And it is a safe bet that you are really unaccustomed to thinking in terms of the logarithmic transformations of odds. But stay focused on the "Logged odds of voting" column. Again apply the linear regression logic. Does a unit change in the independent variable, education, produce a consistent change in the log of the odds of voting? Well, going from low education to middle-low education, the logged odds increases from –2.8 to –1.4, an increase of 1.4. And going from middle-low to middle, the logged odds again increases by 1.4 (0 minus a negative 1.4 equals 1.4). From middle to middle-high and from middle-high to high—each one-unit increase in education produces an increase of 1.4 in the logged odds of voting.

Now there is the odd beauty of logistic regression. Although we may not use a linear model to estimate the effect of an independent variable on the probability of a binary dependent variable, we may use a linear model to estimate the effect of an independent variable on the logged odds of a binary dependent variable. Consider this plain-vanilla regression model:

$$\text{Logged odds } (Y) = \hat{a} + \hat{b}(X).$$

As you know, the regression coefficient, $\hat{b}$, estimates the change in the dependent variable for each unit change in the independent variable. And the intercept, $\hat{a}$, estimates the value of the dependent variable when X is equal to 0. Using the numbers in the "Logged odds of voting" column to identify the values for $\hat{b}$ and $\hat{a}$, we would have

$$\text{Logged odds } (voting) = -2.8 + 1.4 \ (education).$$

Review how this model fits the data. For the low-education group (coded 0 on education), the logged odds of voting would be $-2.8 + 1.4(0)$, which is equal to -2.8. For the middle-low education group (coded 1 on education): $-2.8 + 1.4(1)$, equal to -1.4. For the middle group (coded 2): $-2.8 + 1.4(2)$, equal to 0. And so on, for each additional one-unit increase in education. Clearly, this linear model nicely summarizes the relationship between education and the logged odds of voting.

Now if someone were to ask, "What, exactly, is the effect of education on the likelihood of voting?" we could reply, "For each unit increase in education there is an increase of 1.4 in the logged odds of voting." Although correct, this interpretation is not terribly intuitive—and is likely to occasion a quizzical look from our interlocutor. Therefore, we can use the regression coefficient, 1.4, to retrieve a more understandable number: the change in the odds ratio of voting for each unit change in education. How might this be accomplished? Remember that, as in any regression, all of the coefficients on the right-hand side are expressed in units of the dependent variable. Thus the intercept, a, is the logged odds of voting when X is 0. And the slope, b, estimates the change in the logged odds of voting for each unit change in education. Because logged odds are exponents of e, we can get from logged odds back to odds by raising e to the power of any coefficient in which we are interested. Accordingly, to convert the slope, 1.4, we would raise e to the power of 1.4. This exponentiation procedure, abbreviated *Exp(b)*, looks like this:

$$Exp(b) = Exp(1.4) = e^{1.4} = 4.$$

Now we have a somewhat more interpretable reply: "For each unit change in education, the odds ratio increases by four. Members of each education group are four times more likely to vote than are members of the next-lower education group."

Even more conveniently, we can translate the coefficient, 1.4, into a percentage change in the odds of voting. Here is the general formula:

$$\text{Percentage change in the odds of } Y = 100 * (Exp(b) - 1).$$

For our example:

$$\text{Percentage change in the odds of voting} = 100 * [Exp(1.4) - 1] = 100 * (e^{1.4} - 1)$$
$$= 100 * (4 - 1) = 300.$$

Thus we now can say, "Each unit increase in education increases the odds of voting by 300 percent."

Note further that, armed with the logistic regression equation, "Logged odds (voting) = $-2.8 + 1.4$ (education)," we can estimate the odds of voting—and therefore the probability of

Figure 8-1 Plotted Probabilities of Voting (Y), by Education (X)

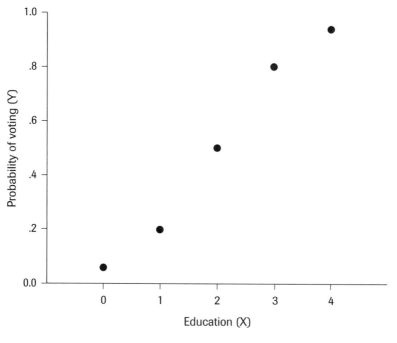

Note: Hypothetical data.

voting—for each value of the independent variable. For the middle-low education group, for example, the logistic regression tells us that the logged odds of voting is −2.8 plus 1.4(1), equal to −1.4. Again, because −1.4 is the exponent of e, the odds of voting for this group would be Exp(−1.4), equal to .25. If the odds of voting is equal to .25, what is the probability of voting? We have already seen that

$$Odds = Probability / (1 − Probability).$$

Following a little algebra:

$$Probability = Odds / (1 + Odds).$$

So for the middle-low group, the probability of voting would be

$$.25 / (1 + .25) = .25 / 1.25 = .20.$$

By performing these reverse translations for each value of X—from logged odds to odds, and from odds to probabilities—we can retrieve the numbers in the "Probability of voting" column of Table 8-2. If we were to plot these retrieved probabilities of Y for each value of X, we would end up with Figure 8-1.

In the beginning we realized that the linear regression logic could not be accurately or appropriately applied to the nonlinear relationship between education and the probability of voting. But after transforming the dependent variable into logged odds, we could apply a linear model. So X bears a nonlinear relationship to the probability of Y, but X bears a linear

Table 8-3 Education and Voting: Logistic Regression Coefficients and Related Statistics

		Intercept $\hat{a}$		Education $\hat{b}$
Logged odds (voting)	=		+	
Coefficient estimates		−1.581		.180
Standard error				.016
Wald				128.85
Significance				.000
Exp(b)				1.197

Source: James A. Davis, Tom W. Smith, and Peter V. Marsden. *General Social Surveys, 1972–2002.* (Chicago: National Opinion Research Center [producer], 2003; Storrs, Conn.: Roper Center for Public Opinion Research, University of Conn./Ann Arbor: Inter-university Consortium for Political and Social Research [distributors], 2003).

Notes: Displayed data are from the 1998 GSS. N = 2,605. Dependent variable is reported turnout in the 1996 presidential election. Independent variable is number of years of formal schooling.

relationship to the logged odds of Y. Furthermore, because the logged odds of Y bears a nonlinear relationship to the probability of Y, the logistic regression model permits us to estimate the probability of an occurrence for any value of X.

An S-shaped relationship, such as that depicted in Figure 8-1, is the visual signature of logistic regression. Just as OLS regression will tell us how well our data fit a linear relationship between an independent variable and the values of an interval-level dependent variable, logistic regression will tell us how well our data fit an S-shaped relationship between an independent variable and the probability of a binary dependent variable.[4] In the hypothetical education-voting example, the relationship worked out perfectly. The logistic regression returned the exact probabilities of voting for each value of education. By eyeballing the "Logged odds of voting" column of Table 8-2, we could easily identify the intercept and regression coefficient of the logistic regression equation. No prediction error. In the practical world of political research, of course, relationships are never this neat.

To apply what you have learned thus far—and to discuss some further properties of logistic regression—we enlist here a real-world dataset, the 1998 General Social Survey (n = 2,605), and reexamine the relationship between education and voting. We estimate the logistic regression equation as follows:

$$\text{Logged odds (voting)} = \hat{a} + \hat{b} \text{ (education)}.$$

The dependent variable is reported turnout in the 1996 presidential election. As in the hypothetical example, voters are coded 1 and nonvoters are coded 0. Unlike the hypothetical example, the independent variable, education, is measured in years of formal schooling. This is a more realistic interval-level variable, with values that range from 0 for no formal education to 20 for 20 years of education. Table 8-3 reports the results obtained from a logistic regression analysis using SPSS.

First consider the numbers in the row labeled "Coefficient estimates." Plugging these values into our equation, we would have

$$\text{Logged odds (voting)} = -1.581 + .180 \text{ (education)}.$$

The coefficients tell us that, for individuals with no formal schooling, the estimated logged odds of voting is equal to -1.581, and each 1-year increment in education increases the estimated logged odds by .180. The value in the bottom-most row, "Exp(b)," translates logged odds back into odds and thus provides a more accessible interpretation. Every unit increase in education increases the odds ratio by 1.197. Individuals at any given level of education are about 1.2 times more likely to vote than are individuals at the next-lower level of education. That is, as we move from one value of education to the next-higher value, we would multiply the odds of voting by about 1.2. Perhaps the most intuitively appealing way to characterize the relationship is to estimate the percentage change in the odds of voting for each 1-year increase in education. As we have seen, this is accomplished by subtracting 1 from the exponent, 1.197, and multiplying by 100. Performing this calculation: $100 * (1.197 - 1) =$ 19.7. Thus the odds of voting increase by about 20 percent for each 1-year increase in the independent variable.

What would the null hypothesis have to say about these results? As always, the null hypothesis claims that, in the population from which the sample was drawn, no relationship exists between the independent and dependent variables, that individuals' levels of education play no role in determining whether they vote. Framed in terms of the logistic regression coefficient, the null hypothesis says that, in the population, the true value of the coefficient is equal to 0, that a one-unit increase in the independent variable produces no change in the logged odds of voting. The null hypothesis also can be framed in terms of the odds ratio, Exp(b). As we have seen, the odds ratio tells us by how much to multiply the odds of the dependent variable for each one-unit increase in the independent variable. An odds ratio of less than 1 means that the odds decline as the independent variable goes up (a negative relationship). (For a discussion of negative relationships in logistic regression, see Box 8-1.) An odds ratio of greater than 1 says that the odds increase as the independent variable goes up (a positive relationship). But an odds ratio of 1 means that the odds do not change as the independent variable increases. Thus an odds ratio equal to 1 would be good news for the null hypothesis, because it would mean that individuals at any level of education are no more likely to vote than are individuals at the next-lower level of education. So if the logistic regression coefficient were equal to 0 or Exp(b) were equal to 1, then we would have to say that the independent variable has no effect on the dependent variable.[5] As it is, however, we obtained an estimated coefficient equal to .180, which is greater than 0, and an odds ratio equal to 1.197, which is greater than 1. But how can we tell if these numbers are statistically significant?

Notice that, just as in OLS regression, logistic regression has provided a standard error for the estimated slope, b. And, again like OLS, the standard error tells us how much prediction error is contained in the estimated coefficient.[6] Thus, according to Table 8-3, each 1-year increase in education produces a .180 increase in the logged odds of voting, give or take .016 or so. Whereas least squares regression computes a test statistic based on Student's t-distribution, logistic regression computes the Wald statistic, which follows a chi-square distribution.[7] Computer programs, such as SPSS, quite helpfully provide a P-value for Wald. Like any P-value, this number tells you the probability of obtaining the observed results, under the assumption that the null hypothesis is correct. A P-value equal to .000 says that, if the null hypothesis is correct, then the probability of obtaining a regression coefficient of .180 is highly remote—clearly beyond the .05 standard. Therefore, we can safely reject the null hypothesis and conclude that education has a statistically significant effect on the likelihood of voting.

Box 8-1 How to Interpret a Negative Relationship in Logistic Regression

As we expected, Table 8-3 reveals a positive relationship between education and the likelihood of voting. Each 1-year increase in schooling increases the logged odds of voting by .180. Alternatively, each increment in education boosts the odds ratio by 1.2— a 20-percent increase for each increment in educational attainment. However, in your own or in others' research you will often encounter negative relationships, situations in which a unit increase in the independent variable is associated with a decrease in the logged odds of the dependent variable. (One of the exercises at the end of this chapter requires that you interpret a negative relationship.) Negative relationships can be a bit trickier in logistic regression than in OLS regression, so let's consider an example. Suppose we were to investigate the relationship between the likelihood of voting and the number of hours respondents spend watching television per day. In this situation, we might expect to find a negative relationship: The more television that people watch, the less likely they are to vote. In fact, we would obtain these estimates:

$$\text{Logged odds (voting)} = 1.013 - .091(\text{TV hours}).$$

Thus each 1-hour increase in daily television watching occasions a decrease of .091 in the logged odds of voting. Obtaining the odds ratio, we would have: $\text{Exp}(-.091) = e^{-.091} = .913$. Positive relationships produce odds ratios of greater than 1, and negative relationships produce odds ratio of less than 1. How would you interpret an odds ratio of .913? Like this: Individuals watching any given number of hours of television per day are only about .9 times as likely to vote as are individuals who watch the next-lower number of hours. For example, people who watch 4 hours per day are .9 times as likely to vote as are people who watch 3 hours per day. Following the formula for percentage change in the odds: $100 * (.913 - 1) = -8.7$. Each additional hour spent in front of the television depresses the odds of voting by about 9 percent.[1]

---

1. Data for this analysis are from the 1998 General Social Survey. The independent variable, number of hours spent watching television, is based on the question "On the average day, about how many hours do you personally watch television?" The logistic regression analysis presented here (n = 2,163) produced a coefficient of –.091, with a standard error of .020 and a Wald statistic of 20.693 (significance = .000).

As you can see, in some ways logistic regression bears a kinship to OLS regression. In running OLS, we obtain an estimate for the linear regression coefficient that minimizes prediction errors. That is, OLS provides the best fit between the predicted values of the dependent variable and the actual, observed values of the dependent variable. OLS also reports a standard error for the regression coefficient, which tells us how much prediction error is contained in the regression coefficient. This information permits us to determine whether X has a significant effect on Y. Similarly, logistic regression minimizes prediction errors by finding an estimate for the logistic regression coefficient that yields the maximum fit between the predicted probabilities of Y and the observed probabilities of Y. Plus it reports a standard error for this estimated effect.

However, a valuable statistic is missing from the analogy between OLS and logistic regression: R-square. As you know, R-square tells the researcher how completely the independent variable (or, in multiple regression, all of the independent variables) explains the dependent variable. In our current example, it certainly would be nice to know how completely the independent variable, education, accounts for the likelihood of voting. Does logistic regression provide an analogous statistic to R-square? Strictly speaking, the answer is no.[8] Even so, methodologists have proposed R-square-like measures that give an overall reading of the strength of association between the independent variables and the dependent variable. To understand these measures, we need to take a closer look at maximum likelihood estimation, the technique logistic regression uses to arrive at the best fit between the predicted probabilities of Y and the observed probabilities of Y.

FINDING THE BEST FIT: MAXIMUM LIKELIHOOD ESTIMATION

By way of introducing maximum likelihood estimation, it is helpful to recall the logic behind proportional reduction in error (PRE) measures of association, such as lambda or R-square. You will remember that a PRE measure first determines how well we can predict the values of the dependent variable *without* knowledge of the independent variable. It then compares this result with how well we can predict the dependent variable *with* knowledge of the independent variable. PRE uses the overall mean of the dependent variable to "guess" the dependent variable for each value of the independent variable. This guessing strategy produces a certain number of errors. PRE then figures out how many errors occur when the independent variable is taken into account. By comparing these two numbers—the number of errors without knowledge of the independent variable and the number of errors with knowledge of the independent variable—PRE determines how much predictive leverage the independent variable provides.

Maximum likelihood estimation (MLE) employs the same approach. MLE takes the sample-wide probability of observing a specific value of a binary dependent variable and sees how well this probability predicts that outcome for each individual case in the sample. At least initially, MLE ignores the independent variable. As in PRE, this initial strategy produces a number of prediction errors. MLE then takes the independent variable into account and determines if, by knowing the independent variable, these prediction errors can be reduced.

Consider a highly simplified illustration, which again uses education (X) to predict whether an individual voted (coded 1 on the dependent variable, Y) or did not vote (coded 0 on Y). MLE first would ask, "How well can we predict whether or not an individual voted *without* using education as a predictor?" For the sake of simplicity, suppose our sample consists of four individuals, as shown in Table 8-4. As you can see, two individuals voted (coded 1) and two did not (coded 0). Based only on the distribution of the dependent variable, what is the predicted probability of voting for each individual? MLE would answer this question by figuring out the sample-wide probability of voting and applying this prediction to each case. Since half the sample voted and half did not, MLE's initial predicted probability (labeled P) would be equal to .5 for each individual. Why .5? Because there is a .5 chance that any individual in the sample voted and a .5 chance that he or she did not vote. Let's label the model that gave rise to the initial predictions Model 1. Table 8-4 shows the predicted probabilities, plus some additional information, for Model 1.

How well, overall, does Model 1 predict the real values of Y? MLE answers this question by computing a **likelihood function**, a number that summarizes how well a model's predic-

Table 8-4 Model 1's Predictions and Likelihoods: Not Using Education to Predict Voting

Individual	Y[a]	Predicted probability of voting (P)	Likelihood
A	1	.5	P = .5
B	1	.5	P = .5
C	0	.5	1 − P = .5
D	0	.5	1 − P = .5

Note: Hypothetical data.

[a] 1 = voted; 0 = did not vote.

tions fit the observed data. In computing this function, MLE first determines a likelihood for each individual case. An individual likelihood tells us how closely the model comes to predicting the observed outcome for that case. MLE then computes the likelihood function by calculating the product of the individual likelihoods, that is, by multiplying them together. The likelihood function can take on any value between 0—meaning the model's predictions do not fit the observed data at all—to 1, meaning the model's predictions perfectly fit the observed data.

Formally stated, the likelihood function is not beautiful to behold.[9] Practically applied to a small set of data, however, the function is not difficult to compute. If a case has an observed value of Y equal to 1 (the individual voted), then the likelihood for that case is equal to P. So individuals A and B, with predicted probabilities equal to .5, have likelihoods equal to P, which is .5. If a case has an observed value of Y equal to 0 (the individual did not vote), then the likelihood for that case is equal to 1 − P. Thus individuals C and D, who have predicted probabilities of .5, have likelihoods equal to 1 − P, or 1 − .5, also equal to .5. The likelihoods for each individual are displayed in the right-most column of Table 8-4. The likelihood for Model 1 is determined by multiplying all of the individual likelihoods together:

$$\text{Model 1 Likelihood} = .5 * .5 * .5 * .5 = .0625.$$

MLE would use this number, .0625, as a baseline summary of how well we can predict voting without knowledge of the independent variable, education.[10]

In its next step, MLE would bring the independent variable into its calculations by specifying a logistic regression coefficient for education, recomputing the probabilities and likelihoods, and seeing how closely the new estimates conform to the observed data. Again, for the sake of illustration, suppose that these new estimates, which we'll call Model 2, yield the predicted probabilities displayed in Table 8-5.

Model 2, which takes into account the independent variable, does a better job than Model 1 in predicting the observed values of Y. By using education to predict voting, Model 2 estimates probabilities equal to .9 and .8 for individuals A and B (who in fact voted), but probabilities of only .3 and .1 for individuals C and D (who in fact did not vote). Just as in the Model 1 procedure, the individual likelihoods for each case are equal to P for each of the voters (for whom Y = 1) and equal to 1 − P for each of the nonvoters (for whom Y = 0). The individual likelihoods appear in the right-most column of Table 8-5. As before, the likelihood function for Model 2 is computed by multiplying the individual likelihoods together:

$$\text{Model 2 Likelihood} = .9 * .8 * .7 * .9 = .4536.$$

Table 8-5 Model 2's Predictions and Likelihoods: Using Education to Predict Voting

Individual	Y[a]	Predicted probability of voting (P)	Likelihood
A	1	.9	P = .9
B	1	.8	P = .8
C	0	.3	1 − P = .7
D	0	.1	1 − P = .9

Note: Hypothetical data.
[a] 1 = voted; 0 = did not vote.

Table 8-6 Model 1 and Model 2 Compared

Model statistic	Model 1	Model 2
Likelihood	.0625	.4536
Logged likelihood (LL)	Ln(.0625) = −2.78	Ln(.4536) = −0.79
Model comparison:		
Model 1 LL minus Model 2 LL	−2.78 − (−0.79) = −1.99	
−2 * (Model 1 LL minus Model 2 LL)	−2(−1.99) = 3.98	

Note: Hypothetical data.

How much better is Model 2 than Model 1? Does using education as a predictor provide significantly improved estimates of the probability of voting? Now, MLE does not work directly with differences in model likelihoods. Rather it deals with the natural log of the likelihood, or **logged likelihood** (LL) of each model. Thus MLE would calculate the natural log of the Model 1 likelihood, calculate the natural log of the Model 2 likelihood, and then determine the difference between the two numbers. Table 8-6 shows these conversions, plus some additional calculations, for Model 1 and Model 2.

Examine the Table 8-6 calculations. As we found earlier, Model 2's likelihood (.4536) is greater than Model 1's likelihood (.0625). This increase is also reflected in the LLs of both models: The LL increases from −2.78 for Model 1 to −0.79 for Model 2. MLE makes the comparison between models by starting with Model 1's LL and subtracting Model 2's LL: −2.78 − (−0.79) = −1.99. Notice that if Model 2 did about as well as Model 1 in predicting Y, then the two LLs would be similar, and the calculated difference would be close to 0.[11] As it is, MLE found a difference equal to −1.99.

So far, so good. But does the number −1.99 help us decide whether Model 2 is *significantly* better than Model 1? Yes, it does. It turns out that, with one additional calculation, the difference between two LLs follows a chi-square distribution. The additional calculation is achieved by multiplying the difference in LLs by −2. Doing so, of course, doubles the difference and reverses the sign: −2 (−1.99) = 3.98. This calculation, usually labeled in computer output as "Change in −2 Log Likelihood" or "Change in −2LL," is a chi-square test statistic, and MLE uses it to test the null hypothesis that the true difference between Model 1 and Model 2 is equal to 0. There is nothing mystical here. It is plain old hypothesis testing using chi-square. If the calculated value of the change in −2LL, equal to 3.98, could have occurred more frequently than 5 times out of 100, by chance, then we would not reject the null hypothesis. We would have to

Table 8-7   Education and Voting: Model Comparison and Summary

Model statistic	Model 1: Education *not* included	Model 2: Education included
Logged likelihood (LL)	−1,627.98	−1,556.59
Model comparison:		
Model 1 LL minus Model 2 LL	−1,627.98 − (−1,556.59) = −71.39	
−2*(Model 1 LL minus Model 2 LL) or		
"Change in −2LL"	142.78	
Significance of change	.000	
Model 2 summary:		
Cox & Snell R-square	.053	
Nagelkerke R-square	.075	

Source: 1998 General Social Survey (GSS).

conclude that the education-voting relationship is not significant. However, if the chances of observing a chi-square value of 3.98 are less than or equal to .05, then we would reject the null hypothesis and infer that Model 2 is significantly better than Model 1. Using the appropriate degrees of freedom and applying a chi-square test, MLE would report a P-value of .046 for a test statistic of 3.98.[12] The P-value is less than .05, so we can reject the null hypothesis and conclude that education is a statistically significant predictor of the probability of voting.

MLE proceeds much in the way illustrated by this example. It first obtains a set of predictions and likelihoods based on a reduced model, that is, a model using only the sample-wide probability of Y to predict the observed values of Y for each case in the data. It then "tries out" a coefficient for the independent variable in the logistic regression model. MLE usually obtains the first "try out" coefficient by running a version of least squares regression using X to predict Y. It enlists this coefficient to compute a likelihood, which it then compares with the likelihood of the reduced model. It then proceeds in an iterative fashion, using a complex mathematical algorithm to fine-tune the coefficient, computing another likelihood, and then another and another—until it achieves the best possible fit between the model's predictions and the observed values of the dependent variable.

MLE is the heart and soul of logistic regression. This estimation technique generates all of the coefficient estimates and other useful statistics that help the analyst draw inferences about the relationship between the independent and dependent variables. Let's return now to the GSS data and consider some of these additional statistics, as reported in Table 8-7. To enhance the comparison between the real-world data and the hypothetical example just discussed, the baseline model—the model estimated without taking into account education— is called Model 1. Model 2 refers to the results obtained after the independent variable, education, is used to predict the likelihood of voting. Note the difference between the LLs of the models: When education is used to predict voting, the LL increases from −1627.98 to −1556.59. Is this a significant improvement? Yes, it is, at least according to the "Model comparison" numbers in the table. Subtracting Model 2's LL from Model 1's LL yields a difference of −71.39. Multiplying the difference by −2, labeled "Change in −2LL," gives us a chi-square test statistic of 142.78, well beyond the realm of the null hypothesis. Thus, compared with how well we can predict the dependent variable without knowledge of the independent variable, knowledge of respondents' education significantly improves our ability to predict the likelihood of voting.

Two additional points should be made about using "Change in –2LL" to evaluate logistic regression models. First, we may follow this procedure to assess the statistical significance of the relationship between the dependent variable and all of the independent variables included in the model. So if Model 2 had several predictors of voting—education, age, and race, for example—then the change in –2LL would provide a chi-square test for the null hypothesis that none of these variables is significantly related to the likelihood of voting. Second, the change in –2LL can be used as an alternative to Wald in evaluating the statistical significance of individual independent variables, provided that each variable is added to the estimation procedure in a stepwise fashion. Thus MLE would estimate the effect of education, report a chi-square statistic, and then add a second variable and tell us if this second variable made a significant improvement in the predictive power of the model. In fact, some methodologists recommend this procedure for testing the significance of individual logistic regression coefficients.[13]

Logistic regression enlists the change in likelihood function in yet another way—as the basis for R-square-type measures of association, two of which are reported in the Table 8-7 "Model 2 summary." These statistics are grounded on the intuitive PRE logic. Model 1's LL represents prediction error without knowing the independent variable. The difference between Model 1's LL and Model 2's LL represents the predictive leverage gained by knowing the independent variable. In conceptual terms, then, we could express the difference between the two models as a proportion of Model 1's LL:

R-square = (Model 1 LL – Model 2 LL) / (Model 1 LL).

If Model 2 did about as well as Model 1 in predicting voting—if the two models' LLs were similar—then R-square would be close to 0. If, by contrast, Model 2's LL were a lot higher than Model 1's LL, then R-square would approach 1.[14] The various R-square measures build on this conceptual framework and seek to adjust for its statistical inadequacies. Cox and Snell's R-square makes an adjustment based on sample size. Cox-Snell is somewhat conservative, however, because it can have a maximum value of less than 1. Nagelkerke's statistic adjusts Cox and Snell's R-square, yielding a measure that is usually higher. By and large, though, these two measures, and several others that you may encounter, give readings of strength that are pretty close to each other.[15]

So what are we to make of an R-square in the .05 to .07 range? Again, unlike least squares regression, MLE is not in the business of explaining variance in the dependent variable. So we cannot say something like, "Education explains about 5 percent of the variation in voter turnout." However, we know that R-square can assume values between 0 and 1, with 0 denoting a very weak relationship and 1 denoting a strong relationship. Thus we can say that education, while significantly related to the likelihood of voting, is not by itself a particularly strong predictive tool. From a substantive standpoint, this is not too surprising. You can probably think of several additional variables that might improve the predictive power of the logistic regression model. Age, race, political efficacy, strength of partisanship—all of these variables come to mind as other possible causes of voting. If we were running OLS, we could specify a multiple regression model and estimate the effect of each of these variables on the dependent variable. Happily, logistic regression also accommodates multiple predictors. We turn now to a discussion of logistic regression using more than one independent variable.

LOGISTIC REGRESSION WITH MULTIPLE INDEPENDENT VARIABLES

Thus far we have covered a fair amount of ground. You now understand the meaning of a logistic regression coefficient. You know how to interpret coefficients in terms of changes in the odds ratio, as well as the percentage change in the odds. You know how to evaluate the statistical significance of a logistic regression coefficient. Plus you have a basic understanding of MLE, and you can appreciate its central role in providing useful statistics, such as the change in –2LL, as well as R-square-type measures of association. So far, however, our substantive examples have been of a simple variety, with one independent variable. Yet political researchers are often interested in assessing the effects of several independent variables on a dependent variable. We often want to know whether an independent variable affects a dependent variable, controlling for other possible causal influences. In this section we show that the logistic regression model, much like the linear regression model, can be extended to accommodate multiple independent variables. We also illustrate how logistic regression models can be used to obtain and analyze the predicted probabilities of a binary variable.

To keep things consistent with the previous examples—but to add an interesting wrinkle—we introduce a dummy independent variable into the education-voting model:

$$\text{Logged odds (voting)} = \hat{a} + \hat{b}_1 \text{ (education)} + \hat{b}_2 \text{ (partisan)}.$$

Education, as before, is measured in years of schooling, from 0 to 20. "Partisan" is a dummy variable that gauges strength of party identification: Strong Democrats and strong Republicans are coded 1 on this dummy, and all others (weak identifiers, independents, and independent leaners) are coded 0. From an empirical standpoint, we know that strongly partisan people, regardless of their party affiliation, are more likely to vote than are people whose partisan attachments are weaker. So we would expect a positive relationship between strength of partisanship and the likelihood of voting.

The coefficients in this model—$\hat{a}$, $\hat{b}_1$, and $\hat{b}_2$—are directly analogous to coefficients in multiple linear regression. The coefficient $\hat{b}_1$ will estimate the change in the logged odds of voting for each 1-year change in education, controlling for the effect of partisan strength. Similarly, $\hat{b}_2$ will tell us by how much to adjust the estimated logged odds for strong partisans, controlling for the effect of education. To the extent that education and partisan strength are themselves related, the logistic regression procedure will control for this, and it will estimate the partial effect of each variable on the logged odds of voting. And the intercept, $\hat{a}$, will report the logged odds of voting when both independent variables are equal to 0, for respondents with no schooling (for whom education = 0) and who are not strong party identifiers (partisan = 0). This point bears emphasizing: The logistic regression model specified above is a linear-additive model, and it is just like a garden-variety multiple regression model. The partial effect of education on the logged odds of voting is assumed to be the same for strong partisans and nonstrong partisans alike. And the partial effect of partisan strength on the logged odds of voting is assumed to be the same at all values of education. (This point becomes important in a moment, when we return to a discussion of probabilities.)

Table 8-8 reports the results of the analysis, using the GSS data. Plugging the coefficient values into the logistic regression model, we find

$$\text{Logged odds (voting)} = -2.022 + .194 \text{ (education)} + 1.539 \text{ (partisan)}.$$

Table 8-8 Education, Partisan Strength, and Voting: Logistic Regression Coefficients and Model Summary

Logged odds (voting)	=	Intercept $\hat{a}$	+	Education[a] $\hat{b}_1$	+	Partisan[b] $\hat{b}_2$
Coefficient estimate		−2.022		.194		1.539
Standard error				.017		.139
Wald				134.739		123.012
Significance				.000		.000
Exp(b)				1.214		4.659

Model summary:	
Change in −2LL	292.655
Significance of change[c]	.000
Cox & Snell R-square	.109
Nagelkerke R-square	.153

Source: 1998 General Social Survey (GSS).
Note: Dependent variable is reported turnout in the 1996 presidential election. N = 2,539.
[a] Education is number of years of formal schooling.
[b] Partisan coded 1 for strong partisans and 0 otherwise.
[c] Degrees of freedom = 2. Both independent variables included in complete model.

Interpretation of these coefficients is by now a familiar task. When we control for partisan strength, each 1-year increase in education increases the logged odds of voting by .194. And, after we take into account the effect of education, being a strong partisan increases the logged odds of voting by 1.539. Turning to the odds ratios, reported in the "Exp(b)" row of Table 8-8, we can see that a unit increase in education multiplies the odds by about 1.2. And, when "partisan" is switched from 0 to 1, the odds ratio jumps by nearly 4.7. In other words, when we control for education, strong partisans are nearly five times more likely to vote than are weak partisans or independents. Framing the relationships in terms of percentage change in the odds: The odds of voting increase by about 21 percent for each incremental change in education and by 366 percent for the comparison between nonstrong partisans and partisans. Finally, according to the Wald statistics (and accompanying P-values), each independent variable is significantly related to the logged odds of voting.

Overall, how well does the model perform? Not too badly. The "Change in −2LL" chi-square statistic (292.655, P-value = .000) says that including both independent variables in the estimation procedure provides significant predictive improvement over the baseline know-nothing model.[16] And Cox-Snell (.109) and Nagelkerke (.153), while not spellbinding, suggest that education and partisanship together do a decent job of predicting voting, especially when compared with our earlier analysis (see Table 8-7), in which education was used as the sole predictor.

These results add up to a reasonably complete analysis of the relationships. Certainly it is good to know size and significance of the partial effects of education and partisan strength on the logged odds of voting, and it is convenient to express these effects in the language of odds ratios and the percentage change in odds. Often, however, the researcher wishes to understand his or her findings in the most intuitively meaningful terms: probabilities. We might ask, "What are the effects of the independent variables on the probability of voting? Although education and partisan attachments clearly enhance the odds of voting, by how much do these variables affect the probability that people will turn out?" These questions are perfectly reasonable, but they pose two challenges. First, in any logistic regression model—including the simple model with one independent variable—a linear relationship exists between X and the logged odds of Y, but a nonlinear relationship exists between X and the probability of Y. As we discussed at the beginning of this chapter, the marginal effect of X on the probability of Y will not be the same for all values of X. Thus the effect of, say, a 1-year increase in education on the probability of voting will depend on where you "start" along the education variable. Second, in a logistic regression model with more than one independent variable, such as the model we just discussed, the independent variables bear a linear-additive relationship to the logged odds of Y, but they bear an interactive relationship to the probability of Y. This means, for example, that logistic regression will permit the relationship between partisan strength and the probability of voting to vary, depending on respondents' levels of education. So logistic regression might find a big marginal effect of partisan strength on the probability of voting among people with less education (who are less likely to vote) but a much weaker effect among the better educated (who are already quite likely to vote). Odd as it may sound, these challenges define some rather attractive features of logistic regression. Properly applied, the technique allows the researcher to work with probabilities instead of odds or logged odds and, in the bargain, to gain revealing substantive insights into the relationships being studied.

WORKING WITH PROBABILITIES

Let's return to the logistic regression model we just estimated and figure out how best to represent and interpret these relationships in terms of probabilities. The model will, of course, yield the predicted logged odds of voting for any combination of the independent variables. Just plug in values for education and the partisan dummy, do the math, and obtain an estimated logged odds of voting for that combination of values. As we saw earlier, logged odds can be converted back into odds and, in turn, odds can be translated into probabilities. These conversions—from logged odds to odds, and from odds to probabilities—form the basis of two commonly used methods for representing complex relationships in terms of probabilities. First, the researcher might calculate and compare the predicted probabilities of voting for a few illustrative values of education and partisan strength. With these calculations in hand, the researcher obtains a **probability profile** of the effects of the independent variables on the probability of voting. The probability profile approach works nicely for models having few independent variables. A second and perhaps more widely used method is to examine the effect of each independent variable on the predicted probability of voting, while holding the other independent variables constant at their sample averages. Using the **sample averages** approach, we could show the effect of partisan strength for people with average education or the effect of education among people with average partisan strength. Let's consider both methods using the GSS data, beginning with the probability profile approach.

The Probability Profile Method

Suppose that we wanted to see what happens to the probability of voting as education increases from 8 years, to 12 years, to 16 years, to 20 years. Suppose further that we would like to find out how partisan strength affects the probability of voting at each of these values of education. To accomplish this, we would use the model's estimates to figure out the logged odds of voting for the first combination of independent variables—respondents with 8 years of education (education = 8) who are not strong partisans (partisan = 0)—and convert this estimate into a probability. To find the probability of voting for strongly partisan people who have 8 years of education, we would recompute the logged odds for partisans (partisan = 1) and convert this value into a probability. We would then move to the next illustrative value of the education variable, 12 years, and repeat the procedure. A complete probability profile, with estimated probabilities for each combination of the four values for "education" and two values for "partisan," would require eight sets of conversions. This sounds like a lot of mathematical drudgery—and it is. Fortunately, any data analysis software worth its salt will do the work for you.[17] But to see how it is done, and to make an interesting substantive comparison, let's work through two conversions. We will translate the logged odds of voting into probabilities of voting for people who share the same level of education, 8 years, but who differ in partisan attachment.

For convenience, here is the logistic regression equation we obtained earlier:

$$\text{Logged odds (voting)} = -2.022 + .194 \text{ (education)} + 1.539 \text{ (partisan)}.$$

Our first illustrative group, people with 8 years of schooling who are not strong partisans, have a value of 8 on the education variable and a value of 0 on the partisan variable. Using the logistic regression model to estimate the logged odds of voting for this group:

$$\text{Logged odds (voting)} = -2.022 + .194 \text{ (8)} + 1.539 \text{ (0)},$$
$$= -2.022 + 1.552 + 0 = -.47.$$

So the estimated logged odds of voting are equal to $-.47$. What are the odds of voting for this group? Well, odds can be retrieved by taking the exponent of logged odds. Doing so: Exp(-.47), which is equal to .625. Thus the odds are .625. Now let's get back to a probability. Recall the formula: Probability = Odds / (1 + Odds). Converting .625 to a probability of voting, we have .625 / 1.625 = .385. So the estimated probability of voting for weak partisans or independents with 8 years of education is equal to .385. Clearly there is a weak probability—a bit more than one chance in three—that these individuals voted. How about their strongly partisan counterparts who have the same level of education? These respondents will have a value of 8 on the education variable and a value of 1 on the partisan variable. For this combination of independent variables, the logged odds are as follows:

$$\text{Logged odds (voting)} = -2.022 + .194 \text{ (8)} + 1.539 \text{ (1)},$$
$$= -2.022 + 1.552 + 1.539 = 1.069.$$

If the logged odds are 1.069, then the odds would be Exp(1.069), equal to 2.912. Finally, the estimated probability is: 2.912 / 3.912 = .744. There are almost three chances in four that these people voted. Pretty remarkable. For people at this low level of educational attainment, partisan attachment has a very large effect on the probability of voting. How large? Subtracting .385 from .744 gives us .359. So for people with 8 years of education, partisan strength increases the probability of voting by a robust .359. What happens to this effect as education increases?

Table 8-9 presents the estimated probabilities of voting for all eight education and partisan groups. First consider the effect of partisan strength on the estimated probability of voting, controlling for education. At the lowest education level, as we have seen, this effect is

Table 8-9 Predicted Probabilities of Voting for Four Values of Education and Two Values of Partisan Strength

Education	Strong partisan?	Predicted probability
8 years	No	.385
	Yes	.744
	Difference[a]	*.359*
12 years	No	.576
	Yes	.863
	Difference	*.287*
16 years	No	.747
	Yes	.932
	Difference	*.185*
20 years	No	.865
	Yes	.968
	Difference	*.103*

Source: 1998 General Social Survey (GSS).

Note: Number of cases (N) for each value of education and partisan strength are as follows: 8 years (63 No/18 Yes/ 81 total cases), 12 years (678/157/835), 16 years (321/84/405), and 20 years (48/19/67).

[a] Predicted probability for strong partisans minus predicted probability for nonstrong partisans.

quite large, .359. At the next chosen illustrative value, 12 years, the effect of the "partisan" variable is fair-sized, too—there is a difference of .287 between the predicted probability for strong partisans (.863) and the probability for people with weak partisan ties (.576). But notice that, as we ascend into higher values of education, most respondents, despite partisan strength, are quite likely to have voted. Thus the marginal effect of the "partisan" variable gets weaker and weaker. At the highest level of education, 20 years, the effect of partisan strength shrinks to .103. We can, of course, turn the analysis around and examine the effect of education, controlling for partisan strength. Viewed in this way, we can see that education has a more potent effect among those lacking a strong partisan commitment. Between the lowest education reference group (.385) and the highest (.865), the probability of voting increases by .48. Among strong partisans, however, this effect is more modest (about .22).

The Sample Averages Method

Constructing a probability profile, as we have just done, provides richness and detail, and it is a good method to use if you have two or three independent variables. However, in doing your own analyses, or in reading the research findings of other researchers, you are quite likely to encounter logistic regression models having many independent variables. Under these circumstances, the probability profile approach becomes a bit cluttered and confusing. Therefore, many researchers use the sample averages method. The sample averages method is centered on this question: If we were to hold all other independent variables constant at their sample-wide means, what is the effect of this particular independent variable on the estimated probability of the dependent variable? Applying this question to our voting example, we might first ask,

"If we hold education constant at its sample mean, what is the effect of partisan strength on the estimated probability of voting?" We also could ask, "If we hold partisan strength constant at its sample mean, what is the effect of education on the estimated probability of voting?" The answers to these questions will help to illustrate the effects of partisan strength and education for the average respondent. Typically, researchers will present the change in the estimated probability of the dependent variable across the full range of a particular independent variable of interest, at the sample means of the other variables in the model. For example, we would want to present the full effect of going from the lowest education code (0 years) to the highest education code (20 years) at the sample average of partisan strength.[18]

How do we proceed? First, we need two numbers, the sample mean of education and the sample mean of partisan strength. For an interval-level variable, such as education, we find the arithmetic average. According to the GSS data, the mean number of years of formal schooling is 13.25 years. For a dummy variable, such as partisan strength, the mean is equal to the proportion of the sample who are strong partisans, that is, the proportion coded 1 on the dummy. In the GSS data, .221 of the sample falls into this category.[19] To figure out the effect of partisan strength at mean levels of education, we would enlist the estimates of the logistic regression model, enter 13.25 as the value of the education variable, and then estimate the probability for nonstrong partisans, respondents coded 0 on partisan strength:

$$\text{Logged odds (voting)} = -2.022 + .194\,(13.25) + 1.539\,(0),$$
$$= -2.022 + 2.571 + 0 = .549.$$

A logged odds equal to .549 translates into a probability of .634. So, for nonstrong partisans with average education, there are a bit more than 6 chances in 10 that they voted. We then would do the calculations again, this time switching "partisan" from 0 to 1:

$$\text{Logged odds (voting)} = -2.022 + .194\,(13.25) + 1.539\,(1),$$
$$= -2.022 + 2.571 + 1.539 = 2.088.$$

A logged odds of 2.088 converts to an odds of 8.069, which returns an estimated probability of .890, or about 9 chances in 10 that these respondents voted. Thus, by subtracting the nonstrong probability, .634, from the strong partisan probability, .890, we can figure out the full effect of partisan strength while holding education constant at its sample mean: .890 − .634 =.256. Table 8-10, which summarizes these calculations, also shows what happens to the estimated probability of voting across the full range of education, at the sample-wide mean of partisan strength. If you opt for the sample averages method, you could use Table 8-10 as a template for presenting your own logistic regression results.

SUMMARY

A political researcher wants to explain why some people approve of gay marriage whereas others disapprove. Thinking that age plays a causal role, she hypothesizes that as age increases, the likelihood of disapproval will go up, that older people will be more likely than younger people to disapprove of gay marriage. A plausible and interesting idea. Consulting her survey dataset, the researcher finds a binary variable that will serve as the dependent variable (respondents who approve of gay marriage are coded 0 on this variable and those who

Table 8-10 Full Effects of Partisan Strength and Education on the Estimated Probability of Voting

	Independent variable (low value, high value)	
Estimated probability at	*Partisan strength* (0,1)	*Education* (0,20)
Low value	.634	.157
High value	.890	.900
Full effect	.256	.743

Source: 1998 General Social Survey (GSS).

Note: For partisan strength, probabilities calculated at education sample mean (13.25). For education, probabilities calculated at partisan strength sample mean (.221).

disapprove are coded 1). She also finds an interval-level independent variable, age measured in years, from 18 to 99. So she has the hypothesis, the data, and the variables. Now what? Which analytic technique is best suited to this research problem? If this researcher is someone other than you, she may need to test her idea by collapsing age into three or four categories, retrieving the tool labeled cross-tabulation from her methods toolbox, and comparing the percentages of disapprovers across the collapsed categories of the independent variable. That might work okay. But what if she decides to control for the effects of several other variables that may shape individuals' approval or disapproval of gay marriage—such as education, sex, and partisanship? Cross-tabulation would become cumbersome to work with, and she may need to settle for an incomplete analysis of the relationships. The larger point, of course, is that this researcher's ability to answer an interesting substantive question is severely limited by the tools at her disposal.

If this researcher is you, however, you now know a far better approach to the problem. Reach into your toolbox of techniques, select the tool labeled logistic regression, and estimate this model: Logged odds (disapproval) = a + b (age). The logistic regression coefficient, b, will tell you how much the logged odds of disapproval increase for each 1-year change in age. Of course, logged odds are not easily grasped. But by entering the value of b into your hand-held calculator and tapping the e^x key—or, better still, by examining the Exp(b) values in the computer output—you can find the odds ratio, the change in the odds of disapproving as age increases by 1 year. You can convert Exp(b) into a percentage change in the odds of disapproval. You can test the null hypothesis that b is equal to 0 by consulting the P-value of the Wald statistic. You could see how well the model performs by examining changes in the magnitude of −2LL and reviewing the accompanying chi-square test. Several R-square-like measures, such as Cox-Snell and Nagelkerke, will give you a general idea of the strength of the relationship between age and the likelihood of disapproving of gay marriage. You can calculate and examine the predicted probabilities of disapproval for a few illustrative age groups and thus achieve a closer understanding of your results. If you are challenged by a skeptic who thinks you should have controlled for education and sex, you can reanalyze your model, controlling for these variables—and any other independent variables that might affect your results. By adding logistic regression to your arsenal of research techniques, you are now well prepared to handle any research question that interests you.

KEY TERMS

binary variable (p. 180)
common logarithms (p. 184)
likelihood function (p. 190)
logged likelihood (LL) (p. 192)
logits (p. 184)
maximum likelihood estimation (MLE) (p. 190)

natural logarithms (p. 184)
odds (p. 182)
odds ratio (p. 183)
percentage change in the odds (p. 183)
probability profile (p. 197)
sample averages (p. 197)

EXERCISES[20]

1. Students of comparative politics are quite interested in questions of democratic development. Under what conditions are countries more likely (or less likely) to develop democratic forms of government? One idea has to do with the equitable—or inequitable—distribution of wealth. According to this reasoning, when economic resources are concentrated in the hands of a few, those controlling the wealth would much prefer a political system not open to popular rule. Thus, as economic inequality goes up, the likelihood of democracy will go down. Does this idea have empirical support? Below are the results of a logistic regression analysis of the relationship between type of government and economic inequality. The binary dependent variable is coded 1 for democratic countries and 0 for nondemocratic countries. The independent variable, economic inequality, is a 10-point scale, with high values denoting greater inequality:

		Intercept		Economic inequality
Logged odds (democracy)	=	a	+	b
Coefficient estimate		3.538		−.944
Standard error				.249
Wald				14.325
Significance				.000
Exp(b)				.389

   A. The logistic regression coefficient tells us that, for each one-unit increase in inequality, the logged odds of democracy declines by .944. Turn your attention to the odds ratio, Exp(b). This coefficient says that a country at one value of economic inequality is only about _____ times as likely to be a democracy as a country at the next-lower level of economic inequality.
   B. Use the value of Exp(b) to compute a percentage change in the odds. According to your calculations, each unit increase in economic inequality decreases the odds of democracy by about how much?
   C. State the null hypothesis for this relationship. What is your inferential decision—reject the null hypothesis or do not reject the null hypothesis?

2. Here is an extension of the idea you examined in Exercise 1. According to this broader idea, the inequitable distribution of any resource within a country will depress the likelihood of democracy. This could be a material resource, such as economic wealth, but it might be a symbolic resource, such as the value attached to language, religion, or ethnicity. So, for example, a country having several linguistic or ethnic groups, all of whom are vying for political power, may have a hard time establishing a democracy, because each disparate group may seek a form of governance that establishes its language or religion as dominant. By contrast, countries in

which nearly all citizens share the same language or ethnicity might avoid these bitter disputes, thus making democracy easier to achieve. This is just an idea. Does it have merit? Here are the results of a logistic regression analysis that add a dummy variable, "homogeneous," to the model you interpreted in Exercise 1. The variable homogeneous takes on a value of 1 for countries having low levels of ethnic and linguistic diversity and a value of 0 for nonhomogeneous countries.

		Intercept		Economic inequality		Homogeneous
Logged odds (voting)	=	a	+	b_1	+	b_2
Coefficient estimate		3.033		−.906		1.033
Standard error				.289		.525
Wald				9.833		3.881
Significance				.002		.049
Exp(b)				.404		2.811

Model summary:

Change in −2LL	22.307
Significance of change	.000
Cox & Snell R-square	.241
Nagelkerke R-square	.322

Parts A–D present interpretations based on these results. For each part, (i) state whether the interpretation is correct or incorrect, and (ii) explain why the interpretation is correct or incorrect. For incorrect interpretations, be sure that your response in (ii) includes the correct interpretation.

A. Interpretation One: If we control for countries' homogeneity, each one-unit increase in economic inequality decreases the likelihood of democracy by about 40 percent.

B. Interpretation Two: If we control for countries' levels of economic inequality, homogeneous countries are about 2.8 times more likely to be democracies than are nonhomogeneous countries.

C. Interpretation Three: Compared with how well the model performs without including measures of economic inequality and homogeneity, inclusion of both of these independent variables provides a statistically significant improvement.

D. Interpretation Four: Economic inequality and homogeneity together explain about 32 percent of the variance in the likelihood of democracy.

9

Thinking Empirically, Thinking Probabilistically

This book has covered only the basics—the essential skills you need to understand political research and to perform your own analysis. Even so, we have discussed a wide range of topics and methodological issues. The first four chapters dealt with the foundations of political analysis: defining and measuring concepts, generating explanations and hypotheses, describing variables, and setting up and interpreting comparisons. In the last four chapters we considered the role of statistics: making inferences, gauging the strength of relationships, performing linear regression analysis, and interpreting logistic regression. As you read research articles in political science, discuss and debate political topics, or evaluate the finer points of someone's research procedure, the basic knowledge imparted in this book will serve you well.

This book also has tried to convey a larger vision of the enterprise of political analysis. Political scientists seek to establish new facts about the world, to provide rich descriptions and accurate measurements of political phenomena. Political scientists also wish to explain political events and relationships. In pursuit of these goals, researchers learn to adopt a scientific mindset toward their work, a scientific approach to the twin challenges of describing and explaining political variables. As you perform your own political analysis, you too are encouraged to adopt this way of thinking. Here are two recommendations. First, in describing new facts, try to think empirically. Try to visualize how you would measure the phenomenon you are discussing and describing. Be open to new ideas, but insist on empirical rigor. Political science, like all science, is based on empirical evidence. This evidence must be described and measured in such a way that others can do what you did and obtain the same results. Second, in proposing and testing explanations, try to think probabilistically. You are well aware of one reason that political researchers must rely on probabilities: Random samples are a fact of life for much political science. Another reason is political science deals with human behavior and human events, and so it is an inexact science. Let's briefly illustrate why it is important to think empirically. Let's also look at the reasons political scientists must think probabilistically.

THINKING EMPIRICALLY

The main projects of political science are to describe concepts and to analyze the relationships between them. But potentially interesting relationships are often obscured by vague, conceptual language. During a class meeting of a voting and elections course, for example, students were discussing the electoral dynamics of ballot initiatives, law-making vehicles used frequently in several states. Controversial proposals, such as denying state benefits to illegal immigrants or abolishing affirmative action, may appear on the ballot to be decided directly by voters. Near the end of the discussion, one student observed: "It appears to me that most ballot initiatives target specific groups. Most ballot initiatives, if they pass, decrease equality. Very few seem designed with egalitarian principles in mind." Now, this is an interesting, imaginative statement. Is it true? Without conceptual clarification, there is no way to tell.

Upon hearing statements such as the one made by this student, you have learned to insist that conceptual terms, like *equality* or *egalitarian principles*, be described in concrete language. How would one distinguish an egalitarian ballot initiative, an initiative that increases equality, from one that is not egalitarian, an initiative that decreases equality? Pressed to clarify her conceptual terms, the student settled on one defining characteristic of the degree of egalitarianism in a ballot initiative. The concept of egalitarianism, she said, is defined as the extent to which a ballot initiative would confer new legal rights on a specific group. So some initiatives, such as those that would legalize marriage between same-sex couples, could be classified as more egalitarian, whereas others, like those making English the state's official language, could be classified as less egalitarian. With a workable measurement strategy in hand, this student could then turn to an empirical assessment of her in-class claim. Using clearly defined terms and reproducible findings, this student's research would enhance our understanding of these vehicles of direct democracy.[1]

An openness that is tempered by skepticism nurtures knowledge of the political world. This means that political scientists must sometimes revisit relationships and rethink established explanations. The search for truth is an ongoing process. Consider another example. For years, scholars of U.S. electoral behavior have measured voter turnout in presidential elections by dividing the number of people who voted by the size of the voting-age population. So if one wanted to describe and compare turnouts between 1960 and 2004, one would calculate the percentage of the voting-age population who voted in each year, and then track the numbers over time. Indeed, measured in this way, turnouts declined steadily from a twentieth-century high in 1960 to a twentieth-century low in 1996. Although turnouts rose in 2000 and 2004, these increases were less than one would expect, based on rising levels of education and the easing of legal restrictions on voting. The relatively low turnout in presidential elections is one of the most heavily researched phenomena in U.S. politics, and it has fostered a search for explanatory factors. Some explanations have linked declining turnout to attitudinal variables, such as a weakened attachment to the political parties or an erosion of trust in government.

However, research by Michael P. McDonald and Samuel Popkin points to a potentially serious measurement problem with using the voting-age population as the basis for calculating turnout.[2] They show that, by using the voting-age population, researchers have been including large groups of ineligible people, such as felons or noncitizens. What is more, the number of ineligible persons has been increasing over time—for example, the percentage of noncitizens among the voting-age population went from 2 percent in 1966 to 7.5 percent in

1998. Once McDonald and Popkin adjust for these and other measurement errors, they show that, although turnout dropped after 1972 (when the eligible electorate was expanded to include 18 year olds), there has been no downward trend.

How will this new measurement strategy affect empirical research on turnout? No doubt, in the coming years political scientists will debate this and other measurements. They will create new explanations and test new hypotheses. Though it is too soon to know what specific substantive findings may emerge from this interplay, we can be sure of one thing: In the end, we will have expanded our knowledge of electoral participation in the United States. Rigorous, empirical debate will guarantee it.

THINKING PROBABILISTICALLY

It is probably safe to say that statistics is among the least alluring topics in political analysis. The dryness of its appeal, however, belies its central importance to the research process. A discussion of random error has come up in several topics in this book—measurement, sampling, hypothesis testing, and statistical significance. We have seen that the accuracy of measurements may be affected by haphazard factors that can be difficult to control. And, in drawing samples from large and unseen populations, political researchers consciously introduce random sampling error. You have learned how to estimate the size of this error. You know how to "give chance a chance" to account for your results. And you can recognize and apply accepted standards for rejecting the null hypothesis, the omnipresent spokesperson for random probability. These are key skills in probabilistic thinking.

But probabilistic thinking is important in political research in a larger sense, one that has less to do with measurement error and random samples. Rather, it involves an important difference between the way the scientific approach is applied in the social sciences, such as political science, and the way it is applied in the physical sciences, such as physics or astronomy. To appreciate this difference, consider political scientist Gabriel Almond's retelling of philosopher Karl Popper's famous "clouds and clocks" metaphor:

> Karl Popper . . . uses the metaphor of clouds and clocks to represent the commonsense notions of determinacy and indeterminacy in physical systems. He asks us to imagine a continuum stretching from the most irregular, disorderly, and unpredictable "clouds" on the left to the most regular, orderly, and predictable "clocks" on the right. As the best example of a deterministic system at the clock-extreme, Popper cites the solar system. . . . As an example of a system near the other, indeterminate, end of the continuum, he cites a cluster of gnats or small flies in which each insect moves randomly except that it turns back toward the center when it strays too far from the swarm. Near this extreme we would find gas clouds, the weather, schools of fish, human societies, and, perhaps a bit closer to the center, individual human beings and animals.[3]

Physical scientists seek to explain phenomena toward the clocks side of the continuum. They develop and test explanations by gathering empirical data and seeing if the data are consistent with their causal explanations. And they set a deterministic standard in evaluating their theories. Causal factor X must be found to determine outcome Y. Political scientists seek to explain political phenomena, activity more toward the clouds side of the continuum. Political scientists, too, propose causal explanations and marshal empirical, reproducible facts to test their theories. But political behavior, like all human activity, is different from the behavior of objects in the physical world. Human behavior is far more complex. It is difficult to know for certain if political behavior Y is being determined by causal factor X or by some other cause of which we are unaware and for which we have not accounted. Indeed, you have learned that the "How else?" question is the centerpiece of controlled comparisons in political research. Only by identifying plausible alternative causes, and controlling for their effects, can we gain confidence in the explanations that we propose. For this reason, political scientists set a probabilistic standard in evaluating their theories. Political scientists do not expect their theories to provide deterministic predictions of political behavior, but they do expect them to predict appreciably better than chance.[4] Thus causal factor X must be found to increase the probability that people will choose political behavior Y instead of political behavior Z.

Probabilistic thinking should always accompany you when you observe the world and propose hypotheses to explain what you see. Consider a final illustration. According to information contained in the 2000 National Election Study, 52.7 percent of major-party voters reported voting for Democrat Al Gore, compared with 47.3 percent who voted for Republican George W. Bush. So, based on these numbers, if you had to predict the vote choice of any randomly chosen major-party voter, you would do fairly well by flipping a coin—heads, they voted Democratic, or tails, they voted Republican. But suppose you knew each individual's party identification, the direction and strength of their psychological attachment to one of the political parties. This knowledge would permit you to predict vote choice with far more certainty than chance alone. The percentage of Gore voters declines systematically as you move across the values of the party identification variable, from a high of 97.6 percent among strong Democrats to a low of 2.1 percent among strong Republicans.[5] Thus partisanship is a powerful predictor, perhaps the most powerful predictor we have in explaining this particular political behavior. But does party identification provide a deterministic explanation of vote choice? No, it does not. After all, some strong Democrats voted for Bush, and some strong Republicans voted for Gore. What are we to make of these individuals, these voters who do not cooperate with our explanation? In political science, unexplained phenomena do not lead us to abandon the search for the underlying causes of human behavior. Quite the contrary, "facts that don't fit" animate the search for better probabilistic explanations. The truth is always out there, waiting for you to discover it.

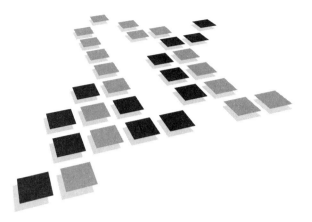

Notes

Chapter 1

1. This example draws on the influential work of Benjamin I. Page and Robert Y. Shapiro, *The Rational Public: Fifty Years of Trends in Americans' Policy Preferences* (Chicago: University of Chicago Press, 1992). Page and Shapiro argue that the concept of public opinion—and its relationship to other important concepts, such as democratic governance—is best studied at the aggregate level.

2. The term *operational definition,* universally used in social research, is something of a misnomer. An operational definition does not take the same form as a conceptual definition, in which a conceptual term is defined in empirical language. Rather, an operational definition describes a procedure for measuring the concept. *Measurement strategy* is probably a more descriptive term than *operational definition.*

3. The research on political tolerance is voluminous. This discussion is based mostly on the work of Samuel A. Stouffer, *Communism, Conformity and Civil Liberties* (New York: Wiley, 1966), and the conceptualization offered by John L. Sullivan, James Piereson, and George E. Marcus, "An Alternative Conceptualization of Tolerance: Illusory Increases, 1950s–1970s," *American Political Science Review* 73 (September 1979): 781–794. For further reading, see George E. Marcus, John L. Sullivan, Elizabeth Theiss-Morse, and Sandra L. Wood, *With Malice Toward Some* (New York: Cambridge University Press, 1995).

4. The term *Hawthorne effect* gets its name from a series of studies of worker productivity conducted in the late 1920s at the Western Electric Hawthorne Works in Chicago. Sometimes called reactive measurement effects, Hawthorne effects can be fairly durable, changing little over time. Test anxiety is an example of a durable reactive measurement effect. Other measurement effects are less durable. Some human subjects may initially respond to the novelty of being studied, and this effect may decrease if the subjects are tested again. The original Hawthorne effect was such a response to novelty. See Neil M. Agnew and Sandra W. Pyke, *The Science Game* (Englewood Cliffs, N.J.: Prentice-Hall, 1994), 159–160.

5. W. Phillips Shively argues that reliability is a necessary (but not sufficient) condition of validity. Using the metaphor of an archer aiming at a target, Shively describes four possible patterns: (A) a random scatter of arrows centered on an area away from the bull's-eye (high systematic error and high random error), (B) arrows tightly grouped but not on the bull's-eye (high systematic error and low random error), (C) a random scatter of arrows centered on the bull's-eye (low systematic error and high random error), and (D) arrows tightly grouped inside the bull's-eye

(low systematic error and low random error). According to Shively, only the last pattern represents a valid measurement. Earl Babbie, however, argues that reliability and validity are separate criteria of measurement. Using a metaphor identical to Shively's, Babbie characterizes pattern C as "valid but not reliable" and pattern D as "valid and reliable." See W. Phillips Shively, *The Craft of Political Research*, 6th ed. (Upper Saddle River, N.J.: Pearson Prentice Hall, 2005), 48–49; Earl Babbie, *The Practice of Social Research*, 10th ed. (Belmont, Calif.: Thomson Wadsworth, 2004), 143–146.

6. There are other ways to evaluate reliability. The *parallel forms method*, for example, is a sophisticated version of the test-retest approach. In this technique, the retest would be accomplished by using an instrument similar in content, but not identical, to the first. Of course, the researcher would need to establish the fact that the two forms are parallel.

7. This example is from Herbert Asher, *Polling and the Public: What Every Citizen Should Know*, 5th ed. (Washington, D.C.: CQ Press, 2001), 88–89. Asher notes that this question has been dropped from the American National Election Study. Face validity is similar to other approaches that you may encounter. *Sampling validity* asks whether the traits being measured fairly represent all the traits that are implied by the concept. Sampling validity is closely related to face validity, because both look at the specific items that comprise the operational measure. A more generic rubric, *content validity*, is often used to describe these approaches to evaluating validity. See David Nachmias and Chava Nachmias, *Research Methods in the Social Sciences*, 2d ed. (New York: St. Martin's, 1981), 140–142.

8. For a discussion of how the construct validity approach has been applied to the GRE, see Janet Buttolph Johnson, Richard A. Joslyn, and H. T. Reynolds, *Political Science Research Methods*, 4th ed. (Washington, D.C.: CQ Press, 2001), 86–87.

9. The interviewer asks, "Generally speaking, do you think of yourself as a Republican, a Democrat, an Independent, or what?" Respondents are given six choices: Democrat, Republican, Independent, Other Party, No Preference, and Don't Know. Those who choose Democrat or Republican are asked, "Would you call yourself a strong Democrat [Republican] or a not very strong Democrat [Republican]?" Those who choose Independent, Other Party, No Preference, or Don't Know are asked, "Do you think of yourself as closer to the Republican Party or to the Democratic Party?" Interviewers record these responses: Closer to Republican Party, Neither, or Closer to Democratic Party. Of the 1,807 people who were asked these questions in the 2000 National Election Study, 1,776 were classified along the 7-point scale, 9 identified with another party, 17 were apolitical, and 5 did not give complete responses. See Nancy Burns, Donald R. Kinder, Steven J. Rosenstone, Virginia Sapiro, and the National Election Studies, *American National Election Study, 2000: Pre- and Post-election Survey*, 2nd version (Ann Arbor: University of Michigan, Center for Political Studies [producer], 2001; Inter-university Consortium for Political and Social Research [distributor], 2002).

10. Bruce E. Keith, David B. Magleby, Candice J. Nelson, Elizabeth Orr, Mark C. Westlye, and Raymond E. Wolfinger, *The Myth of the Independent Voter* (Berkeley: University of California Press, 1992).

11. Herbert F. Weisberg, "A Multidimensional Conceptualization of Party Identification," *Political Behavior* 2 (1980): 33–60.

12. The measurement problem illustrated by Table 1-2 is known as the *intransitivity problem*. For a concise review of the scholarly debate about intransitivity and other measurement issues, see Richard G. Niemi and Herbert F. Weisberg, *Controversies in Voting Behavior*, 4th ed. (Washington, D.C.: CQ Press, 2001), chap. 17.

13. This helpful hint comes from Robert A. Bernstein and James A. Dyer, *An Introduction to Political Science Methods*, 3d ed. (Englewood Cliffs, N.J.: Prentice-Hall, 1992), 3.

14. The following discussion refers to a variable by its name. For example, "the variable, age" means the same thing as "the variable named age."

15. A higher level of measurement is sometimes discussed: ratio-level variables. A ratio variable has all the properties of an interval-level measure, plus it has a meaningful zero-point—the complete absence of the attribute being measured. As a practical matter, you will probably never encounter a research situation in which the distinction between interval and ratio measurements makes a difference.

Chapter 2

1. The education-turnout explanation also suggests that people with less education are less politically aware and less efficacious than people with more education, and that awareness and efficacy are linked to turnout. An explanation can, and usually does, suggest more than one empirical relationship. In this chapter we discuss this aspect of explanations.

2. The 1996 National Election Study asked respondents, "Do you favor or oppose a ban on the sale of all handguns, except those that are issued to law enforcement officers?" Some 47 percent said they favored such a ban; 53 percent said they opposed it.

3. This is the origin of the term *dependent variable*. In a causal explanation, the values of the dependent variable are said to "depend on" the values of the independent variable.

4. Some researchers prefer the term *direction* instead of *tendency*. The problem with *direction* is that it has both logical and empirical meanings. If one were to propose that women and men have different opinions on gun control, then one would not be stating direction. If one were to say that women are more likely than men to favor gun control, one would be stating direction. This logical usage makes perfect sense. But to say that the gender–gun opinions relationship has a "positive direction" or "negative direction" does not make sense, because gender is not a quantitative variable. The term *tendency* is used in this chapter in order to avoid confusion in Chapter 3, when *direction* is used to describe empirical relationships between quantitative variables.

5. Robert D. Putnam, *Bowling Alone: The Collapse and Revival of American Community* (New York: Simon & Schuster, 2000).

6. Leslie Lenkowsky, "Still 'Bowling Alone'?," *Commentary* (October 2000): 57.

7. Like many explanations for social or political variables, Putnam's explanation does not rely on a single independent variable. The changing age composition is very important to Putnam's explanation, but he also suggests that another long-term social trend, the rise in television as the primary source of entertainment, is causally linked to the decline in organized social and community interaction. Putnam regards the decline in civic organizations as a serious matter. He argues that such face-to-face interaction fosters social trust and participatory skills, essential elements for a healthy democratic society. These assertions are, of course, open to empirical test.

8. Malcolm Gladwell, *The Tipping Point: How Little Things Can Make a Big Difference* (Boston: Little, Brown, 2000), 5, 14.

9. As an example of an archetypical connector, Gladwell cites Lois Weisberg, commissioner of cultural affairs for the city of Chicago. By Gladwell's count, Weisberg has hundreds of contacts spanning ten different professional and social contexts: actors, writers, doctors, lawyers, park-lovers, politicians, railroad buffs, flea market aficionados, architects, and people in the hospitality industry. The point about connectors like Weisberg "is that by having a foot in so many different worlds, they have the effect of bringing them all together." *The Tipping Point*, 51.

10. Gladwell also discusses the role of other causal factors in the spread of contagions. A disease needs to change form, becoming less virulent, "sticking around" so that it can infect more people. Also, the behavior that supports the contagion must be a widely shared social norm within the demographic context in which it takes its highest toll.

11. Gladwell, *The Tipping Point*, 56–57.

12. Ibid., 33.

13. These typical errors in hypothesis writing are pointed out by Robert A. Bernstein and James A. Dyer, *An Introduction to Political Science Methods*, 3d ed. (Englewood Cliffs, N.J.: Prentice-Hall, 1992), 11–12.

14. Edward R. Tufte, *Data Analysis for Politics and Policy* (Englewood Cliffs, N.J.: Prentice-Hall, 1974), 4. This story is a medical school recollection of E. E. Peacock Jr., quoted in *Medical World News* (September 1, 1972): 45.

15. To avoid confusion, in this chapter the terms *true experiment* or *experimental design* will always refer to research that follows the experimental research design. The terms *natural experiment* or *natural experimental design* will always refer to research that fits the natural experimental research design.

16. Random assignment does not completely guarantee that the two groups are identical, of course. By chance, subjects picked for the test group might still differ from control subjects. Random processes are well understood, however, and we know how to adjust for chance differences. Random selection is discussed at length in Chapter 5.

17. This description draws on Shanto Iyengar and Donald R. Kinder, *News That Matters: Television and American Opinion* (Chicago: University of Chicago Press, 1987); and Shanto Iyengar, Mark D. Peters, and Donald R. Kinder, "Experimental Demonstrations of the 'Not-So-Minimal' Consequences of Television News Programs," in *Experimental Foundations of Political Science,* ed. Donald R. Kinder and Thomas R. Palfrey (Ann Arbor: University of Michigan Press, 1993), 313–331.

18. Iyengar and Kinder, *News That Matters,* 18–19.

19. Iyengar, Peters, and Kinder, "Experimental Demonstrations," 321. These researchers are very much aware of questions about external validity. They suggest that the problem of external validity can be addressed by using a variety of methods, so-called methodological pluralism, to investigate the role of media.

20. Philip H. Pollock III and Bruce M. Wilson, "Evaluating the Impact of Internet Teaching: Preliminary Evidence from American National Government Classes," *PS: Political Science and Politics* 35, no. 3 (September 2002): 561–566.

Chapter 3

1. The terms *cases, subjects, units,* and *units of analysis* will be used interchangeably in this discussion.

2. *Variation, dispersion,* and *spread* all refer to the distribution of cases across the values of a variable.

3. For interval-level variables, there is a precise statistical measure of dispersion, the standard deviation. The statistical understanding of variation is fundamental to many aspects of political research—sampling, inferential statistics, measures of association, to name a few. In Chapter 5 we will discuss the standard deviation and look at how it is applied to problems of sampling and inference.

4. The use of statistics in hypothesis testing is discussed in Chapter 6.

5. To avoid confusion in terminology, we should note that a *proportion* is the raw frequency divided by the total frequency. A *percentage* is a proportion multiplied by 100. Barring rounding error, proportions total to 1.00 and percentages total to 100.

6. In describing a variable, whether one chooses to display the percentage of cases or the number of cases along the vertical axis of a bar chart is largely a matter of individual preference. In either case, the relative heights of the bars will be the same. When comparing the distributions of a variable for two or more subsets of cases—for example, comparing the distribution of religious attendance for whites with the distribution of religious attendance for blacks—percentages must be used, because the subsets have unequal numbers of cases.

7. The survey has a total of 1,714 respondents. Because two respondents did not report their ages, they have to be dropped from the calculations. Missing cases are not included in the calculation of percentages or means.

8. Statistically speaking, a distribution that is perfectly symmetrical, one that has no skew, has a skewness equal to zero. Most data analysis packages report a measure of skewness that takes on a positive value or a negative value, indicating the direction of skew. These computer programs also provide a companion statistic (called the standard error of skewness) that allows the researcher to determine if the skewness of the distribution departs too much from zero.

9. The interviewer begins with this preamble: "We are faced with many problems in this country, none of which can be solved easily or inexpensively. I'm going to name some of these problems, and for each one I'd like you to tell me whether you think we're spending too much money on it, too little money, or about the right amount." The interviewer then names a series of programs and policies. The variable displayed in Table 3-4 and Figure 3-4 was constructed by summing the number of "spending too little" responses to "assistance to big cities," "drug rehabilitation," "education," "the environment," "assistance to the poor," "health," and "assistance to blacks."

10. Another graphic display, the histogram, is often used to depict interval-level variables. Histograms

are similar to bar charts. Whereas a bar chart shows the percentages (or frequency) of cases in each value of a variable, a histogram shows the percentage or frequency of cases falling into intervals of the variable. These intervals, called bins, compress the display, removing choppiness and gaps between the bars. Both bar charts and histograms work about equally well in helping the researcher to describe an interval-level variable.

11. Analysis and interpretation of interval-level dependent and independent variables is covered in Chapter 7. Chapter 8 covers research situations in which the dependent variable is a two-category nominal or ordinal variable and the independent variable is interval level.

12. The National Election Study's 7-point party identification scale was discussed in Chapter 1. The scale classifies respondents as Strong Democrat, Weak Democrat, independent-leaning Democrat, pure independent, independent-leaning Republican, Weak Republican, and Strong Republican. For the purpose of illustrating cross-tabulation analysis, the Weak and Strong Democrats are grouped together, as are the Weak and Strong Republicans. Independents are composed of the leaners and the pure independents.

13. Freedom House, a nonprofit organization, ranks countries on two separate 7-point scales: political rights and civil liberties. The variable being discussed here was created by summing these scores for each country. The final variable was rescaled to range from 0 (fewest political rights and freedoms) to 12 (most political rights and freedoms). For a discussion of Freedom House's methodology, see http://www.freedomhouse.org/ratings/index.htm.

14. The general preference for the format illustrated by Table 3-8 is shaped by practical considerations. For one thing, computer output for mean comparison analyses almost always takes the single-column form, with the values of the independent variable appearing on the left and the means of the dependent variable appearing on the right. Also, in interpreting mean comparisons there are fewer potential sources of confusion than in interpreting cross-tabulations—there is, after all, only one summary measure to compare across values of the independent variable. This permits more flexibility in the presentation of means. This is a general preference, not a rule. If the Table 3-7 format suits you better, then go ahead and construct mean comparisons according to that format.

15. In the real world of political research, relationships are rarely symmetrical. Figure 3-8 is no exception. You can see that respondents on the Republican side of the scale's midpoint are more likely to vote than are their counterparts on the Democratic side. Still, the relationship roughly approximates a V- or U-shaped pattern.

Chapter 4

1. When a relationship is spurious, researchers sometimes refer to the relationship as an "artifact" of a rival cause, as an artificial creation of an uncontrolled variable.

2. This popular example is retold by Royce Singleton Jr., Bruce C. Straits, Margaret M. Straits, and Ronald McAllister, *Approaches to Social Research* (New York: Oxford University Press, 1988), 81.

3. In interpreting controlled comparisons using cross-tabulation analysis, particularly when one of the variables is nominal level, there is no universally accepted term for a set of relationships herein labeled *additive*. However, the term *additive* does have apposite usage in regression analysis, in which relationships are often modeled as "linear-additive." The "linear" part of linear-additive says that (controlling for Z) each unit increase in X has a consistent effect on Y, and that (controlling for X) each unit increase in Z has a consistent effect on Y. The "additive" part of linear-additive says that one determines the combined effects of X and Z on Y by summing or "adding up" their individual effects. Regression analysis is discussed in Chapter 7. In the current discussion, the term *additive* conveys the idea that each variable, the independent variable and the control variable, makes a distinct and consistent contribution to the explanation of the dependent variable.

4. Of the two interchangeable terms that describe this scenario—specification and interaction—specification perhaps has more intuitive appeal. The word *specification* tells us that the control variable Z specifies the relationship between X and Y, that the X→Y relationship depends on the specific value of Z. *Interaction*, which is frequently used in regression analysis (see Chapter 7),

imparts the idea that the independent effects of X on Y and Z on Y, when combined, interact to produce an effect on Y that is greater than the effect of each independent variable alone. Medication labels, for example, often warn that the effect of the drug on drowsiness, combined with alcohol, will be greater than simply adding the independent effect of taking the drug to the independent effect of consuming alcohol. To keep the presentation consistent, the term *interaction* is used throughout this book. However, interaction and specification are synonymous terms, and you will encounter both terms in political research.

5. For this example, education has been collapsed into two categories. "Low" education is defined as high school or less, and "high" education is defined as more than high school.

6. The 7-percentage-point racial difference would be termed a first-order partial, because one other variable, education, has been controlled. As more variables are taken into account, the designation increases in order. Comparing whites and blacks, controlling for education *and* gender, for example, would produce a second-order partial.

7. To get a more complete picture of all the relationships, researchers often set up a separate cross-tabulation for the overall relationship between Z and X. In this example, a cross-tabulation would show race and education to be strongly related, with 57.9 percent of blacks having "low" education, compared with 42.7 percent of whites. It is worth pointing out that this information also can be gleaned from a control table, though a little estimation (or a hand-held calculator) may be required. Notice, for example, that of the 171 blacks in Table 4-2, 99—greater than half—are in the low-education category. But for whites, a quick comparison of the numbers—561 in "low," 753 in "high"—tells us that substantially fewer than half fall into the low-education category.

8. The interviewer frames the feeling thermometer questions with this preamble: "I'd like to get your feelings toward some of our political leaders and other people who are in the news these days. I'll read the name of a person and I'd like you to rate that person using something we call the feeling thermometer. Ratings between 50 degrees and 100 degrees mean that you feel favorable and warm toward the person. Ratings between 0 degrees and 50 degrees mean that you don't feel favorable toward the person and that you don't care too much for that person. You would rate the person at the 50-degree mark if you don't feel particularly warm or cold toward the person."

Chapter 5

1. See, for example, John Harwood and Cynthia Crossen, "A Close Contest, Plunging Responses Tax Already-Inexact Science of Polls," WSJ.com (Dow Jones and Company, Inc.), September 29, 2000.

2. Richard Morin, "New Woes Surface in Use of Estimates," *The Washington Post*, November 4, 2004, A29.

3. The terms *population characteristic* and *population parameter* are synonymous and will be used interchangeably in this chapter.

4. Of course, purely random sampling is impractical for large populations. However, researchers have devised several random-based techniques for large sampling frames. An excellent treatment may be found in Herbert Asher, *Polling and the Public: What Every Citizen Should Know*, 6th ed. (Washington, D.C.: CQ Press, 2004). Also see S. K. Thomson, *Sampling* (New York: Wiley, 1992).

5. As a statistical matter, the population variance is calculated just as shown here—by summing the squared deviations from the mean and dividing by N, the population size. As a practical matter, however, you are more likely to encounter calculations of the sample variance, defined as the summation of the squared deviations divided by the sample size minus one, or $n - 1$. Most spreadsheets and data analysis packages reasonably assume that the user is working with a sample and, so, report sample statistics, not population parameters. For example, SPSS, a popular data analysis package, reported a variance equal to $20.45 and a standard deviation of $4.52 for the population of wage earners in Table 5-1. More to the point, if you are exercising your ability to calculate the variance and standard deviation of a list of numbers—and then checking your work against software-generated values—then make sure to divide the sum of the squared deviations by $n - 1$.

6. Statisticians typically detest imprecision, but this rule of thumb is acceptable because it is conservative; that is, it slightly widens the bandwidth of the random error associated with the 95 percent confidence interval.

Chapter 6

1. The term *P-value* is widely, though not universally, used. Computer output commonly reports P-values under the heading "significance" or its abbreviation, "sig." *P-value* and *significance* are synonymous terms. Both terms tell you the probability of obtaining the observed results if the null hypothesis is correct.
2. Statistically, one can think of a random sample of, say, 100 cases as equivalent to 100 random samples of size n = 1. Assigning each individual outcome the value 1 if it falls into a specific category of a variable, and coding it 0 if it does not fall into that category, we find the mean value by summing the 100 0's and 1's and dividing by 100. The result, of course, is a proportion.
3. Alan Agresti and Barbara Finlay, *Statistical Methods for the Social Sciences,* 3d ed. (Upper Saddle River, N.J.: Prentice-Hall, 1997), 255. Chi-square is one member of a large family of nonparametric statistics, tests that make fewer assumptions about the population from which the sample is drawn.
4. This intuitive way of getting expected frequencies works okay, but it can introduce a fair amount of rounding error. A more precise method of obtaining expected frequencies is to multiply the column total by the row total and divide by the sample size. For example, the expected frequency (f_e) for the "low attendance–never allow" cell would be the total number of cases in the "low" column, 802, multiplied by the number of cases in the "never allow" category of the dependent variable, 200, divided by the sample size, 1,679: (802 * 200) / 1,679 = 95.5.
5. George W. Bornstedt and David Knoke, *Statistics for Social Data Analysis,* 2d ed. (Itasca, Ill.: F. E. Peacock, 1988), 124–126.
6. Bornstedt and Knoke analyze the birth-month distribution of 1,462 individuals from the 1984 General Social Survey. They obtain a calculated χ^2 of 11.39. For 11 degrees of freedom, the upper limit of random error, using the .05 threshold, is 19.68. Since a χ^2 of 11.39 could occur more frequently than five times out of 100 by chance, one cannot say that some months are more prevalent than are other months for being born.
7. Yate's correction is an adjustment often seen in computer calculations. It consists of either adding or subtracting .5 from an observed frequency to reduce the difference between f_o and f_e.
8. Inconsistency between the pattern of the data and the sign of an ordinal statistic is extremely common in computer analysis. Most data analysis packages arranged tables so that the lowest numeric codes of both variables define the upper-left cell of a table, and the highest numeric codes define the lower-right cell. The sign of an ordinal statistic follows this "model" of a positive relationship, upper left to lower right. If one ordinal variable is coded so that lower numeric values indicate more of the attribute being measured, as is campaign interest in Table 6-8 (people who are "very interested" are coded 1), then an inconsistent sign will result.
9. One of the Somer's d statistics, the one calculated using education level as the dependent variable, is not appropriate, because education is the independent variable in the hypothesis being tested. The "symmetric" version, as well as the "asymmetric" statistic calculated using campaign interest as the dependent variable, are appropriate for the hypothesis.
10. Statisticians refer to such measures as strong measures, because they require a fair-sized relationship before they will provide an estimate. So lambda is a strong nominal-level PRE measure.
11. For whites, $\chi^2 = 6.50$, and for blacks, $\chi^2 = 7.60$. Both have P-values of less than .05 (1 degree of freedom).
12. Cramer's V essentially *is* χ^2, adjusted for sample size (n). It is the square root of the expression χ^2 / ((n)(min(r – 1, c – 1)), where min(r – 1, c – 1) tells us to plug in the number of rows minus 1 or the number of columns minus 1, whichever is smaller. There is still another non-PRE measure based on chi-square, the contingency coefficient (C) that some researchers prefer. It returns values that are similar to Cramer's V. Since the interpretation of Cramer's V is somewhat more straightfor-

ward, it is generally recommended. For a discussion of the nuances, see Borhnstedt and Knoke, *Statistics for Social Data Analysis*, 310–311.

13. Information on workday voting and nonworkday voting in 58 democracies was obtained from Lawrence LeDuc, Richard G. Niemi, and Pippa Norris, "Introduction: Comparing Democratic Elections," pp 1–39 in LeDuc, Niemi, and Norris, eds., *Comparing Democracies 2: New Challenges in the Study of Elections and Voting* (London: Sage Publications, 2002). See Table 1.3, pp. 13–15. Turnout data are from the Shared Global Database (Revised Fall 2004), Pippa Norris, John F. Kennedy School of Government, Harvard University, Cambridge, Mass. Retrieved from http://ksghome .harvard.edu/~pnorris/Data/Data.htm. For each country, turnout is the average of all national legislative elections held during the 1990s.

14. Michael L. Ross, "Does Oil Hinder Democracy?" *World Politics* 53 (April 2001): 325–361. This quote page 325. This exercise compares the 15 most highly oil-dependent economies, as identified by Ross (Table 1, p. 326), with 20 other countries, which were randomly selected from the Shared Global Database (Revised Fall 2004), Pippa Norris, John F. Kennedy School of Government, Harvard University, Cambridge, Mass. The dependent variable, based on the Freedom House political rights and civil liberties scales (2003–2004), also was obtained from the Shared Global Database.

Chapter 7

1. In practice, regression is often used when the dependent variable is an ordinal-level measure that has many categories.

2. All of the statistics presented in this chapter were generated through computer analysis using SPSS, a powerful data analysis software package widely used in academic and business environments. SPSS is a product of SPSS, Inc. The SPSS homepage is http://www.spss.com/.

3. The numerator is equal to Σ (X – the mean of X)(Y – the mean of Y). So for each observation, one would find its deviation from the mean of the independent variable, multiply this result by its deviation from the mean of the dependent variable, and then sum these products across all the observations. The denominator is based on the total sum of squares—squared deviations from the mean— of each variable considered separately. It is equal to the square root of the expression: Σ (X – the mean of X)^2 $\times$ Σ (Y – the mean of Y)^2.

4. The regression coefficient summarizes change in the dependent variable for each unit change in the independent variable. Computationally, $\hat{b}$ is equal to Σ (X – mean of X)(Y – mean of Y) divided by Σ (X – mean of X)^2. The numerator summarizes the covariation of X and Y. The denominator summarizes variation in X. The result is the average amount of change in Y for each unit change in X.

5. The standard error of the estimated regression slope is based on how closely the predicted values of Y approximate the actual values of Y. Logically enough, if the regression line produces predicted values that are close to the actual values, the standard error of $\hat{b}$ is small. As the size of the prediction errors increases, so does the slope's standard error. The statistical properties of the standard error of $\hat{b}$ will not be discussed here. For a highly readable explanation, see Edward R. Tufte, *Data Analysis for Politics and Policy* (Englewood Cliffs, N.J.: Prentice-Hall, 1974), 65–73.

6. OLS regression determines â by the formula (mean of Y) – $\hat{b}$ (mean of X).

7. For all of this chapter's examples using the state data to illustrate inference, we will assume a random sample.

8. We encountered TSS before, in the Chapter 5 discussion of the variance and standard deviation. As a building block of R-square, the calculation of TSS is identical. R-square determines the deviation from the mean of the distribution for each observation, squares this deviation, and then sums the squared deviations across all the cases.

9. Some methodologists label the two components of TSS as *regression sum of squares* and *residual sum of squares*. Our labels are based on those used by Michael S. Lewis-Beck, *Applied Regression: An Introduction* (Thousand Oaks, Calif.: Sage Publications, 1980).

10. Another measure of goodness of fit for the regression line, which has the unfortunate label *standard*

error of the estimate, is less commonly used. Its appearance in computer output is a potential source of confusion, however, because its name sounds similar to a statistic that we use all the time, the *standard error of the regression coefficient*. This is a confusion that should be avoided.

11. This point is emphasized by Michael S. Lewis-Beck. See Lewis-Beck, *Applied Regression*, 25.

12. Regression analysis also produces a standard error and t-statistic for the Y-intercept. The standard error of the Y-intercept can be used to test the null hypothesis that the true value of the Y-intercept in the population, α, is equal to 0. The usefulness of these statistics depends on the research problem at hand. In the current example, we are not interested in testing the hypothesis that α, the turnout rate of non-Southern states, is 0. So the standard error of â, and its accompanying t-ratio, have been omitted from Table 7-3.

13. This brief exposition shows the main ideas behind the modeling of interaction. For an excellent guide to more advanced applications, see James Jaccard and Robert Turrisi, *Interaction Effects in Multiple Regression*, 2d ed. (Thousand Oaks, Calif.: Sage Publications, 2003).

14. The regression results in Exercises 3 and 4 were obtained from an analysis of the 1998 GSS. The GSS asks respondents whether or not a woman should be able to obtain a legal abortion under each of seven circumstances. The abortion scale was created by summing the number of "No" responses. The religious attendance dummy in Question 4 was coded 1 for people who attend "every week" or "more than once a week," and coded 0 otherwise. For the regression in Question 3, n = 1,578. For Question 4, n = 1,557. The abortion scale used in Exercises 3 and 4 differs from the pro-choice scale analyzed in Tables 7-6 and 7-7. The pro-choice variable, on which higher scores denote stronger pro-choice attitudes, is based only on the GSS items tapping respondents' approval of abortion under circumstances clearly related to choice, and not involving health considerations. The abortion scale used in the exercises was created from all of the GSS items, and it was coded such that higher scores denote stronger pro-life opinions.

Chapter 8

1. Methodologists have developed several techniques that may be used to analyze binary dependent variables. One popular technique, probit analysis, is based on somewhat different assumptions than logistic regression, but it generally produces similar results. Logistic regression, also called logit analysis or logit regression, is computationally more tractable than probit analysis and thus is the sole focus of this chapter. For a lucid discussion of the general family of techniques to which logistic regression and probit analysis belong, see Tim Futing Liao, *Interpreting Probability Models: Logit, Probit, and Other Generalized Linear Models* (Thousand Oaks, Calif.: Sage Publications, 1994).

2. There are two statistically based problems with using OLS on a binary dependent variable, both of which arise from having only two possible values for the dependent variable. OLS regression assumes that its prediction errors, the differences between the predicted values of Y and the actual values of Y, follow a normal distribution. The prediction errors for a binary variable, however, follow a binomial distribution. More seriously, OLS also assumes *homoscedasticity* of these errors, that is, that the prediction errors are the same for all values of X. With a binary dependent variable, this assumption does not hold up. An accessible discussion of these problems may be found in Fred C. Pampel, *Logistic Regression: A Primer* (Thousand Oaks, Calif.: Sage Publications, 2000), pp. 3–10.

3. Because of this natural log transformation of the dependent variable, many researchers use the terms *logit regression* or *logit analysis* instead of logistic regression. Others make a distinction between logit analysis (used to describe a situation in which the independent variables are not continuous but categorical) and logistic regression (used to describe a situation in which the independent variables are continuous or a mix of continuous and categorical). To avoid confusion, we use *logistic regression* to describe any situation in which the dependent variable is the natural log of the odds of a binary variable.

4. Logistic regression will fit an S-shaped curve to the relationship between an interval-level independent variable and the probability of a dependent variable, but it need not be the same S-shaped pattern shown in Figure 8-1. For example, the technique may produce estimates that trace a "lazy S,"

with probabilities rising in a slow, nearly linear pattern across values of the independent variable. Or perhaps the relationship is closer to an "upright S," with probabilities changing little across the high and low ranges of the independent variable but increasing rapidly in the middle ranges.

5. If the logistic regression coefficient, $\hat{b}$, were equal to 0, then the odds ratio, $\text{Exp}(\hat{b})$, would be $\text{Exp}(0)$, or e^0, which is equal to 1.

6. Computer output also will report a standard error and test of significance for the intercept, $\hat{a}$. This would permit the researcher to test the hypothesis that the intercept is significantly different from 0. So if we wanted to test the null hypothesis that the logged odds of voting for individuals with no formal education (who have a value of 0 on the independent variable) was equal to 0—that is, that the odds of voting for this group was equal to 1—we would use the standard error of the intercept. Much of the time such a test has no practical meaning, and so these statistics have been omitted from Table 8-3.

7. The Wald statistic (named for statistician Abraham Wald) divides the regression coefficient by its standard error and then squares the result. The value of Wald follows a chi-square distribution with degrees of freedom equal to 1.

8. The estimation procedure used by logistic regression is not aimed at minimizing the sum of the squared deviations between the estimated values of Y and the observed values of Y. So the conventional interpretation of R-square, the percentage of the variation in the dependent variable that is explained by the independent variable(s), does not apply when the dependent variable is binary.

9. The likelihood function $= \Pi \{P_i^{Yi} * (1 - P_i)^{1-Yi}\}$. The expression inside the brackets says, for each individual case, to raise the model's predicted probability (P) to the power of Y, and to multiply that number by the quantity 1 minus the predicted probability raised to power of $1 - Y$. The symbol Π tells us to multiply all these individual results together. The formula is really not as intimidating as it looks. When Y equals 1, the formula simplifies to $(P * 1)$, since P raised to Y equals P, and $(1 - P)$ raised to $1 - Y$ equals 1. Similarly when Y equals 0, the formula simplifies to $1 - P$.

10. The baseline model is also called the reduced model, because its predictions are generated without using the independent variable. Informally, we could also call it the "know-nothing model," because it does not take into account knowledge of the independent variable.

11. A likelihood model that uses the independent variable(s) to generate predicted probabilities is called the full model or complete model. In making statistical comparisons between models, some computer programs work with the log of the likelihood ratio, denoted $\ln(L1 / L2)$, in which L1 is the likelihood of Model 1 (reduced model) and L2 is the likelihood of Model 2 (complete model). Taking the log of the likelihood ratio is equivalent to subtracting the logged likelihood of Model 2 from the logged likelihood of Model 1: $\ln(L1 / L2) = \ln(L1)$ minus $\ln(L2)$.

12. Degrees of freedom is equal to the difference between the number of independent variables included in the models being compared. Since Model 2 has one independent variable and Model 1 has no independent variables, degrees of freedom is equal to 1 for this example. We can, of course, test the null hypothesis the old-fashioned way, by consulting a chi-square table. The critical value of chi-square, at the .05 level with 1 degree of freedom, is equal to 3.84. Since the change in −2LL, which is equal to 3.98, exceeds the critical value, we can reject the null hypothesis.

13. The Wald statistic, commonly used to test the significance of logistic regression coefficients, is somewhat controversial. Some methodologists argue that, if the estimated logistic regression coefficients are large or if dummy independent variables are being used, Wald may underestimate the effect of an independent variable and thus bias inference too strongly toward Type II error. These researchers recommend a procedure based more directly on changes in the likelihood function. For a discussion of potential problems with the Wald statistic, see Scott Menard, *Applied Logistic Regression Analysis*, 2d ed. (Thousand Oaks, Calif.: Sage Publications, 2002), pp. 43–48. See also J. Scott Long, *Regression Models for Categorical and Limited Dependent Variables* (Thousand Oaks, Calif.: Sage Publications, 1997).

14. Logged likelihoods can be confusing. Remember that likelihoods vary between 0 (the model's predictions do not fit the data at all) and 1 (the model's predictions fit the data perfectly). This means that the logs of likelihoods can range from very large negative numbers (any likelihood of

less than 1 has a negatively signed log) to 0 (any likelihood equal to 1 has a log equal to 0). So if Model 2 had a likelihood of 1—that is, it perfectly predicted voter turnout—then it would have a logged likelihood of 0. In this case, the conceptual formula for R-square would return a value of 1.0.

15. Cox and Snell's R-square and Nagelkerke's R-square are included in SPSS logistic regression output. Another measure, popular among political researchers, is Aldrich and Nelson's Pseudo R-square: (Change in $-2LL$) / (Change in $-2LL + N$), in which N is the sample size. Menard has proposed yet another measure, based on the correlation between the logistic regression's predicted probabilities of Y and the actual values of Y. Reassuringly, the Aldrich-Nelson statistic for the GSS data is equal to .052, and Menard's proposed measure returned a value of .051, both close to Cox-Snell (.053) and a bit lower than Nagelkerke (.075). See John H. Aldrich and Forrest D. Nelson, *Linear Probability, Logit, and Probit Models* (Thousand Oaks, Calif.: Sage Publications, 1984), pp. 54–58; and Menard, *Applied Logistic Regression Analysis*, pp. 24–27.

16. The logged likelihoods for the reduced model and the complete model are not shown in Table 8-8. Rather, only the chi-square test statistic of interest, the change in $-2LL$, is reported. Note that, because no independent variables are included in the baseline model and two independent variables are included in the complete model, there are 2 degrees of freedom for the chi-square test.

17. If requested by the user, SPSS will enlist the logistic equation estimates to calculate and save predicted probabilities of the dependent variable for each case in the dataset. These predicted values become a new variable, which can be further examined and analyzed.

18. Researchers have proposed and debated a variety of ways to present and interpret estimated probabilities. For a discussion of several approaches, see Pampel, *Logistic Regression: A Primer*, pp. 28–30.

19. It may seem odd to consider a 0-1 variable as having a mean or average in the conventional sense of the term. After all, respondents are coded either 0 or 1. There is no respondent who is coded ".221" on partisan strength. However, means can also be thought of as random probabilities, termed *expected values* by statisticians. If you were to pick any respondent at random from the GSS dataset, what is the probability that the case you chose would be a strong partisan? The answer is .221, the expected value, or mean value, of this variable.

20. Data used in these exercises are from the Shared Global Database (Revised Fall 2004), Pippa Norris, John F. Kennedy School of Government, Harvard University, Cambridge, Mass. Retrieved from http://ksghome.harvard.edu/~pnorris/data/data.htm. Using Norris's definition, democratic countries are coded 1 and nondemocratic countries are coded 0. Economic inequality is measured by the gini coefficient, divided by 10. This measure, based on information provided by the World Bank, can vary between 0 (most equal) and 10 (least equal). The variable homogeneous is based on the cultural homogeneity index (1980), which Norris obtained from the State Failure Project Phase III. Countries having homogeneity scores at or above the median value are coded 1 on homogeneous. Those having homogeneity scores below the median are coded 0. Numbers of cases (n): 102 for Exercise 1 and 81 for Exercise 2.

Chapter 9

1. This dialogue occurred during classroom discussion of Richard J. Ellis, "The States: Direct Democracy," in *The Elections of 2000*, ed. Michael Nelson (Washington, D.C., CQ Press, 2001), 133–159.

2. Michael P. McDonald and Samuel Popkin, "The Myth of the Vanishing Voter," *American Political Science Review* 95, no. 4 (2001): 963–974.

3. Gabriel A. Almond, *A Discipline Divided: Schools and Sects in Political Science* (Thousand Oaks, Calif.: Sage Publications, 1990), 33.

4. Charles A. Lave and James G. March, *An Introduction to Models in the Social Sciences* (New York: Harper and Row, 1975), 34.

5. The percentages of Gore voters for all values of party identification are as follows: strong Democrats, 97.6 percent; weak Democrats, 89.5 percent; independent-leaning Democrats, 78.5 percent; independents, 50.0 percent; independent-leaning Republicans, 14.5 percent; weak Republicans, 14.1 percent; and strong Republicans, 2.1 percent (2000 National Election Study).

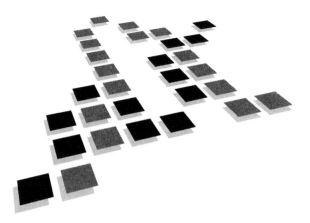

Index

Page references ending in *n* refer to the Notes.